Cambridge English

FUN for Movers

TEACHER'S BOOK

Anne Robinson
Karen Saxby

4th edition

Cambridge University Press
www.cambridge.org/elt

Cambridge Assessment English
www.cambridgeenglish.org

Information on this title: www.cambridge.org/9781316617557

© Cambridge University Press 2016

First published 2006
Second edition 2010
Third edition 2015
Fourth edition 2016

20 19 18 17 16 15 14 13

Printed in Malaysia by Vivar Printing

A catalogue record for this publication is available from the British Library

ISBN 978-1-316-61753-3 Student's Book with online activities with audio and Home Fun booklet
ISBN 978-1-316-63195-9 Student's Book with online activities with audio
ISBN 978-1-316-61755-7 Teacher's Book with downloadable audio
ISBN 978-1-108-72815-7 Presentation Plus

Contents

Introduction

Welcome to *Fun for Movers Fourth edition*

Fun for Movers Fourth edition is the second in a series of three books written for learners aged between 7 and 13 years old. *Fun for Starters Fourth edition* is the first book in the series and *Fun for Flyers Fourth edition* is the third.

Who is *Fun for Movers Fourth edition* for?

Fun for Movers is suitable for:

- learners who need comprehensive preparation for the *Cambridge English: Movers (YLE Movers)*, in addition to their general English course
- mixed classes where some of the learners are preparing to take the *Cambridge English: Movers* test, and who need motivating and fun English lessons
- small and large groups of learners
- monolingual and multilingual classes

Fun for Movers supports the development of good learning habits and language practice in meaningful, fun, creative and interactive ways. It is ideal for learners who have been studying English for between two and three years, and who need to consolidate their language and skills.

The key features include:

- complete coverage of the vocabulary and grammar on the *Cambridge English: Movers* syllabus
- thorough preparation for all parts of the *Cambridge English: Movers* test
- a focus on all four skills, with an emphasis on those areas most likely to cause problems for young learners at this level
- recycling of language and topics
- fun activities that practise English in a meaningful way
- opportunities for learners to personalise the language and make the tasks relevant to them

Cambridge English: Young Learners

For more information on *Cambridge English: Young Learners*, please visit https://www.cambridgeenglish.org/exams-and-tests/. From here, you can download the handbook for teachers, which includes information about each level of the Young Learners exams. You can also find information for candidates and their parents, including links to videos of the Speaking test at each level. There are also sample test papers, as well as games, and links to the Teaching Support website.

Course components

Student's Book with downloadable class audio and online activities

The Student's Book has been updated to include:

- even more opportunities for test practice. In most units, there will be at least one authentic test-style task. The instructions for these tasks are shown in (blue lozenge), while instructions for tasks which provide more general test practice are shown in black.
- new illustrations, designed to stimulate learner engagement
- a variety of fun activities, such as games, puzzles, drawing and colouring, to ensure your learners are involved in, and enjoy, their English lessons
- recordings for the listening tasks, which are available via the access code at the front of the book, so that learners can practise at home.
- online activities, available via the access code at the front of the book, which provide further practice of the grammar and vocabulary featured in the Student's Book as well as exam preparation activities
- projects that encourage learners to explore topics in more depth and produce work more independently

Teacher's Book with downloadable class audio

In the fourth edition of the Teacher's Book, you can find:

- clear signalling of *Cambridge English: Movers* test practice tasks and authentic test-style tasks that appear in each unit. These are listed in the information boxes at the start of each unit, under **Movers practice** or **Movers test**. In the unit notes, an icon like this Listening**2** indicates the part of *Cambridge English: Movers* that an authentic test-style task replicates.
- useful tips to guide and support learners in their preparation for each part of the test.
- materials and equipment needed to teach each unit. This means less preparation is needed, as you can see at a glance the audio resources or numbers of photocopies you need for each lesson.
- suggested wording of classroom language at the learners' level of English
- support for teaching pronunciation activities in a fun and motivating way for learners of this age
- ideas for maximising the involvement of learners in their learning process
- ideas for extending activities into simple, fun projects that give learners the chance to explore topics more independently and consolidate their English in creative ways
- additional resources, visuals and lesson ideas for teachers, and interactive games and activities to accompany *Fun for Movers*.

Online audio

The audio is available to download by following the instructions and using the access code at the front of the Student's Book.

Presentation plus

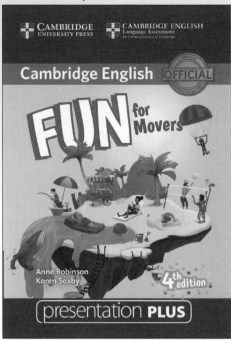

New for the fourth edition, Presentation plus is a digital version of the Student's Book and all the audio to complete the listening tasks. The integrated tools enable you to make notes, highlight activities and turn the Student's Book into an interactive experience for your learners. The Presentation plus includes:

o   all the Student's Book pages
o   all the audio for the Student's Book
o   pdfs of the Teacher's Book, including a complete practice test with the Listening audio
o   unit tests – one per unit, testing the key language covered in each unit

An app for mobile phones and tablets

For further practice of the list of vocabulary for the *Cambridge English: Movers* tests, download our new app and encourage your learners to practise their vocabulary while having fun!

Online activities

The online activities provide students with extra practice in grammar, vocabulary and exam tasks. All of the students online work can be tracked and reviewed by the teacher. It has also been fully updated to reflect task types and new words in the word list.

For access to Fun for Movers online content, contact your local Cambridge representative.

How is the Student's Book organised?

Contents
This lists the Student's Book unit numbers and titles.

50 units
Each unit is topic-based and designed to provide between 75 and 90 minutes of class time. Language is presented and practised throughout the unit and the final activity usually provides freer, fun practice of the unit's key content language. In most units, at least one task will provide *Cambridge English: Movers* test practice. The title instructions for these tasks are shown in blue lettering. The title instructions for all other tasks are shown in black lettering.

Ideas for project work on topic are included in many units and signalled by a 🧳 icon, as are fun activities to practise specific phonemes or other key aspects of pronunciation.

Pairwork activities
Learners will use these in specific unit tasks.

Unit wordlist
This is a list of the key words which appear in each unit (organised by topic or word class).
Listings are not repeated if they have already featured in a previous unit.

List of irregular verbs
This includes all the irregular verbs in the *Cambridge English: Movers* test. Space is provided for learners to write translations.

How is the Teacher's Book organised?

Contents
This shows where to find each section of the Teacher's Book.

Introduction
This will help you use *Fun for Movers Fourth edition.* It includes:

o   a **quick guide** to how units in the Teacher's books are organised (page 6)
o   suggestions for **games and activities** (page 6)
o   suggestions for how to use **pictures in the Student's Book** (page 7)
o   suggestions for **using dictation** (page 8)

Checklist for **Cambridge English: Movers** *Test preparation* (page 9)
o   a quick guide to what learners have to do in each part of the Movers test and units where each part is covered in the Student's Book. 'Test' indicates those activities that reflect the format of the Movers Listening, Reading and Writing or Speaking test. 'Practice' indicates activities that prepare for a particular part of Movers, but do not reflect the identical format of the test.

Map of the Student's Book (pages 10–13)
o   an overview of the content and organisation of all the units in the Student's Book.

Topics and grammar indexes (pages 14–15)

Unit guides / Teacher's notes
The teacher's notes for each of the 50 units. See below for a detailed guide to these.

Photocopiable activities (pages 116–127)
o   these relate to specific units as indicated in the teacher's notes.

Photocopiable practice test (pages 129–152)
o   a complete Movers practice test (Listening, Reading and Writing, Speaking) to photocopy and use with learners. Audioscripts, a sample Examiner's script for the Speaking and a key are also provided.

How is each unit organised?

Topics, and non-Movers words

This is a list of all the topics, covered in the unit. Any words that appear in the unit but not in the Movers wordlist are also listed here.

Equipment needed

This lists any equipment, for example: audio resources and/or material needed for the unit, including including the number of photocopies needed for any activities. Pages to be photocopied are found at the back of the Teacher's Book.

Instructions

These are usually labelled A, B, C, etc. and correspond to the different activities which appear in the Student's Book. There are some activities that appear only in the teacher's notes and are not labelled A, B, C, etc.

Audioscripts

The audioscripts for each Listening are at the end of the activity where they are used.

Project work

There are a number of suggestions for projects. The instructions for these generally appear at the ends of units.

Listening tasks

In the Listening tasks with a icon, the lengths of the pauses in the audio are the same as in the Young Learners English Tests the first time they are played.

When the audio is heard the second time in the *Cambridge English: YLE Tests*, the pauses are slightly shorter, allowing time to add any missing answers and/or to check answers.

For all other Listening tasks in this book, the lengths of pauses are approximate. You may want to re-start or stop the audio to allow your learners less or more time in which to complete tasks.

46   A day on the island

Pronunciation practice Sentence stress (*The pirate in the big boat has a black hat on his head*). See C.

Equipment needed
- Movers Audio 46A.

A ▶ **Listen and draw lines.**   Listening Part 1

> **Movers tip**
> In Listening Part 1, candidates have to name the people so, before they listen, they should look at the people in the picture and think about what they are doing and wearing, where they are, etc. If two people are doing the same or wearing the same clothes, they should look for other differences because this might be tested.

- Learners look at the picture. Ask: *Would you like to go to this beach? What can you do at this beach?* Learners answer. For example: go sailing / fishing / play games / read comics / find shells / sleep.
- Say: *Find five things that start with the letter 's'.* (**Suggestions:** sand, sea, shell, sun, shoes, shark, shorts). Say: *There's a line from the name Jack to one of the boys on the beach. What colour is that boy's T-shirt?* (red and white) *What's he doing?* (looking for something) *Where is he looking?* (on the sand near/under the plant)
- Play the audio stopping after the example. Ask: *What's Jack looking for?* (his glasses)
- Learners listen to the rest of the conversation and draw lines from the names to the people in the picture. Play the audio twice.

> **Check answers:**
> Lines should be drawn between:
> 1 Sally and girl hiding behind rock.
> 2 Peter and boy lying on ground with his eyes closed.
> 3 Sam and boy calling the parrot.
> 4 Vicky and girl holding her foot.
> 5 Alex and boy pirate on boat.

- Say: *You didn't need one of the names. Which one?* (Grace)

Audioscript

Look at the picture. Listen and look. There is one example.
Boy: Look at the picture.
Woman: Yes, they are, but what's the matter with that boy?
Boy: Oh! You mean Jack. He's looking for his glasses. He dropped them near that plant.
Woman: Oh yes! I can see them now.
Can you see the line? This is an example. Now you listen and draw lines.

106

One
Boy: Look at Sally!
Woman: Where?
Boy: There. She's the girl who's hiding behind that big rock.
Woman: Oh yes! I can see her. She's playing with her friend.
Two
Boy: There's Peter.
Woman: Which one's he?
Boy: There. I think he's sleeping in the sun.
Woman: I think he's awake, but his eyes are closed because it's sunny.
Three
Woman: Who's that boy? The boy who's calling the parrot?
Boy: Oh, that's Sam.
Woman: Why's he doing that?
Boy: Because the parrot's not in its cage. Look! The door's open.
Woman: Oh dear!
Four
Boy: Vicky doesn't look very happy.
Woman: Which one's she?
Boy: She's the girl who's holding her foot.
Woman: Did she hurt her foot on that shell?
Boy: Yes, I think she did.
Five
Boy: And there's Alex. He's very funny.
Woman: The boy on the boat?
Boy: Yes!
Woman: I like his pirate hat!
Boy: Me too!

B **Look and read and write.**   Reading & Writing Part 6

- Learners look at the picture in **A** again. Read out the first example: *The pirate on the ship is wearing a black hat.* Read out the second example: *What is the person in the small boat doing? Fishing* Ask: *Where's the small boat?* Learners point to the boat. Ask: *Is there a man in this boat? Is he fishing?* (yes)
- Say: *Read 1–4 and write 1–5 words. Then, write two sentences on the lines in 5 and 6 about people or things in the picture in A!* Learners write words and sentences.

> **Check answers:**
> (Suggestions) **1** some glasses / a headache   **2** the coconut tree
> **3** a (bird) cage   **4** behind the rock

- Ask: *What colour are the glasses?* (blue and black). Explain that they can write words like blue, big, etc to complete the sentences. Ask: *Is the cage big or little?* (little) *Is the rock little or big?* (big) Explain that they can add adjectives to their answers to the questions.
- Ask different learners to read out one of the sentences they wrote in 5 or 6. Encourage learners by saying: *Well done! Brilliant!*

Suggestions
Simple sentences: One person is looking for his glasses. There are no big waves in the sea. You can see the sun in the sky.
Compound sentences: The boy is sad because he hurt his foot on the shell. One person is asleep because he's tired. The ship has only got one sail and there's only one person on the ship.

C **Listen and say.**

- Say: *Look at the sentence in C. Some words in this sentence are more important than the other words.* Read out the sentence making sure that you stress the bold words: *The pirate in the big boat has a black hat on his head!*
- Ask one learner to only read out the bold words: *pirate, big boat,*

Fun and games

The following games and activities can be done in class to practise or revise a wide range of vocabulary or grammar.

Bingo

Learners make a grid of six or nine squares, in two or three rows of three. They write a word in each square. Read out words, one by one. If learners have the word, they cross it out or cover it with a small piece of paper. The first learner to cross out or cover all their words is the winner. Check that learners have heard the right words by asking them to say the words and comparing them with your list of words.

Seven lives ('Hangman')

Draw (or stick) seven body outlines on the board.

ХХХХХХХ

Choose a word. Draw one line on the board for each letter in the word, for example: __ __ __ __ __ __. (*shorts*) Learners put up their hands to say letters. If the letter is in the word, you write it on the line. If the letter is not in the word, you remove one of the bodies from the board. The game finishes when the learners complete the word or they lose all seven lives. Learners then play in groups, drawing lines for their own words.

The long sentence

Choose a simple sentence which can grow if words are added to the end of it.
For example:
Teacher: *In my bedroom, there's a bed.*
Learner 1: *In my bedroom, there's a bed and a table.*
Continue round the class, with each learner repeating the sentence and all the words which have been added, before then adding another word. The winner is the person who remembers all the words in the correct order when everyone else has been eliminated.

Guess what I'm drawing

One learner chooses a word and draws a picture of it on the board, one line at a time. After each line, the learner asks: 'What is it?' The other learners have to guess what it is. This can then be played in groups with learners drawing the lines on paper.

Spell it!

Choose a group of words (they could be from a particular topic, like body or animals, or they could be unrelated.) Tell learners to listen and write the letters as you say them (for example: P-E-). If they think they know the word, learners say 'Stop!' and say the remaining letters (for example: A-R) and the word (pear). If they are right, they get a point for each letter they gave. If they are not right, continue to spell out the word, letter by letter.

Change places

Learners sit in a circle. Say sentences starting with the words: *Change places if …* For example: *Change places if you got up at 8 o'clock today.* All the learners who got up at 8 o'clock have to stand up and move to sit in a different place.

Group or order the words

Take any group of words (related or not) and ask learners to group or order them:

o   **from longest to shortest.**
    Learners either write the words in order according to the number of letters they have, or learners write the words in order according to the number of vowels they have.

o   **from smallest to biggest.**
    Learners write the words starting with the smallest thing / animal / food etc.

o   **in alphabetical order.**
    Learners write the words in alphabetical order.

- o **in colour groups.**
  Learners write words in groups according to their colour.
- o **in sound groups**
  Learners write words in groups according to pronunciation similarities (stress patterns, vowel sounds etc).

Backs to the board

- o Make teams of 4–8 learners, depending on the size of the class.
- o Put one chair for each team at the front of the class. A learner from each team comes and sits on a chair, with their back to the board.
- o Write up a word on the board (for example: *page*). One team gives clues to the learners on the chairs so that they can guess the word.
- o The first learner from the chairs at the front to stand up gives an answer. If they are right, they get a point for their team. If they are wrong, they sit down and another team gives a clue. Again the first person to stand up gives an answer. Teams get a point for every correct answer.
- o When the word has been guessed, different learners from each team come to the front of the class and sit down and the activity is repeated.

Fun with pictures

You can use the pictures in the Student's Book in many different ways to revise and practise language. Here are some suggestions.

Which picture?

In pairs or small groups, one learner chooses a picture from any page in *Fun for Movers Third edition*. The other learner(s) have to ask questions to discover which picture. For example: *Are there any people? Is it inside? Is it the only picture on the page?* Once the other learner(s) have found the picture, they choose a picture and are asked questions.

Differences

Tell learners to look at two different pictures in the Student's Book, for example: page 15 (Unit 5) and page 99 (Unit 47). In pairs, they find similarities and differences between the two pictures. (For example: *In both pictures, we can see a bike. In the first picture, there are two bikes, but in the second picture, there is only one bike.*)

Yes or no?

In small groups, learners write sentences about a picture in the Student's Book. Some sentences should be true for the picture and some should be false. They either pass their sentences on to another group or they say the sentences to the other group. The other group has to say or write *yes* for the true sentences and *no* for the false ones.

Listen and draw

Learners work in pairs or small groups. One learner looks at one of the pictures in the Student's Book. This person describes the picture to the other learner(s), who listen and try to draw the picture.

Where's the treasure?

Tell learners to imagine that there is some treasure hidden somewhere in the picture. Learners have to find it by asking questions. For example: page 56 (Unit 26) *Is it behind one of the pictures?* (no) *Is it inside the clock?* (yes!)

Which one is different and why?

Three of the pictures are similar in some way and one of the pictures is different (for example: it's sunny / raining / sunny / sunny).

Pairs or groups work together. Learners in one pair or small group could choose, for example, the pictures in Unit 1A (page 6), Unit 5F (page 15), Init 15C (page 35) and Unit 16D (page 37). The other pair or group then looks at the four pictures and says why one picture is different from the others. (The classroom picture on page 35 is different because in this picture there's no ball / the children aren't doing sports / the children are inside, not outside.)

Say something more!

- o Divide the class into groups of 6–8 and ask them to sit in circles. All learners look at the same picture in the Student's Book (for example: page 86, Unit 41). One learner starts and says a sentence about the picture. For example: *The people are at a party.* The learner next to that learner says another sentence about the picture. For example: *Three people are dancing.*
- o Continue round the circle. If a learner repeats a sentence that someone else has said, they are eliminated (or lose a point).
  Variation: Each learner has to repeat the previous sentences and then add a new one.

What are they saying?

Pairs decide what different animals or people could be saying to each other in the picture. For example: page 23, Unit 9: *What's the mother horse saying to the baby horse?* or page 29, Unit 12: *What's the boy saying to the people at the door? What's the man saying to the people at the door?*

Tell me more about these people.

Learners work in pairs to imagine and talk or write about the people in the picture. For example: page 10, Unit 3: *What's this boy's name? How old is he? What does he like doing? What's his favourite animal / game / colour? etc.*

How many words?

Teams look at a picture and write as many different words as they can for things they can see. For example: page 24, A, Unit 10. *Roofs, windows, street, balconies,* etc. The winners are the team with the most correctly spelt words.

Fun with dictations

Dictations don't have to be boring! They are great for practising spelling, word order and prediction. Here are some different ways you can use dictation in class.

Word dictations

- Spell a word, letter by letter. Learners listen and write the letters. When a learner thinks they know the word you are spelling, they shout *Stop!* and say the word and the remaining letters. If the learner is correct, give them a point for every remaining letter they guessed.

- Dictate the letters of a word, but not in the right order. Learners have to write the letters, then un-jumble them and write the word, correctly spelt, as quickly as possible.

- Dictate all the consonants from a word (indicating the gaps for vowels). Learners have to complete the word with *a-e-i-o-u.*

Sentence dictations

- Dictate the key words from a sentence which has appeared in the unit or text. Learners have to write the full sentence so that it is similar (or identical) to the original sentence.

- Dictate a sentence a word at a time. (For example: a definition sentence like those which appear in Movers Reading and Writing Part 1.) Learners write the words and shout *Stop!* when they think they can complete the sentence (or say what is being defined).

- Dictate only the start of sentences. Learners complete the sentences with their own words. For example: Teacher: *This morning I put on* … Learner (writes): *my clothes.*

- Learners listen to a sentence. They only write the longest word (with the most letters) in the sentence.

- Learners listen to a sentence. They say how many words were in the sentence. For example: *I don't know him very well but he's quite nice.* (12)

Checklist for Cambridge English: Movers preparation

Paper	Part	Task	Unit
Listening Approx. 25 minutes	**1**	Draw lines between names outside a picture to figures inside.	*Practice:* 1, 9, 17, 26, 31, 41, 47 *Test:* 5, 15, 29, 46
	2	Write words or numbers.	*Practice:* 12, 30 *Test:* 2, 14, 39, 40
	3	Multiple matching. Write a letter in each box.	*Practice:* 28, 30, 33, 38 *Test:* 16, 22, 42
	4	Multiple choice. Tick the correct picture.	*Practice:* 4, 19, 47 *Test:* 10, 21, 36, 50
	5	Colour objects and write.	*Practice:* 1, 3, 6, 14, 18, 20, 22, 23 *Test:* 12, 31, 47
Reading and Writing 30 minutes	**1**	Match words to definitions by copying the word.	*Practice:* 2, 5, 6, 8, 11, 15, 17, 20, 23, 26, 27, 41, 44, 50 *Test:* 7, 18, 21, 35, 45
	2	Multiple choice. Read the dialogue and circle the best response.	*Practice:* 16, 22, 24, 41, 42, 43, 47, 49 *Test:* 10, 13, 19, 33, 48
	3	Picture gap fill. Choose words and write one word in each gap. Choose the best name for the story.	*Practice:* 9, 10, 14, 17, 21, 25, 28, 32, 34, 35, 36, 43 *Test:* 15, 20, 25, 38, 41, 48
	4	Multiple choice. Choose words to complete the factual text.	*Practice:* 2, 3, 36, 42, 43, 44, 47 *Test:* 8, 11, 16, 32, 39
	5	Complete sentences about the story by writing 1–3 words in each gap.	*Practice:* 2, 3, 4, 13, 17, 28, 35, 36, 43, 44 *Test:* 9, 37, 40, 45
	6	Complete sentences and answer questions about a picture. Write two sentences.	*Practice:* 1, 5, 12, 15, 19, 41, 49 *Test:* 18, 22, 26, 31, 34, 46
Speaking 5–7 minutes	**1** Two similar pictures	Describe four differences between pictures.	*Practice:* 12, 19, 23, 24, 26, 27, 32, 45, 46, 49 *Test:* 13, 34, 38, 42, 43, 44
	2 Picture story	Describe the pictures.	*Practice:* 31, 32, 38 *Test:* 7, 12, 35, 44
	3 Picture sets	Identify the odd one out and give reasons.	*Practice:* 2, 11, 13, 20, 29, 50 *Test:* 3, 25, 27, 37, 46
	4 Open-ended questions	Answer personal questions.	*Practice:* 1, 5, 7, 8, 9, 10, 11, 14, 15, 16, 17, 18, 24, 28, 29, 30, 31, 33, 36, 37, 38, 39, 40, 41, 43, 44, 45, 47, 48, 49 *Test:* 21

Map of the Student's Book

Unit	Topic	Grammar	Exam Practice
1 Watch us! We're moving!	sports and leisure, names	present simple and continuous, *be good at, like/love + ing*	Listening Parts 1 and 5, Reading and Writing Part 6, Speaking Part 4
2 Animals, animals …	animals, body and face	conjunctions, *can*, possessives, *have got*	Reading and Writing Parts 1 and 4, Speaking Part 3 Test: Listening Part 2
3 Fun at the farm	animals, the world around us	conjunctions, present simple, questions	Listening Part 5, Reading and Writing Part 5 Test: Speaking Part 3
4 Your hair looks great!	body and face, colours, names	relative clauses, *be called, have got*	Listening Part 4, Reading and Writing Part 5
5 The woman in the red dress	clothes, colours, body and face	*in* (to describe 'wearing'), *with* (to describe features), *Who's … -ing?*, prepositions of place	Reading and Writing Parts 1 and 6, Speaking Part 4 Test: Listening Part 1
6 My neck, my shoulders	body and face, colours	questions, comparative adjectives, prepositions of place, verb + infinitive, imperatives	Listening Part 5, Reading and Writing Part 1
7 What's the weather like?	weather, school	questions, conjunctions, prepositions of place	Speaking Part 4 Test: Reading and Writing Part 1, Speaking Part 2
8 The hottest and coldest places	weather, animals	comparative and superlative adjectives, past simple	Reading and Writing Part 1, Speaking Part 4 Test: Reading and Writing Part 4
9 Me and my family	family, names	possessive *'s'*, superlative adjectives, *a lot of*	Listening Part 1, Reading and Writing Part 3, Speaking Part 4 Test: Reading and Writing Part 5
10 People in our street	the home, body and face	comparative and superlative adjectives	Reading and Writing Part 3, Speaking Part 4 Test: Listening Part 4, Reading and Writing Part 2
11 Things we eat and drink	food and drink, colours	conjunctions, simple present	Reading and Writing Part 1, Speaking Parts 3 and 4 Test: Reading and Writing Part 4
12 Party things	food and drink, the home	prepositions, determiners, imperatives, obligation and need, *shall, there is / there are*	Listening Part 2, Reading and Writing Part 6, Speaking Part 1 Test: Listening Part 5, Speaking Part 2
13 Different homes	home, work	prepositions and adverbs of place and direction, present simple and continuous, past simple, *there is / there are*	Reading and Writing Part 5, Speaking Part 3 Test: Reading and Writing Part 2, Speaking Part 1

Unit	Topic	Grammar	Exam Practice
14 Our homes	the home, the world around us	prepositions of place, conjunctions	Listening Part 5, Reading and Writing Part 3, Speaking Part 4 Test: Listening Part 2
15 At our school	school, sports and leisure	determiners, past simple, questions, relative clauses, *there is / there are*	Reading and Writing Parts 1 and 6, Speaking Part 4 Test: Listening Part 1, Reading and Writing Part 3
16 Let's do some sport!	sports and leisure, time	prepositions of place, simple past, questions	Reading and Writing Part 2, Speaking Part 4 Test: Listening Part 3, Reading and Writing Part 4
17 Our hobbies	sports and leisure, family and friends	*go + -ing, like + -ing*, relative clauses, pronouns	Listening Part 1, Reading and Writing Parts 1, 3 and 5, Speaking Part 4
18 At the hospital	health, work	relative clauses	Listening Part 5, Speaking Part 4 Test: Reading and Writing Parts 1 and 6
19 What is the matter?	health, body and face?	questions, past simple, *have got*	Listening Part 4, Reading and Writing Part 6, Speaking Part 1 Test: Reading and Writing Part 2
20 Where?	places, the world around us	past simple, conjunctions	Listening Part 5, Reading and Writing Part 1, Speaking Part 3 Test: Reading and Writing Part 3
21 Here and there in town	places, family and friends	infinitive of purpose, past simple	Reading and Writing Part 3 Test: Listening Part 4, Reading and Writing Part 1, Speaking Part 4
22 A trip to the city	places, time, transport	*I think/know …* , adverbs, comparative adverbs, comparative adjectives	Listening Part 5, Reading and Writing Part 2 Test: Listening Part 3, Reading and Writing Part 6
23 The world around us	the world around us	adverbs of frequency, determiners, plurals, present simple	Listening Part 5, Reading and Writing Part 1, Speaking Part 1
24 Travelling, texting, phoning	the world around us, transport	present simple and continuous, past simple, conjunctions	Reading and Writing Part 2, Speaking Parts 1 and 4
25 Which one is different?	the home, animals	present and past simple, verb + infinitive, adjective order	Test: Reading and Writing Part 3, Speaking Part 3
26 Guess who lives here?	the home, sports and leisure	prepositions of place, superlative adjectives	Listening Part 1, Reading and Writing Part 1, Speaking Part 1 Test: Reading and Writing Part 6
27 Seeing differences	body and face, the world around us, clothes	plurals, conjunctions, impersonal *you*, relative clauses	Reading and Writing Part 1, Speaking Part 1 Test: Speaking Part 3

Unit	Topic	Grammar	Exam Practice
28 Our busy holidays	time, sports and leisure, family and friends	adverbs of frequency, prepositions and determiners in time expressions, verb + *ing*	Listening Part 3, Reading and Writing Parts 3 and 5, Speaking Part 4
29 About us	family and friends, names, sports and leisure	adverbs of manner, past simple, present simple, conjunctions	Speaking Parts 3 and 4 Test: Listening Part 1
30 About me	topic review	questions, present simple, past simple, *can*	Listening Parts 2 and 3, Speaking Part 4
31 Why is Sally crying?	family and friends, animals	relative clauses, conjunctions, present simple and continuous, past simple	Listening Part 1, Speaking Parts 2 and 4 Test: Listening Part 5, Reading and Writing Part 6
32 Mary goes shopping	food and drink, numbers	quantifiers, countable, singular and plural nouns, present continuous, present simple, conjunctions, *there is / there are*	Reading and Writing Parts 2 and 4, Speaking Parts 1 and 2 Test: Reading and Writing Part 6
33 Last weekend, last week	places, time	past simple, questions	Listening Part 3, Speaking Part 4 Test: Reading and Writing Part 2
34 What did you do then?	time, friends and family, sports and leisure	past simple, prepositions of time and place	Reading and Writing Part 4 Test: Reading and Writing Part 6, Speaking Part 1
35 What a morning!	school, sports and leisure	past simple, conjunctions, prepositions of time and place	Reading and Writing Parts 3 and 5 Test: Reading and Writing Part 1, Speaking Part 2
36 Could you do it?	sports and leisure, time	past simple, *have (got) to, could/ couldn't*, conjunctions	Reading and Writing Parts 3 and 4, Speaking Part 4 Test: Listening Part 4
37 Mr Must changes his job	work	past simple, *have (got) to, like doing something, when* clauses	Speaking Part 4 Test: Reading and Writing Part 5, Speaking Part 3
38 Playing and working	work, the home	past simple, adverbs of time, conjunctions	Listening Part 3, Speaking Parts 2 and 4 Test: Reading and Writing Part 3, Speaking Part 1
39 We've got lots of things to do	work, the home, time	prepositions of time, adverbs of frequency, questions	Speaking Part 4 Test: Listening Part 2, Reading and Writing Part 4
40 People who help us	work, animals, body and face	past simple questions and short answers, conjunctions, relative clauses	Speaking Part 4 Test: Listening Part 2, Reading and Writing Part 5

Unit	Topic	Grammar	Exam Practice
41 I had a great birthday!	family and friends, food, names	past simple, *would like*	Listening Part 1, Reading and Writing Parts 1, 2 and 6, Speaking Part 4 Test: Reading and Writing Part 3
42 An exciting week for Alex!	time, school, food and drink	suggestions: *Shall I? How about?, must,* comparative adjectives	Reading and Writing Parts 2 and 4 Test: Listening part 3, Speaking Part 1
43 My holidays	sports and leisure, transport, weather	past simple, adverbs of frequency, prepositions, questions, verb + infinitive	Reading and Writing Parts 2, 3 and 5, Speaking Part 4 Test: Speaking Part 1
44 Along the beach	the world around us, sports and leisure	past simple, prepositions of time and place, *before* and *after* + noun	Reading and Writing Parts 1 and 5, Speaking Part 4 Test: Speaking Parts 1 and 2
45 Treasure!	the world around us, food and drink	*when* clauses, past simple, present continuous	Speaking Parts 1 and 4 Test: Reading and Writing Parts 1 and 5
46 A day on the island	the world around us, sports and leisure	prepositions of place, verbs + *-ing*, present and past question forms and short form answers	Speaking Part 1 Test: Listening Part 1, Reading and Writing Part 6, Speaking Part 3
47 The different things we do	the home, sports and leisure	past simple, verb + *ing*	Listening Parts 1 and 4, Reading and Writing Parts 2 and 4, Speaking Part 4 Test: Listening Part 5
48 We want to do this one day	transport, the world around us	*Would you like?, Yes, I would / No, I wouldn't* and other *Yes/No* short form answers, verb + infinitive	Speaking Part 4 Test: Reading and Writing Parts 2 and 3
49 Ask me another question	topic review	prepositions of place, questions, *What's it like?*	Reading and Writing Part 2, Speaking Parts 1 and 4
50 Well done!	topic review	grammar review	Reading and Writing Part 1, Speaking Part 3 Test: Listening Part 4

Fun for Movers topic index

Topics	Units
Sports and leisure, names	1 Watch us! We're moving!
Animals, body and face, clothes and colours	2 Animals, animals … 3 Fun at the farm 4 Your hair looks great! 5 The woman in the red dress 6 My neck, my shoulders
Weather	7 What's the weather like? 8 The hottest and coldest places
The home, family, food and drink	9 Me and my family 10 People in our street 11 Things we eat and drink 12 Party things 13 Different homes 14 Our homes
School, sports and leisure	15 At our school 16 Let's do some sport! 17 Our hobbies
Health	18 At the hospital 19 What's the matter?
Places and time	20 Where? 21 Here and there in town 22 A trip to the city
The world and the home	23 The world around us 24 Travelling, texting, phoning 25 Which one is different? 26 Guess who lives here? 27 Seeing differences
Family and friends, time	28 Our busy holidays 29 About us 30 About me 31 Why is Sally crying?
Time, numbers, school	32 Mary goes shopping 33 Last weekend, last week 34 What did you do then? 35 What a morning! 36 Could you do it?
Work	37 Mr Must changes his job 38 Playing and working 39 We've got lots of things to do 40 People who help us
Leisure time - today and yesterday	41 I had a great birthday! 42 An exciting week for Alex 43 My holidays 44 Along the beach 45 Treasure! 46 A day on the island
Transport, the world around us	47 The different things we do 48 We want to do this one day 49 Ask me another question 50 Well done!

Fun for Movers grammar index

Grammar	Grammar	Units
adverbs	frequency	22, 23, 28, 39, 43
	manner	29
	time	38
	place	13
articles		17, 18
	be called	4
	be good at	1
	can / can't / could	2, 4, 30, 36
comparative and superlative	adjectives	6, 8, 9, 10, 22, 26, 42
	adverbs	22
conjunctions		2, 3, 7, 10, 14, 20, 24, 27, 29, 31, 35, 36, 38, 40
determiners		12, 15, 23, 28
	have got	2, 4, 10, 19, 25, 31, 41
	I think/know …	22
imperatives		6, 12
modal verbs (*must / have to / need*)		12, 36, 37, 42
plurals		23, 27, 32
possessives		2, 9
prepositions	place	5, 6, 7, 12, 13, 14, 16, 26, 34, 35, 44, 46, 49
	time	28, 34, 35, 39, 44
pronouns		8, 17, 32
questions		3, 6, 7, 15, 16, 19, 30, 33, 39, 43, 46, 49
	short answers	40, 46, 48
relative clauses		4, 15, 17, 18, 27, 31, 40
Suggestions: *Shall I? / How about?*		12, 23, 31, 42
	there is / there are	7, 12, 13, 15, 23, 27, 31, 32
verb tenses	present simple	1, 3, 10, 13, 23, 24, 25, 29, 30, 31, 32
	present continuous	1, 13, 24, 25, 31, 32, 45
	past simple	8, 13, 15, 16, 19, 20, 21, 24, 25, 29, 30, 31, 33, 34, 35, 36, 37, 38, 40, 41, 44, 45, 47
verb forms	infinitive of purpose	21, 27
	verb + infinitive	6, 25, 43, 48
	verb + *ing*	1, 17, 28, 37, 46, 47
***when* clauses**		37, 45
	would like	2, 3, 31, 41, 42, 48

1 Watch us! We're moving!

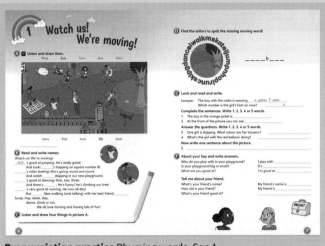

Pronunciation practice Rhyming words. See A.

Equipment needed

- Movers Audio 1A.
- (Optional) a picture of ice skates and roller skates. See A.
- (Optional) magazines for the project idea.

A ▶ Listen and draw lines.

- Tell learners to cover the lower half of the page with a book or piece of paper. They should only be able to see the picture and the ten names.
- Learners look at the picture. Ask questions:
  Where are these children? (in a playground/park)
  How many children can you see? (nine)
  Can you see any grown-ups, too? (yes, one!)
  Are there any animals in the playground? (yes)
  What are they? (a bird, a dog and a sheep)
- Explain that especially in America, people sometimes use the word 'kids' to mean children, then ask: *What are the kids doing?*
  If necessary, pre-teach any action verbs that are new at this level (hop, skate, skip and dance). You may also like to teach/revise 'roller skates' and 'ice skates' and the verbs 'to roller skate' and 'to ice skate'. Ask: *Is the girl wearing roller skates or ice skates here?* (roller skates). *Do any of you like roller skating? Where do you go roller skating? In the park?* Learners answer.
- Say: *These children need names!* Ask: *How many names can you see?* (ten) Say: *You don't need one of the names.*
- Say: *Now listen and draw lines between the children and their names.* Play the audio once. Learners draw lines.
- If learners need a second listening, play the audio again.

Check answers:
Lines should be drawn between:
1 Jack and jumping boy.
2 Sue and hopping girl.
3 Jane and roller skating girl.
4 Sam and skipping girl.
5 Dan and dancing boy.
6 Pat and climbing boy.
7 Tom and running boy.
8 Jill and walking girl with J on clothes.
9 May and walking girl with M on clothes.

- Ask: *Which name isn't an answer?* (Eva)
  Tell learners that one of the boys' names is almost the same as what he's doing.
  Ask: *Who is that?* (Dan) *What's Dan doing?* (He's dancing!)
- Point to the teacher and say: *Let's give the teacher a name, too.* Learners choose a name for the teacher, write it on the dotted line under the children's names and draw a line to her.
- Ask different learners how they can mime the actions (jump, hop, roller skate, skip, dance, climb, run and walk) while sitting! Say: *Only move your body, arms and head.* Repeat with some of the other children's names.
- When everyone can mime the actions, say: *Now look at the children's names and listen!*
  My name's Dan! What does Dan like doing? Learners dance with their upper bodies only.
  Say: *Now I'm Sam! What does Sam like doing?* Learners mime skipping with their upper bodies only. Repeat with some of the other children's names.

Rhyming words

- Learners listen to the audio a second time (or third time if they needed a second hearing for the naming activity). Play the audio, pausing at the end of each line. Ask: *What's the last word?*
- Write the last words on the board: *great, eight, Sue, blue, round, playground, Sam, am, three, tree, Pat, hat, day, May, run, fun.*
- Say: *Some of these words sound the same. Some have the same last letters, too. Which words have the same letters at the end?* (S**ue**/bl**ue**, **round**/play**ground**, S**am**/**am**, th**ree**/t**ree**, P**at**/h**at**, d**ay**/M**ay**, r**un**/f**un**).
  Ask: *Do great and eight have the same letters at the end?* (yes, but only the 't'). Show learners that the ends of both these words sound like /eɪt/ but the letters that spell that sound are very different ([gr]eat/eight).
- Learners work in small groups. Ask: *Can you think of more words that sound like three/tree? And words that sound like day and May?* Give groups time to think of words or to find rhyming words in their word lists and then ask for their ideas.
  Suggestions: be, he, me, pea, see, sea, we; grey, play, say, they.
- Groups try to make a rhyming sentence using these words: three, tree(s), me, pea(s), see(s), sea.
  This will be difficult for some learners so offer help if necessary.
  Suggestions: Can you see me in the sea?
  I'm in the sea, come and swim with me!
  There are three peas in those trees!
  One, two, three, come and play with me!

Audioscript

Watch us! We're moving!
Jack's good at jumping. He's really great!
And look! Sue's hopping on square number 8!
Can you see Jack? Can you see Sue?
Yes, I can! Sue's dress is blue.

Jane's roller skating! She's going round and round.
And watch Sam skipping in our new playground.
Can you see Jane? Can you see Sam?
Are you looking? Yes, I am!

Dan's good at dancing … one, two, three!
And there's Pat. He's funny! He's climbing our tree.
Can you see Dan? Can you see Pat?
Yes, I can. Pat's wearing a hat!

Tom's very good at running. He runs all day!
But Jill likes walking (and talking) with her best friend, May.
Jump, hop, skate, skip … dance, climb or run,
We all love moving and having lots of fun!

B Read and write names.

o Practise 'be good at -ing'. Say, for example: *I'm good at writing. I'm not good at drawing.* Ask 2–3 learners: *What are you good at?*
Note: Remember answers for your following questions.

o Ask *Who?* questions about children in the class, for example: *Who's sitting next to (Maria)? Who likes wearing white clothes?* (Tomas) *Who's good at writing?* (Chantal) *Who's good at climbing?* (Serpil)

o Say: *Now look at the poem.* Ask: *What's the name of this poem?* (Watch us! We're moving!) Say and model: *Move your arms!* (Learners copy you and all wave their arms in the air.) *Now move your feet!* (Learners copy you and all shuffle their feet.)

o Learners find the moving verbs in the poem and colour, circle or underline them.

o Say: *Two people like doing one thing. Their names are … ?* (Jill and May) Write on the board: *Jill and May like walking.* Explain that after 'like' or 'love' we use the '-ing' form of the verb.

o In pairs, learners write the children's names in the poem. They put up their hands to show they have finished. Check answers then ask different learners to each read out one of the first ten lines. Learners could read out the last line in chorus.

> **Check answers:**
> Sue, Jane, Sam, Dan, Pat, Tom, Jill/May

C Listen and draw four things in picture A.

o Say: *Find your pencils.* Point to the picture again and say: *Listen and draw four things in this picture now. Don't worry. You don't have to be good at drawing!*

o Read out slowly, pausing between instructions to give learners time to draw:
Find the sheep. It's a bad sheep! It's eating the teacher's favourite flower. Draw the flower in the sheep's mouth.
Find Jane. Jane likes wearing funny hats. Draw a funny hat on Jane's head.
Can you see Dan's school bag? Draw another bag there. That's right. Draw another bag there.
Now the balloon. Draw a face on the balloon. Put a really happy face on the balloon.

o Give learners a minute to admire each other's drawings!

o Check answers by asking questions:
What's on the balloon? (a happy face) *What's on Jane's head?* (a funny hat) *What's next to Dan's school bag?* (another bag) *What's in the sheep's mouth?* (a flower)

o Learners work in pairs. Each learner adds two more things to their drawings and then shows them to their partner. Learners then ask and answer questions about the drawings. For example, Learner A asks: *In my picture, what's on Tom's T-shirt now?* Learner B looks and answers, for example: *an apple!* Learner B then asks Learner A questions about their drawing.

D Find the letters to spell the missing moving word.

o Say: *Find the moving words. Draw circles round them.*

o Learners find the seven verbs. (run, skip, dance, walk, skate, jump and hop)

o Say: *There are seven more letters here.* Ask different learners to say a letter and write them on the board: c g l m i n i

o Point to the lines and the 'b' in the middle of them and the letters on the board. Ask: *Which moving word can you spell with these letters?*

o Pairs find the word and write *climbing* on the lines. Say: *When we say 'climbing', we don't hear one of the letters. Which one?* (b)

E Look and read and write.

> **Movers tip**
> In Reading and Writing Part 6, candidates need to complete two sentences and then answer two questions about a big picture. They then need to write two sentences about the picture. In this practice task, they only need to write one sentence. They can write about what they can actually see in the picture or what they imagine is happening.

o Point to the boy in the yellow T-shirt in the picture in **A** and read out the first example sentence: *The boy with the radio is wearing … (a yellow T-shirt)* Point to the girl who's hopping in the picture and read out the second example: *Which number is the girl's foot on now?* (eight)

o Point to sentences 1 and 2 and questions 3 and 4. Say: *Write short answers* (between one and five words) to complete these sentences and answers.

> **Check answers:**
> (Suggestions) **1** running (after a sheep) **2** a blue bike
> **3** (They're) red. **4** She's roller skating / smiling.

o Point to the picture in **A** and say: *Let's say and write sentences about this picture.* Prompt learners by asking questions if necessary, for example, *Where are these people?* (These people are in a park.)

o Point to the woman, the boy in the tree, the football, the bag, the bird, etc and ask learners to say sentences. Do this in open class or with learners working in pairs. Write their sentences on the board.
Note: With stronger classes, different learners say a sentence, and then come to the front of the class and write their sentence on the board.
Suggestions: (simple and compound sentences)
These people are in a park.
There are nine children in the picture.
The teacher is a woman.
A boy is climbing a tree.
The boy wants to catch the sheep because it's eating all the flowers.
I think the boy in the yellow T-shirt likes playing football.
One girl has M on her T-shirt and another girl has J on her T-shirt.
Learners choose a sentence from the board and copy it on the line next to 5 in **E**.

F About you! Say and write answers.

> **Movers tip**
> In Speaking Part 4, candidates do not read any of the questions. They only hear them. They answer three simple questions, then a 'Tell me' question. For the 'Tell me' question, they should try to think of three simple answers. The examiner will only use prompts for the 'Tell me' question (as shown in **F**), if candidates need support.

o Ask different learners one of the first three questions and then ask one strong learner the three 'Tell me about' questions.

o In pairs, learners then take turns to ask and answer the questions and then complete the written answers.

o Walk round and help learners who need more support.

> 📁 **Moving!**
> o Learners find and cut out pictures of children or adults doing different moving verbs in magazines or draw and colour their own pictures.
> o In groups of 3–4, learners make a collage of them and label each picture in the collage with sentences like: *Look! He's dancing. This person's swimming. She's really good at jumping.*
> o If possible, display these collages on the classroom wall. Alternatively, learners add their pictures to their project file.

2 Animals, animals ...

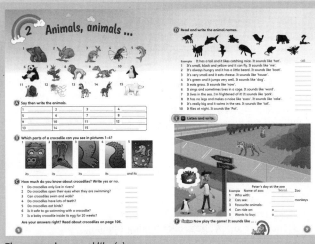

Flyers words: *sound like* (v)

Equipment needed

- Movers Audio 2E.
- Small cards or slips of paper for learners to write single words on (six per learner). See F.
- Picture of a kangaroo. See F.

A Say then write the animals.

Note: Some animals on the Movers wordlist might not be found in your part of the world. Use pictures to teach these animals and ask learners if they've seen these animals in books, on TV, in films or at a zoo.

- Ask different learners:
  What's your favourite animal?
  Are you afraid of any animals? Which ones?
  Which animals are beautiful / ugly / funny / dangerous?

- Most of the animals in these pictures are Movers words apart from 'bear', 'lizard', 'jellyfish', 'zebra', 'donkey' and 'polar bear'. Use the pictures to teach/revise any animal words that learners don't already know. Then ask: *What's the animal in picture one?* Learners say together: *It's a bear!*
  Ask *What's the animal in picture … ?* questions about three or four more animal pictures. Show learners that you want them to answer in groups. Groups answer together.

- Ask individual learners similar questions. Different learners answer. Continue until learners know all the animal words or tire of the activity.

- Write all the animal words on the board in a random order. Point to 'bear'. Ask: *What number is next to the bear in your pictures?* (one) Learners write *bear* on the line next to 1. Say: *A bear is brown or black but a polar bear isn't brown or black. It's…?* (white)

- In pairs, learners continue finding and copying the correct animal word for numbers 2–15.

> **Check answers:**
> **2** rabbit **3** kangaroo **4** fly **5** dolphin **6** panda **7** parrot
> **8** lion **9** lizard **10** penguin **11** snail **12** jellyfish **13** zebra
> **14** donkey **15** polar bear

- Clean the board to practise the animal vocabulary by using one of the following race games:

- **Writing race:** In their notebooks, pairs write all the animals as quickly as possible in alphabetical order. Check answers by asking different pairs to spell one of the animal words: *bear, dolphin, donkey, fly, jellyfish, kangaroo, lion, lizard, panda, parrot, penguin, polar bear, rabbit, snail, zebra.*

- **Biggest to smallest:** In pairs or small groups, learners quickly decide how to order the animals from biggest to smallest and then write their list. Accept any reasonable order, for example: *bear, polar bear, panda, kangaroo, dolphin, donkey, zebra, lion, penguin, jellyfish, rabbit, parrot, lizard, snail, fly.*

Make groups

- Write on the board: *lions, lizards.* Draw a circle round these two words.
  Say: *Lions and lizards can run quickly.*

- Write on the board: *rabbits, kangaroos.* Draw a circle round these two words.
  Say: *Rabbits and kangaroos can …?* (jump/hop)

- In groups of 3–4, learners choose animals which have something in common and write them in a circle. Ask one learner from each group to come to the board and write the animals in a circle. The other groups have to say what the connection is.
  Suggestions: They eat meat. They can fly. They can swim. They have / haven't got legs / a tail.

B Which parts of a crocodile can you see in pictures 1–4?

- Point to the crocodile's eyes in picture 1. Ask: *What are these?* (the crocodile's eyes)
  Point to the crocodile's nose in picture 1. Ask: *What's this?* (its nose)
  Point to the whole of the crocodile's head and ask: *And what's this?* (its head)
  Learners write *head* on the line under picture 1.

- Learners look at pictures 2, 3 and 4 and say which part of the crocodile they can see. Ask different learners to come to the board and write the answers. Learners then copy the answers on the lines.

> **Check answers:**
> **2** mouth/teeth **3** leg/foot **4** tail

- Ask questions about a crocodile:
  Is a crocodile's mouth big or small? (big)
  Is a crocodile's tail long or short? (long)
  Are a crocodile's legs ugly or beautiful? (Learners' own answer!)

- Point to picture 5. Ask: *What's this?* (A baby crocodile.) Point to the egg and ask: *Do you know that crocodiles come from eggs?*
  Learners write *baby* on the line under the last picture.

C How much do you know about crocodiles?

- Learners read the seven questions. In pairs, they decide if the answers are 'yes' or 'no'. They can write their answers in pencil so if they are wrong they can easily correct them.

Are your answers right? Read about crocodiles on page 106.

- Learners work in A and B pairs. Learner A keeps their book open on page 8. Learner B turns to page 106. Pairs can then see both the questions and the text about crocodiles. Ask one pair to read out the first piece of information about crocodiles: *Crocodiles eat fish, birds, animals and sometimes they eat people too! They do not eat grass or plants.*
  Ask: Which *question does this answer?* (Question 5 – *Do crocodiles eat birds?*) Say: *So what's the answer to this question?* (yes) Learners write *yes* on the line next to question 5.
  Read 1–7 with learners and check answers.

> **Check answers:**
> Question 1 (answer is found in text 4) *No*
> Question 2 (answer is found in text 5) *Yes*
> Question 3 (answer is found in text 2) *Yes*
> Question 4 (answer is found in text 6) *Yes*
> Question 6 (answer is found in text 7) *No*
> Question 7 (answer is found in text 3) *No*

○ Teach/Revise 'like + ing' form of the verb.
  Write on the board: *Crocodiles don't like ....grass or plants*.
  Point to the gap and ask: *Can I write eat, eats or eating here?* (eating)
  Ask a learner to come to the board and write *eating* in the gap.
  Ask different learners: *What do/don't you like eating?*

ⓓ Read and write the animal names.

○ In pairs, learners look at the animals. Ask different pairs: *Which animals can you see?* Each pair says one animal: *a cat, a shark, a frog, a bird, a cow, a snake, a goat, a bat, a whale, a mouse, a bee.*

○ Say the following sentences. Learners listen and say which animal in the pictures the sentence can describe. For example: *This animal has got four legs.* Learners put up their hands to answer. (a cat, a frog, a cow, a goat, a mouse)
  This animal doesn't have legs. (a shark, a snake, a whale)
  This animal can fly. (a bird, a bat, a bee)
  This is a big animal. (a shark, a cow, a whale)

○ If necessary, remind learners what *sounds like* means.
  Write on the board: *mat   hat*. Say: **Mat** sounds like **hat**.
  Write on the board: *take   make*. Say: **Take** sounds like **make**.

○ Learners look at the example (hat/cat) then, in pairs, they read out 1–10 and write the answers. If learners need more help, read out the sentences yourself and ask learners what the answers are before they write them.
  Note: The animal answers all appear in the pictures in **D**.

> **Check answers:**
> **1** bee   **2** goat   **3** mouse   **4** frog   **5** cow   **6** bird   **7** shark
> **8** snake   **9** whale   **10** bat

ⓔ ▶ Listen and write.   Listening **2** Part

○ Say: *Peter's at the zoo today. Do you know the name of the animal that's standing by his feet?* (It's a penguin!) *Do you like penguins?* Learners answer.

○ Ask: *What's Peter doing?* (phoning someone) *Who's he talking to? Guess!* (learners guess). Say: *That's right!* if a learner guesses he's talking to his grandma.

○ Say: *Let's listen to Peter and his grandma now. Write the answers. Only write one word or number. There's one example.*

Audioscript

Listen and look. There is one example.
Boy: Hello Grandma! I'm at the zoo!
Woman: Hello Peter! Wow! Which zoo?
Boy: I'm at World Zoo. You spell that W-O-R-L-D.
Woman: World Zoo. It's great there!
Boy: I know!
Can you see the answer?
Now you listen and write.

One
Woman: Who are you with?
Boy: I'm here with Mum.
Woman: So you're there with Mum. That's nice.
Boy: Yes, I'm talking to you on her phone.
Woman: Oh!

Two
Woman: Where are you now?
Boy: We're by the cafe.
Woman: What can you see?
Boy: I'm looking at five monkeys. They've got really funny faces!
Woman: Five monkeys! I love monkeys.
Boy: Me too!

Three
Woman: Are monkeys your favourite animals?
Boy: No, they aren't.
Woman: So which animals do you like best?
Boy: The dolphins. They're very good at jumping!
Woman: Yes, dolphins can swim very well, too!
Boy: I know, Grandma!

Four
Boy: You can ride some animals here!
Woman: Which animals?
Boy: You can ride a horse. It's really big!
Woman: You can ride a horse there?
Boy: Yes, Grandma! I'm not frightened of that … .

Five
Boy: There's a shop here, too.
Woman: What can you buy there?
Boy: Well I want to buy a book. I'd like a new book!
Woman: Good idea!
Boy: Oh Grandma! There's a penguin. It's standing by my foot… .
Woman: What?
Boy: Sorry Grandma! I've got to go now. Bye!

> **Check answers:**
> **1** Mum   **2** 5/five   **3** dolphins   **4** horse   **5** (new) book

○ Write on the board:
  What's your favourite animal?
  Have you got a pet? What kind of animal is your pet?
  Would you like another pet? Which kind?
  Do you like going to the zoo? Which animals do you like watching there?

○ Learners ask and answer the questions in groups of 3–4. Walk round and help groups with vocabulary if necessary.

○ Then, ask groups about their favourite animals and pets.

ⓕ Now play the game! It sounds like …

○ Divide the class into three groups A, B and C. Give each learner six different pieces of card or paper to write different words on.

○ Draw three large circles on the board. Mark these A, B and C.
  In circle A, write: *word hair coat buy mat lake*
  In circle B, write: *cat snake goat bear bird fly*
  In circle C, write: *make hat there boat eye third*
  Point to group A and to circle A and say: *Write these words on your pieces of paper.* Do the same with group B and group C. Learners write the words.

○ Learners take their cards and sit in groups of three (an A, a B and a C learner).

○ Hold up your picture of a kangaroo. Say: *kangaroo sounds like …?* (point to your shoe) *shoe!*
  Say to B learners: *Say one of your words now.* Say to A and C learners: *Have you got a word that sounds the same? Say it!*
  Show learners what to do if necessary. Using one group, ask a B learner to find the word 'cat'. Ask A and C learners to find their rhyming words. Learners find 'mat' and 'hat'.

  Alternative suggestion:

○ Learners work in pairs. In their notebooks, they copy an animal word from circle B then find two more rhyming words (one from circle A and one from circle C) to make a set of three words.
  You could warn learners that two sets are easy because the words have the same letters in them. But three are more difficult!

> **Check answers:**
> cat: mat/hat;   snake: lake/make;   goat: coat/boat;
> bear: hair/there;   bird: word/third;   fly: buy/eye.

3   Fun at the farm

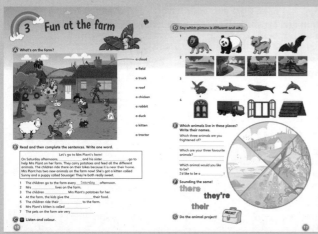

Pronunciation practice *there / they're / their, your/you're, by / bye / buy.* See F.

Equipment needed

○ Magazines with pictures of animals. See G.
○ Colouring pencils or pens. See C.
○ Movers Audio 3C.

A What's on the farm?

○ Ask: *Do you live near a farm? Which animals can you sometimes see on a farm?*
  Suggestions: cows, sheep, goats, horses, rabbits, ducks, chickens, dogs

○ Learners look at the picture. Teach any new vocabulary if necessary. Say: *Draw lines from the eight words to these things in the picture.* Learners work in pairs. Check answers.

○ Ask two learners to choose names for the boy and the girl in the picture. Write the names on the board then ask:
  Who's playing with the puppy? Who's jumping in the water?
  Ask more questions about the picture:
  How many clouds/chickens can you see? (three/five)
  How many potatoes are on the ground? (four)
  Where's the rabbit / woman / truck? (next to [or near] the tree / window / cow)
  And where's the tractor? In the…? (field)
  What's your favourite animal in the picture?

○ Teach/revise: 'cloudy' and 'sunny'. Point to the picture and ask: *Is it a cloudy day or a sunny day?* Point to your classroom window and say: *Look outside. Is it a cloudy day or a sunny day here today?*

B Read and then complete the sentences. Write one word.

○ Read the text out loud. Pause for learners to say and write the names they chose for the children.

○ Ask: *When do the children go to the farm?* (on Saturday afternoons)
  Who lives there? (Mrs Plant)
  What do the children carry for Mrs Plant? (mime carrying a sack of potatoes) Write the words *food* and *feed* on the board. Point to the two spellings so learners see the similarity. Explain that 'feed' means the same as 'give food to something or someone'.
  Do the children go there on the bus? (no)
  What's the name of Mrs Plant's kitten? (Sunny)
  Say: *That's a nice name for a kitten. Is Cloudy a nice name for a kitten, too? What are your favourite names for cats and dogs?*
  Learners answer.

○ In pairs, learners read the sentences and add the missing word. Make sure they understand that just <u>one</u> word is missing.

○ Walk round and give support where needed.

> **Check answers:**
> 1 Colour sheep - blue.
> 2 Colour door - red.
> 3 Colour puppy - yellow.
> 4 Colour grass - purple.

C ▶ Listen and colour.

○ Write on the board: *sheep   door   puppy   tall grass*

○ Tell learners in pairs to find these things in the picture in **A**. Walk around and check they are correctly identifying these four things. Ask: *What colour are these things?* (white)

○ Ask: *Have you got your colouring pencils?* Check that learners have blue, red, yellow and purple colouring pens or pencils amongst others. Say: *Now listen and colour.*

○ Play the audio twice, pausing for 15 seconds after each item to give learners time to colour.

> **Check answers:**
> sheep – blue, door – red, puppy – yellow, grass – purple

Audioscript

Look at the picture. Listen and colour.

One
Girl:	Can I colour the sheep in this picture?
Man:	Yes! Would you like to colour it blue?
Girl:	That's a funny colour for a sheep!
Man:	Yes, it is! Do you like that colour?
Girl:	Yes, I do.

Two
Man:	Now colour the door for me. Can you see it?
Girl:	The door of the house?
Man:	Yes, that's right.
Girl:	Shall I colour it with my red pencil?
Man:	Yes! Good idea!

Three
Girl:	Can I colour the puppy now?
Man:	Yes. Which colour shall we make the puppy?
Girl:	Can I make it yellow because I love that colour?
Man:	OK. I like that colour too.

Four
Man:	And now, please colour the tall grass. Can you see it?
Girl:	Yes. It's near the girl.
Man:	That's right. Colour that tall grass purple.
Girl:	OK. I'm doing that now.
Man:	Great! Well done!

D Say which picture is different and why.   Speaking Part 3
Animal groups

○ Write on the board: *swim, fly, hop, run, jump, climb.*
  Check understanding, asking different learners to mime each verb. Learners copy the words into their notebooks leaving room after each verb to write three more words.

○ Say: *When people or animals do these things, they all move!* Ask: *Can people do <u>all</u> these things? Can they swim, fly, run, hop, jump and climb?* (no) *What can't people do?* (fly)

○ Learners work in pairs or groups of three. Say: *Think of three animals that do these moving verbs. Write the animals on the line next to their verb.* You might like to teach/revise 'bee', 'donkey', 'penguin' and 'zebra' to add to learners' list of known animals.

Tell learners they should try not to write the same animal more than once. When they have finished, groups should hold up their hands.

Suggestions: (four given for each group)
swim: shark, dolphin, whale, fish;
fly: bat, duck, fly, parrot;
run: lion, tiger, giraffe, sheep;
hop: kangaroo, rabbit, bird, monkey;
jump: goat, frog, horse, dog;
climb: cat, goat, spider, bear

> **Movers tip**
> In Speaking Part 3, it doesn't matter which difference candidates talk about as there is often more than one possible answer. The important thing is to talk, and to give a reason for the difference.

O Before you begin this activity, practise 'because'.
Write on the board: *crocodile, giraffe, spider, whale*
Ask: *Which one is different?* (a spider) *Why?* (It's very small).
Write the model answer on the board: *A .... is different because it ....*
Point to the answer and say: A spider is different because it's very small.
Ask: *Can you think of a different answer?* (a whale) *Why?*
Say: *A whale is different because … ? It hasn't got legs / can't walk.*
Ask: *And another answer?* (a crocodile) *Why?* Point to the model answer on the board and your teeth. Learners say in chorus: *A crocodile is different because it's got lots of big teeth!*

O Learners look at the four rows of pictures and think of odd-one-out reasons for the four groups. They can either write sentences to express the differences or talk about them. Ask different learners to say the differences.

Suggested answers:
1 A bat is different because it can fly.
2 The park is different because it's sunny / not cloudy there.
3 The rabbit is different because it can't swim.
4 The truck is different because it isn't part of a house.

E Which animals live in these places? Write their names.

O Say: *You're an animal and you live in the sea. What kind of animal are you? Choose an animal but don't say anything.*
Note: Learners can look back at Units 1 and 2 for ideas. Learners don't have to move around the classroom, but they can pull faces or use their arms to mime movement through water. You may want to choose an animal and move too!
Note: After asking each of the four following questions, write any acceptable answers on the board in random order. Do <u>not</u> write the answers in their groups.

O Ask: *What are you?*
Suggestions: fish, dolphins, sharks, whales

O Say: *You're not in the sea now. You're walking in the jungle. Be careful!* Ask: *Which animals are near?*
Suggestions: monkeys, snakes, tigers, spiders, lizards, bats

O Say: *You're hiding in some tall grass in Africa. Shh! Which animals can you see?*
Suggestions: giraffes, lions, lizards, hippos, elephants, crocodiles, parrots, frogs, spiders

O Say: *You live on a farm.* Ask: *Which animals live on your farm too?*
Suggestions: horses, cows, sheep, ducks, chickens, goats, dogs, cats, flies

O In pairs, learners copy the animals that are on the board into the appropriate parts of the circle. Walk round, check spellings and accept any reasonable answers.

O Learners write three animals they are frightened of, three of their favourite animals and an animal they would like to be on the lines.

F Sounding the same!

O Point to 'there', 'they're' and 'their' and ask: *How do we say these words?* Learners may suggest different pronunciations, but explain there is no difference in these words when we hear or say them. They are all pronounced /ðeə/.

O Learners work in pairs. Ask: *How many 'there', 'they're' or 'their' words can you find on these two pages? Draw circles round them!*

O Give learners a minute or so to find the words and draw their circles. Ask different pairs to read out the sentences in which these words appear.

O Write on the board:
.... *are the cats!*
.... *wearing hats!*
Are .... *hats red, yellow or blue?*

O Learners copy the sentences into their notebooks, completing them with *there, they're* or *their*. Make sure they use capital letters where necessary. (*There are the cats. They're wearing hats! Are their hats red, yellow or blue?*) Learners could then draw two cats wearing red, yellow or blue hats. Learners decide which colour(s) to choose.

Optional extension:
Show learners that 'your' and 'you're' /jɔː/ and 'by', 'bye' and 'buy' /baɪ/ also sound exactly the same.

G Do the animal project!

O Learners choose an animal from this unit. Give them magazines with pictures of animals to cut out, or ask them to draw their chosen animal and look in books or on the internet for information about it. You might like to ask learners questions about their animal. For example:
Where does this animal live? Does it live in trees, in caves, in the sea?
What does it look like? What colour is it? Is it big, small, fat, thin?
What kind of animal is it? Is it strange, funny, beautiful, ugly?
What does it eat? Does it eat meat, leaves, fruit, fish?
How does it move? Has it got legs? Can it fly? Can it live under the water?
Which animals is it afraid/frightened of?

O Learners could then make a poster about each of their animals, using their pictures and their answers to the questions. Learners could add their posters to their project file. Alternatively, display the posters on the classroom walls if possible.

4 Your hair looks great!

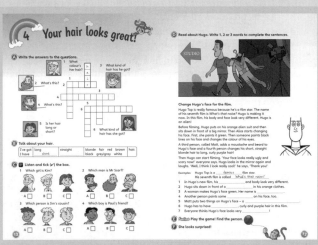

Not in YLE wordlists: *suit*

Equipment needed

- Movers Audio 4C.
- 20 small squares of blank paper or card for each pair of learners. See E.
- Copies of photocopiable page 116 for each pair of learners. See F.

A Write the answers to the questions.

- Learners look at the crossword. Say: *All the answers are about people's hair.* If necessary, teach/revise words that learners will need for their answers. Use the pictures to help you.
- Learners fill in the answers by answering the questions about each picture. Ask different learners to spell one of the answers. Write the answers on the board.

> **Check answers:**
> **1** blonde **2** beard **3** curly **4** moustache **5** short **6** straight

B Talk about your hair.

- Point to the first box in the table. Say: *When we talk about our hair, we can start our sentence with 'I've got' or 'I have'.*
- Point to the second box in the table.
  Say: *When we want to talk about our hair we can say 'it's long' or … ?* (short) *first.*
  Point to 'short' on the line under 'long'.
  Point to a learner in the class who has short hair.
  Ask: *Is (Paolo)'s hair long?* (No, it's short.)
  Point to a learner with long hair. Ask: *Is (Elisa)'s hair long?* (Yes, it is.)
- Point to the line under 'straight' in the third box.
  Say: *After long or short, we can say hair is straight or … ?* (curly)
  Learners write *curly* on the line.
- Point to the fourth box. Say: *These are all … ?* (colours) Point to your own hair and say: *We can have red, brown, black, grey or white … ?* (hair)
  Note:
  1. Show learners that 'grey' and 'gray' are different spellings of the same colour. 'Gray' is used in American English.
  2. Point out that 'blonde' can be spelt with or without its final 'e'.
  3. Explain that 'fair' is another way of describing hair that's blonde or very light brown.
- Point to the girl in picture 1 in **A**. Say: *She's got long, straight blonde hair. Her hair is long, straight and blonde.*
  Point out the words in the boxes in **B** so learners can see the correct order (length/type of hair/colour): *long, straight blonde hair.*

- Learners work in pairs. They write a sentence about each of the other pictures in **A** in their notebooks.
- Ask different learners to read out one of their sentences.
- Learners circle one word from each box in the table that describes their own hair. Ask different learners to read out their completed sentence. For example: *I've got short, curly, black hair.*
  Optional extension:
  Explain in learners' own language that they are going to imagine a new friend. Tell them they are going to do this with their eyes closed. Say you are going to ask questions about their new friend but they shouldn't answer your questions out loud. They should just 'see' the answers in their imagined picture of their new friend.
- Say slowly (pausing for about five seconds after each question for learners to imagine the answers):
  Close your eyes. You are not in this classroom now. Where are you?
  You're looking at your new friend. Is your new friend a boy or a girl?
  Look at your new friend's face. Is your new friend happy? Sad? Tired?
  What's your new friend's hair like? Is it long? Short? Black? Fair?
  Listen! What is your new friend saying to you?
  Open your eyes now.
- Divide learners into groups of 3–4. Say: *Talk about your new friends.* Learners take turns to tell others in the group about their imagined new friend. Ask one or two confident learners to tell the whole class about their imagined new friend.

C ▶ Listen and tick the box.

- Learners look at the first group of three pictures. Ask them to describe each picture and to notice the differences between them.
  Suggestions:
  A A girl with long, blonde (fair) straight hair.
  B A girl with short, blonde (fair) curly hair.
  C A girl with short, brown straight hair.
- Play the audio. Listen to 1. Ask: *Which girl is Kim?* (C) Learners put a tick in box 1C.
  Write on the board: *Kim is the girl with … .*
  Ask learners to finish the sentence about Kim. (*short, brown, straight hair*)
- Learners listen to the other conversations and put a tick in the correct boxes. Play the audio a second time to allow learners to complete and check their answers.

> **Check answers:**
> **2** C **3** B **4** B

- Write three more sentence heads on the board for 2, 3 and 4:
  2 *Mr Scarf is the man with …*
  3 *Jim's cousin has …*
  4 *Paul's friend is the boy with …*
  Learners complete the sentences about the people in the pictures they ticked in **C**.

> **Check answers:**
> **2** fair hair, a moustache and glasses **3** curly fair/blond hair
> **4** short black hair and glasses

Audioscript

Listen and tick the box.

One	*Which girl is Kim?*
Girl:	Look, Dad! Kim's playing football with the boys!
Man:	Is she the girl with long blonde hair?
Girl:	No, Kim's got brown hair and it's short, not long.
Man:	Oh yes, I see her. Wow! She's good!

Two	*Which man is Mr Scarf?*
Woman:	Excuse me. Is that Mr Scarf? The man with the beard?
Boy:	Mr Scarf hasn't got a beard, but he's got a moustache.
Woman:	Oh. Is that him, the man with fair hair?
Boy:	Yes, that's right.
Three	*Which person is Jim's cousin?*
Man:	Is that your brother, Jim? The boy who's standing next to your mum?
Boy:	Yes, Mr Cook. My hair is straight, but he's got curly brown hair.
Man:	And who's the boy with curly fair hair?
Boy:	That's my cousin. His name's John.
Four	*Which boy is Paul's friend?*
Woman:	That's a good drawing, Paul. Is this you? The boy with the curly brown hair?
Boy:	Yes, Miss Best. And my friend Nick is in my drawing too, but his hair is straight.
Woman:	The boy who's wearing glasses? Is that him?
Boy:	That's right!

D Read about Hugo. Write 1, 2 or 3 words to complete the sentences.

> **Movers tip**
>
> In Reading and Writing Part 5, structures found in the text and in the question sentences may be different. However, the words that candidates need to complete the sentences must be copied from the text. Candidates should not change these words in any way.

In Reading and Writing Part 5, there are three pictures (not two as here). However, this text does provide good practice for finding one, two or three words to complete each sentence about Hugo's day.

○ Ask: *Do you like going to the cinema? Do you know the names of any film stars? Who is your favourite film star? What does s/he look like? Why do you like them?*
Teach/revise: 'be called'.
Point to the text in **D** and say: *This is about a person. He's a film star and he's called Hugo Top.*
Point to the line drawing in **D** and say: *This is Hugo Top's face.* Ask questions about Hugo. Learners guess answers.
How old is Hugo Top? (about 30?)
Where does Hugo live? (in Hollywood?)

○ Say: *You can do some drawing on Hugo Top's face and head but first, let's read about him.*

○ Read the first two sentences: *Hugo Top is really famous because he's a film star. The name of his seventh film is 'What's that noise?'* Learners look at the two examples. Ask: *How many words are there in the first answer?* (1) *How many words are there in the second answer?* (3) *How many words can you write in the other answers?* (1, 2 or 3)

○ Learners work in pairs. They read the text and questions and find words to complete sentences 1–7.

> **Check answers:**
> **1** face **2** (big) mirror **3** Alice **4** (black) lines
> **5** moustache and beard **6** long **7** ugly (and scary)

○ Teach/revise: 'scary' or 'frightening'.
Ask: *What kind of film is 'What's that noise?' A funny film? A sad film? A happy film? A scary/frightening film?* Learners make up their own minds.

Change Hugo's face for the film.

○ Say: *People change Hugo's face. When he comes to work, he has short, blonde hair. He hasn't got a moustache or a … ?* (beard). *At the end of the story, how is his face different?* Ask different learners for answers. (His face is green. He's got black lines on his face. His eyes are a different colour. He's got a moustache and a beard. He's got long, purple hair.)

○ Learners look at the picture of Hugo's face. Say: *How does Hugo look in 'What's that noise?' Draw and colour his face.*
Learners draw and colour Hugo's face and hair. They can choose any colour for his eyes.

○ Learners show each other their pictures.

E Play the game! Find the person.

○ Learners work in pairs. Check that each pair has about 20 small squares of paper or card.
Demonstrate the game. Tell one learner to choose one of the pictures of people in **A** or **C** in this unit. The learner does not say which person they choose!

○ For example: Learner A chooses picture 4C.
Ask: *Is it a man or boy?* (yes)
Take six squares of paper and cover the pictures of the three girls in **A** and the three girls in **C**. Each pair of learners also covers these pictures.
Ask: *Has he got glasses?* (no)
Everyone puts squares over pictures 2C and 4B in **C**.
Ask: *Has he got a beard?* (no)
Everyone covers picture 2 in **A** and picture 2B in **C**.
Ask: *Has he got curly hair?* (yes)
Everyone covers the boys and men with straight hair. (picture 4 in **A** and pictures 2A, 3C and 4A in **C**)
Picture 3 in **A**, and pictures 3A, 3B, 4C in **C** are still not covered, so the next question needs to be about colour.
Ask: *Has he got brown hair?* (yes)
Everyone covers picture 3 in **A** and picture 3B in **C**.
We can see pictures 3A and 4C in **C**. Point to the boy's T-shirt in each picture. Ask: *Has he got a blue T-shirt?* (yes) Cover picture 3A.
Now, the only picture we can see is 4C – the right answer!

○ Play the game once with the whole class. One pair of learners chooses a picture but they don't say which picture. The other learners ask *yes/no* questions to discover which picture the pair chose.

○ Learners then play the game in groups of four. One pair chooses the picture, the other pair asks questions.

F She looks surprised!

○ Revise the following words: happy, sad, pretty, ugly, tired, surprised, angry, old, young.

○ Changing your expression a few times, ask: *How do I look? Do I look happy? Surprised? Tired?* Learners answer: *Yes, you look happy / surprised / tired.*

○ Give each pair of learners the photocopy of page 116.
Pairs decide how each person looks and write:
She/He looks + adjectives under the nine different faces.
Pairs of learners form groups of 4. Groups spread their 18 cards face down on a desk or table. One learner starts by turning over two cards. If they show the same person and the same characteristic, the learner says for example: *He looks old.* The learner can then keep the two cards and turn over two more cards. If the cards are not the same, the learner puts them back in the same place and the next learner turns over two cards. The winner is the learner with the most cards.
Alternatively, learners could find different faces in newspapers, magazines or comics, cut them out and stick them on to card. They could do this for homework and bring their pictures and sentences to the next class.

5 The woman in the red dress

Pronunciation practice Can /kən/ and can't /kɑːnt/. See D.

Equipment needed

o Movers Audio 5F.

o A baseball cap. See A.

A Find the words for the pictures and write them on the lines.

o Say: *Look at the small pictures. What are these? Are they things we can wear?* (yes)

o Ask: *Am I wearing a baseball cap?* (no) Take the baseball cap you've brought to the class and, as you put it on your head, describe the action. Say: *I'm putting on my baseball cap.* Ask: *Am I wearing a baseball cap now?* (yes) You may also wish to teach/revise 'take off'. Tell learners that 'caps' and 'baseball caps' are the same shape and note that in the test, learners might read or hear 'cap' or 'baseball cap' to mean the same thing.

o Say: *Find eight words in the box for the pictures. Draw circles round them and then write the words under their pictures.*

> **Check answers:**
> **2** sweater **3** coat **4** shirt **5** socks **6** swimsuit
> **7** shorts **8** boots

o Ask different learners questions about their clothes:
Who's wearing a shirt today?
Who's wearing a sweater?
Are you wearing socks?
What colour are your socks?
Have you got a coat with you today?
What are your favourite clothes?

B Find the words in the box for five more things people wear.

o Teach/revise: 'a pair of' to describe trousers, jeans, socks, shoes and glasses. Explain that 'a pair' means 'two' and that in English, we think about wearing trousers and jeans on two legs, socks and shoes on two feet and glasses on two eyes!
Learners find and circle five more clothes words in the box in **A** and write an answer in each of the five boxes.

> **Check answers:**
> (a pair of) trousers, skirt, (a pair of) glasses, (baseball) cap, dress

C Choose the correct words from A or B. Write them on the lines.

o Read out the first sentence: *In cold weather, you can wear this round your neck.* Ask: *What do you wear round your neck in cold weather?* (a scarf) Point to 'scarf' on the line in 1.
Ask: *What colour is the scarf in A?* (red and white)

o Learners read the other sentences and write the answers.

> **Check answers:**
> **2** coat **3** socks **4** swimsuit **5** glasses

D Say the words.

o Learners look again at the sentences in **C**. Ask: *Is the word 'can' here?* (yes) *How many 'can's' can you see?* (five).

o Say: *I can read and I can write too!* Carefully pronounce the 'can' here as /kən/.

o Write: *I can read. I can write.* on the board. Rub out or draw a line through the 'a's in both the 'can's. Explain that when we follow 'can' by another verb, we say 'can' more quickly. We lose the sound of its middle letter.

o Practise /kən/ further by asking learners in turn to tell you something that they can do. For example: *I can ride a bike! I can make cakes!*

o Write (or draw) on the board a scarf and a hat. Point to the scarf and say: *You can wear this round your neck.* Point to the hat and say: *You can't wear this round your neck.* Carefully stress 'can't' in this sentence and pronounce it /kɑːnt/.

o Ask the class: *Can you swim? Is your answer 'yes'? Then stand up.*
Point to the 'Yes, I can swim!' answer in the book. Ask again: *Can you swim?*
Learners answer *Yes, I can swim!* in chorus.
Ask the class: *Can you fly? Is your answer 'no'? Then stand up.*
Point to the 'No, I can't fly!' answer in the book. Ask again: *Can you fly?*
Learners answer *No, I can't fly!* in chorus.

o Practise /kɑːnt/ further by asking learners in turn to tell you something else that they can't do. For example: *I can't drive a car! I can't stand on my head!*
Note: This is the British received pronunciation of 'can't' and of the weak form of 'can'.

E Write the words from A and B in the table.

o Write the three headings on the board:
top half   bottom half   top and bottom half
Point to the picture of the scarf in **A**. Ask: *Where do I wear a scarf? On my feet?* (no!) *Round my neck?* (yes!) Write *scarf* under 'top half'.

o Point to the picture of the boots in **A**. Ask: *Where do we wear boots, on the top or bottom half of our body?* (bottom) Write *boots* under 'bottom half'.

o Point to the picture of the coat in **A**. Ask: *Where do we wear a coat? On the top and bottom of our body.* Write *coat* under 'top and bottom half'.

o Learners then write the other words from **A** and **B** in the boxes in **E**. Check answers by asking different learners to come to the board and write words under 'top half', 'bottom half' or 'top and bottom half'.

> **Check answers:**
> **top half:** glasses, (baseball) cap, sweater, shirt
> **bottom half:** boots, skirt, trousers, shorts
> **top and bottom half:** dress, swimsuit

o Now point to one of the helmets in the picture in **F** and ask: *What's this?* (a helmet) *Where do I wear a helmet? On my head or on my feet?* (head) Learners write helmet in the box under 'top half'.

F ▶ Listen and draw lines.   Listening Part **1**

○ Learners look at the picture in **F** and point to the people as you describe them.

1 *The man with a beard.*
2 *The boy who's wearing a pair of glasses.*
3 *The girls who are wearing helmets.*
4 *The girl in the purple skirt and pink T-shirt.*

○ Ask: *Where's the woman in the red dress?* Learners point at the mother on the seat. Ask: *What's she sitting on?* (a seat)

Teach/revise the difference between 'a seat' and 'a chair'.

At this level, you could say we use the word 'seat' to describe something we sit on in a car, bus, train, plane and places like schools, shops or cinemas. 'Seats' are for anyone to sit on outside their homes. 'A chair' is something we sit on at home.

> **Movers tip**
> In Listening Part 1, there may be eight or nine people in the picture and seven names. Candidates only hear six names, which identify six of the people, so one name is not used and not all of the people will be named.

○ Learners read out the seven names. Help learners with pronunciation if necessary. Ask: *Which names are for boys or men?* (Fred, Mark, Tom and Peter) *And which names are for girls or women?* (Anna, Lucy and Jane)

○ Point to the name *Peter* and the red line.

Say: *Can you see this boy? His name's Peter. What's he wearing?* (a white T-shirt and shoes, red shorts and a pair of glasses)

Guess! Which person is Anna / Fred / Mark, (etc)?

Learners guess the names of the people in the picture.

○ Say: *Listen to a boy and a woman. They're talking about the people in the picture.* Play the example.

○ Learners listen to the rest of the audio and draw lines between five more names and five other people in the picture.

> **Check answers:**
> Lines should be drawn between:
> 1 Anna and small girl sitting down eating ice cream.
> 2 Mark and monster.
> 3 Tom and man with beard.
> 4 Jane and girl skating with long red hair.
> 5 Lucy and girl on bike with pink skirt.

Audioscript

Look at the picture. Listen and look. There is one example.
Boy: Hi, Grandma. Look at this picture in my story book!
Woman: Wow! Who are all these people?
Boy: Well, the kid who's wearing glasses is called Peter.
Woman: I like his white T-shirt.
Boy: Me too! He's really good at football!
Can you see the line? This is an example. Now you listen and draw lines.

One
Woman: Who's that girl? The one who's eating an ice cream?
Boy: The small girl on the green seat?
Woman: That's right. She looks happy!
Boy: Well it's her birthday today! Her name's Anna. She's two now!

Two
Boy: And there's Mark!
Woman: Where?
Boy: There! He's got three eyes and four feet!
Woman: What? Oh do you mean the monster?
Boy: That's right. He looks like an alien!
Woman: Yes, he does!

Three
Woman: What about that man? The one with the beard.
Boy: He's one of the boys' grandfathers. He's watching the game.
Woman: And his name?
Boy: He's called Tom. Everyone in the book likes him because he tells silly stories. He's really funny.

Four
Boy: Two of the girls are roller skating. Can you see them?
Woman: Where? Oh yes. They look really cool. Are they sisters?
Boy: No. One of them is called Jane.
Woman: Which one?
Boy: The one in the white trousers. She's got long red hair. Look!

Five
Boy: And look at Lucy!
Woman: The girl on the bike?
Boy: Yes. The one with black hair.
Woman: And the pretty pink skirt?
Boy: Yes, Grandma. That's right.

G Look and read and write.

○ Learners look at the picture in **F**.

Say: *Listen to some sentences about this picture. When you think the answer is 'yes', sit down. When you think the answer is 'no', stand up!*

○ Say: *This is a picture of a beach.* (no – learners stand up)
You can see nine people in this picture. (yes – learners sit down)
An old man is in the park. (yes – learners continue to sit)
It's a very cold day. (no – learners stand up)
Two people are sitting on the seat. (yes – learners sit down)
The monster's body is blue. (no – learners stand up)
Only one girl is wearing roller skates. (no – learners continue to stand) Say: *Sit down again now!*

○ Learners read the two examples then sentences 1 and 2 and questions 3 and 4 and write words on the lines. Remind learners they can write between one and five words.

> **Check answers:**
> (Suggestions) **1** the (boys' new) football   **2** (white) beard
> **3** (It's) green   **4** (They're) wearing helmets

> **Movers tip**
> In Reading and Writing Part 6, candidates may get higher marks if they write compound sentences like the ones in the suggested answers for 5 and 6 here.

○ For a test practice, learners write two sentences about the picture.
If your learners need support before writing sentences, point to sentence 1 and say: *This sentence is about the monster/alien.*
Point to sentence 2 and say: *This sentence is about …?* (the old man)
Point to the baby and ask learners to say a sentence about the baby.
Suggestions: The baby's happy. The baby's got an ice cream.

○ Write on the board: *The baby's happy. The baby's got an ice cream.*
Say: *The baby's happy. Why?* (because she's got an ice cream)
Write on the board: *The baby's happy because she's got an ice cream.*
Point to the sentences on the board: *The baby's happy. The baby's got an ice cream.* and say: *These sentences are good.*
Point to the compound sentence and say: *This sentence is great! I like it! It tells me two things about the baby!*
Write on the board: *because   and*

○ Ask learners to tell you sentences about other people in the picture using 'because' or 'and'.
Suggestions:
The monster is really happy **because** it loves playing football.
The mother is sitting under the tree **because** it's a sunny day.
The boy in the red shorts is happy **because** he likes kicking the ball.
Two boys are playing football **and** they're very good at this sport.
Two girls are roller skating **and** one of them has got an ice cream.
Two girls are riding their bikes **and** they are wearing helmets.

25

6   My neck, my shoulders

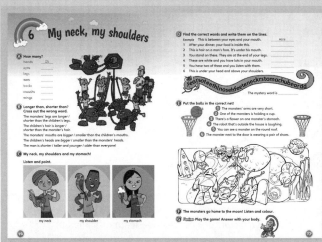

Flyers words: *wing, touch*

Not in YLE wordlists: *mystery*

Equipment needed

o   Colouring pencils or pens. See B and F.

Ⓐ How many?

o   Write on the board: *play*

Add *'er'* to the end of 'play' and say: *A player is a person who plays something.*

A tennis player plays …? (tennis) *A basketball player plays …?* (basketball)

Ask: *How many basketball players can you see in the picture?* (ten: five children and five monsters)

Learners look at the picture. Ask:

What can you see in the picture? (five monsters, seven children [four girls, three boys], a man)

What game are they playing? (basketball)

What colour are the monsters' bodies? (purple)

Are the monsters fat or thin? (fat)

What colour are the players' T-shirts? (yellow)

Are all the players happy? (no)

Can the children catch the ball? (no)

How many hands can you see? (26) Point to '26' on the line next to *hands*.

Are the monsters good at playing basketball? (yes)

o   Learners work in pairs. They look at the picture and the other body words and count, then write, how many they can see.

> **Check answers:**
> eyes 31   legs 26   ears 16   backs 13   mouths 13   wings 10

Ⓑ Longer than, shorter than? Cross out the wrong word.

o   Teach/revise '-er' comparative adjectives. Write on the board: *eye, monster, basketball.* Ask: *Which is a short word? It's only got three letters.* (eye)

Which is a really long word? (basketball)

How many letters are there in 'basketball'? (ten)

How many letters are there in 'monster'? (seven)

Point to 'monster' and then 'eye' on the board. Say: *Look! This word is longer than this word.*

Point to 'basketball' and then 'monster'. Say: *Look! This word is longer than this word.*

o   Point to a learner whose hair is longer than yours and then point to your hair. Say:

(Tania)'s hair is longer than my hair.

Point to a learner whose hair is shorter than yours. Say: *But (Carl)'s hair is shorter than my hair.*

o   Ask one learner: *How old are you, (Eva)?* Learner replies. Ask the class: *Is Eva older or younger than I am?* (younger)

Ask two learners of different heights to come to the front of the class. Ask: *Who's taller? Is (Juan) taller than (Bora)?* Learners answer.

Show learners two classroom objects of very different sizes, for example a book and a rubber. Ask: *Which is bigger? Is the book bigger or smaller than the rubber?* (It's bigger.)

o   Write these six comparatives on the board: *longer, shorter, older, younger, bigger, smaller.* Point and ask: *Which two letters are at the end of longer, shorter, older, taller, bigger and smaller?* ('er') Leave these words on the board.

o   Learners work in pairs. Say: *Look at the picture in A and the sentences in B. Cross out the wrong word in each sentence.*

o   Check answers by asking different pairs to read out one sentence.

> **Check answers:**
> legs are shorter, hair is longer, mouths are bigger, heads are smaller, man is taller and older

o   Add *fatter, thinner, happier,* and *sadder* to the board. Give each learner a sheet of paper and make sure they have their colouring pencils or pens. Say: *Now you draw a monster or an alien. You choose. Draw a child too.* Learners do their drawings. Give them plenty of time for this and walk around offering help if necessary. These five simple monster drawings may give you some extra ideas.

o   When learners have finished their drawings, they talk together and compare drawings in pairs. For example:

Learner 1:   *My monster's fatter than your monster.*

Learner 2:   *My child is taller than your child.*

Learner 1:   *My monster's tail is longer than your monster's tail.*

Learner 2:   *My child's feet are shorter than your child's feet.*

Learner 1:   *My monster's happier than your monster.*

o   Ask 2–3 pairs to show their different drawings and to talk about them to everyone else in the class.

C My neck, my shoulders and my stomach!

o   Learners look at the pictures. Teach/revise: 'neck', 'shoulder' and 'stomach'.
o   Learners draw lines from the words to the girl's neck, the boy's shoulder and the girl's stomach.
o   Say: *Show me! Where's your neck?* (Learners point to their necks.) *And where are your shoulders?* (Learners point to their shoulders.) *And your stomach?* (Learners point to their stomachs.)
o   Teach/revise: 'head', 'teeth', 'beard', 'neck', 'moustache', 'feet'.
o   Tell learners to follow your instructions. Read out the following:
    *Put one hand on your **stomach**.*
    *Now put one hand on your **head**.*
    *Now point to your **teeth**.*
    *Now draw a **beard** on your face!* (Learners use a finger as an imaginary pencil.)
    *Now point to your **neck**.*
    *Now draw a **moustache** under your nose.* (Learners use a finger as an imaginary pencil.)
    *Now make a loud noise with your **feet**!*
    *Now put both your hands on your **shoulders**.*

D Find the correct words and write them on the lines.

> **Movers tip**
>
> In Reading and Writing Part 1, candidates need to understand definitions and match them with six nouns. Grammatical clues (for example *this, these, it* or *they*) can help them choose the correct form. Nouns are usually singular or uncountable but some might be plural.

o   Say: *Find seven face or body words in the snake.* Learners colour each part of the snake that shows a face or body word a different colour.
o   The eight letters that are at the start and end of the snake and in between each word make up another body word. Ask: *What are the eight letters?* (s o l h e r u d) *What face or body word can these letters make?* (shoulder) Learners write *shoulder* to complete the mystery word sentence.
o   In pairs, learners read the definitions and copy the right words from the word snake onto the lines.

> **Check answers:**
> **1** stomach   **2** beard   **3** feet   **4** teeth   **5** ears   **6** neck

E Put the balls in the correct net!

o   Use the pictures either side of the sentences to teach/revise 'net'. Say: *A ball's falling into one net. What colour is that net?* (green)
o   Say: *Look at the picture of the monsters on the moon. Look at the sentences, too.* Ask: *How many sentences are there?* (six) Say: *Some sentences about the picture are wrong! Put their numbers in the red net. Some sentences are right. Put their numbers in the green net.*
o   Working in pairs or on their own, learners draw numbered circles 1–6 in the correct nets.

> **Check answers:**
> **red net**: wrong answers 1, 3, 4   **green net**: right answers 2, 5, 6

F The monsters go home to the moon! Listen and colour.

o   Say: *Find your coloured pencils now. Listen and colour different parts of the picture.*
o   Read each instruction slowly, pausing for about 15 seconds between each instruction to allow learners time to colour. Say:
    Can you see the stars? Colour the smaller star please. Make it orange.
    There's a plant outside the monsters' home. Its leaves are long and thin. Colour that plant blue.
    The monster has got the basketball cup in its hand. Make the cup red.
    Can you see the small monster? It's looking out of the window. Colour its face pink.
    And now colour the robot's legs. Colour the robot's legs yellow.
o   In pairs, learners compare their pictures.

> **Check answers:**
> small star – orange, thin-leaved plant – blue, cup – red, face in window – pink, robot's legs – yellow

o   Learners colour the rest of the picture.
    Ask: *Is the robot happy?* (no)
    Why? (He has to clean the cup / He wanted the children to win, etc.)

G Play the game! Answer with your body.

o   Show learners how to say *yes* and *no* with different parts of their body. Say:
    *For **yes**, wave both hands above your head.*
    *For **no**, move your shoulders up and down.*
    Demonstrate these movements as you give the instructions.
o   Practise this in class prompting learners with *yes* or *no* until everyone is doing this correctly.
o   Ask learners three or four questions (see below). Learners answer with their bodies.
o   Repeat using different body answers. Say:
    *For **yes**, smile and show me your teeth. For **no**, cross your arms in front of your body.*
    Suggested questions:
    Do you like cheese?
    Can you ride a bike?
    Do you live in an apartment?
    Do you clean your teeth every day?
    Have you got a robot at home?
    Do you like painting?
    Are you wearing shoes?
    Is today Wednesday?
    Are your hands longer than your back?
    Are your feet shorter than your hands?
    Is your nose thinner than your neck?
    Are your legs fatter than your arms?
    Is this classroom bigger than your bedroom?
    Is our school smaller than your home?
    Are you happier now because it's the end of the lesson?
o   Learners work in pairs and write three more questions. Pairs work with pairs asking questions and answering with their bodies in the same way.

7 What's the weather like?

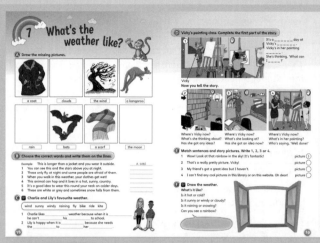

Equipment needed

- Pictures of different types of weather (the sun, snow, rain, wind, clouds, a rainbow). See A.
- Movers Audio 7C and 7F.
- Colouring pens or pencils. See A.

A Draw the missing pictures.

- Before learners look at **A**, show learners pictures of different types of weather.

  Show a picture of the sun in a sunny landscape first. You could use the picture on page 96). Ask:

  What can you see in this picture? (the sun)

  What's the weather like? (It's sunny.)

  Show pictures of snow, rain, wind and clouds and ask:

  What can you see in this picture? What's the weather like?

  Write the nouns and sentences on the board.

snow	It's snowing.
rain	It's raining.
wind	It's windy.
clouds	It's cloudy.

  Note: You could use the weather pictures in Unit 8 if you can't find alternative pictures.

- Say: *When we talk about the weather and there's rain or snow, we say 'It's raining.' or 'It's snowing.'*

  When we talk about the sun, clouds or wind, we can say 'It's sunny.' 'It's cloudy.' or 'It's windy.'

  Write *sun/sunny cloud/cloudy wind/windy* on the board, pointing to the final 'y' and to the double 'n' in 'sunny'.

- Show learners a picture of a rainbow (or draw one on the board). Ask: *What's this?* (a rainbow) Say: *Can you see the word 'rain' in 'rainbow'? We see a rainbow at the end of the rain. When we talk about a rainbow, we can say 'There's a rainbow!'*

- Teach/revise: 'moon'. Say: *In the day we see the sun. At night we see … ?* (the moon). *What colour is the moon?* (white) Draw a circle in the air and ask: *Is the moon sometimes round?* (yes) *Can we always see the moon at night? Can we always see the sun in the day?* (no) Say: *We can't we see the moon or the sun when it's very … ?* (cloudy)

- Write on the board: *yellow animals   pink clothes   blue weather*
  Learners work in pairs. Say: *Look at the pictures and words in A.*
  Find the animal words. Colour the animal words yellow.
  Find the clothes words. Colour the clothes words pink.
  Find the weather words. Colour the weather words blue.

- Learners colour the word boxes yellow, pink or blue. When pairs have finished, ask: *How many animal words are there?* (two) *What are they?* (a kangaroo, bats)

There are some clothes here too. Are there three? (no) *Two?* (yes)
What are they? (a coat, a scarf)

And there are some weather words. How many can you see? (four)
What are they? (clouds, the wind, rain, the moon).

Three of the words don't have any pictures. What must we see in these pictures? (clouds, rain, the moon).

- Learners draw the three missing pictures.

B Choose the correct words and write them on the lines.

Reading & Writing Part 1

> **Movers tip**
>
> In Reading and Writing Part 1, candidates have to match pictures of nouns with their definitions. Point out that answers usually come from three different topic sets. They should know that one of the pictures is not needed for one of the answers.

- Ask: *How many pictures are there in A?* (eight) *How many questions are there in B?* (7) Say: *Find and write the answers to the questions in B. All the words you need are under the pictures in A.*

  > **Check answers:**
  > **1** the moon   **2** bats   **3** rain   **4** a kangaroo   **5** a scarf   **6** clouds

- Say: *Look at the example. Which words help us find this answer?* (longer jacket, wear) In pairs, learners choose and circle words which helped them find answers 1–6. Pairs take it in turns to tell the class which words they've circled.

  Suggestions:
  1 stars, night   **2** fly, night, afraid   **3** weather, wet
  4 animal, hop, hot, sunny   **5** wear, round, neck, colder days
  6 white, grey, snow falls

- Write on the board: *You can sometimes see this on the _ _ _ of the water on really _ _ _ _ days.* ....

  Tell learners to look at page 111. Point to the boy who's ice skating in the second picture of the bottom row. Ask: *What's this boy doing?* (ice skating / skating)

  Point to the ice in the picture and ask: *What's this?* (ice) *Where's the ice? On the …?* (top of the water). *Do you see ice on the top of water on very hot days?* (no) *You can sometimes see ice on the top of water on really…?* (cold days)

  Ask a learner to come to the board and write the words 'top' and 'cold' in the sentence. Ask another learner to come to the board and write 'ice' on the answer line.

C ▶ Charlie and Lily's favourite weather.

- Point to the pictures of the children. Say: *This is Charlie and this is Lily.* Point to the first four words in the box and ask: *What kind of weather does Charlie like? Listen to Charlie now.*

- Play the first part of the audio. Learners listen and answer the question. (Charlie likes sunny weather.)

  Learners write 'sunny' on the first line in 1 and cross out the word 'sunny' in the box.

- Ask: *Why does Charlie like sunny weather?*

  Play the audio again. Learners listen and answer. (Because he can't ride his bike to school when it's raining.) Learners write *raining, ride* and *bike* on the three lines in 1. They cross out these words in the box.

- Continue in the same way for Lily. Check Lily's answers by asking different learners to spell the missing words: windy, wind, fly, and kite.

- Write on the board, leaving gaps as shown:
  We like .... weather because we love ....
  Point at the sentence on the board and say: *I like cloudy, wet weather because I love walking in the rain. How about you?*

Learners work in pairs to complete their own sentence.

For example: *We like sunny weather because we love going to the beach. We like windy weather because we love sailing on the sea.*

Audioscript

One

Boy:	Oh no! It's raining. I don't like the rain!
Woman:	Really? Why, Charlie?
Boy:	Because I can't ride my bike to school when it's raining.
Woman:	Oh! Do you like sunny weather then?
Boy:	Yes! I love sunny weather!

Two

Man:	Are you happy today, Lily?
Girl:	Yes. I'm happy because it's windy today.
Man:	Why do you like windy weather?
Girl:	Because I need the wind to fly my kite!

D Vicky's painting class. Complete the first part of the story.

Speaking Part 2

o Point to the girl with the blank painting in the first picture.

Say: *This is Vicky. How old is she? Who thinks she's 10? Or is she 11?* Learners choose.

o Learners look at the first part of the story. In pairs, they guess what the missing words are and write them on the lines in pencil. Tell learners to make sure their answers have the correct number of letters in them. Don't check the answers yet.

> **Movers tip**
>
> In Speaking Part 2, candidates look at pictures and tell a story. If they can talk about the pictures by answering questions like *Where is s/he now? What's s/he doing now? What can s/he see now?* they will give good descriptions of each picture and tell a good story.

o Point to the story pictures. Say: *These pictures show a story. It's called 'Vicky's painting class'. Just look at the pictures first.*

o Point to the first picture again and read out the first part of the story slowly and clearly: *It's a cloudy day at Vicky's school. Vicky's in her painting class. She's thinking, 'What can I draw?'* Learners check their guessed answers against the words they've heard. Ask: *Who got all four words right? Anyone?* Repeat the first part of the story again so learners can correct their words if they want to.

Now you tell the story.

o Ask different learners to answer the questions for pictures 2, 3 and 4. Write their story on the board.

Suggestion: *Vicky's in the library now. She's thinking about her picture but she hasn't got any ideas.*

Vicky's at home now. She's looking at a rainbow. Now she's got a good idea.

Vicky's in her classroom again. There's a rainbow in Vicky's picture. Her teacher's saying, 'Well done!'

Note: In the test, candidates only hear part of the story, and there are no written prompts or questions as there are under each of the pictures here. The examiner will ask questions if candidates can't think what to say. In this early test practice, seeing the kinds of questions the examiner might ask, will help learners think of their own answers.

E Match sentences and story pictures. Write 1, 2, 3 or 4.

o Point to and read the first sentence: *Wow! Look at that rainbow in the sky! It's fantastic!* Ask: *Which picture does this sentence go with?* (picture 3) Point to the circled 3 on the line after the word 'picture'. Ask: *Who says this?* (Vicky)

o Learners read the other sentences and write the correct picture number. Ask: *Who says sentence 2?* (the teacher) *Who says sentences 3 and 4?* (Vicky)

> **Check answers:**
> **2** 4   **3** 1   **4** 2

Optional extension:

If you would like to extend this story activity, learners could now add more details to the story working in small groups. Write prompts on the board to help them with ideas if necessary, for example: *walks home, talks to mum, has dinner, goes to bed, dreams about a rainbow, gets up, gets dressed, rides bike to school.* They could also add the direct speech from **E** and other direct speech if they want to.

o Groups could then write the completed story and tell their version to the rest of the class.

o Learners could then read out their conversations and/or role play the story!

F Draw the weather.

o Ask: *What's the weather like now?* Learners draw in the window what they can see from the classroom window and label their picture by writing an answer to the questions in the speech bubble. They can use words in the prompts to help them write their sentence.

Suggestion: It's cold, cloudy and it's raining.

Alternatively, they can imagine a weather scene that they can see from another window and label it differently.

Listen and draw. What's the weather like?

o Draw four small window frames on the board and number them 1, 2, 3 and 4. Check learners understand the meaning of 'first', 'second', 'third' and 'fourth'. Say: *Now you draw windows like these in your notebooks. Write the numbers too.*

o Learners copy the windows and numbers. Say: *Now listen and draw the weather!*

o Play the audio twice. Learners listen and draw the weather in each window. Learners show each other their weather windows. Check answers by asking four confident learners to come to the board and draw the weather in each window.

Audioscript

First window (sound of rain)

Oh dear! It's raining again! Look at all that rain!

Second window (sound of birds singing)

What a nice day. It's so sunny! Where are my sunglasses?

Third window

Bbbbrrr. It's really cold but the snow looks beautiful! Let's go outside and play in the snow now!

Fourth window (sound of strong wind)

It's windy and it's really cloudy today. There are lots and lots of big grey clouds above our school.

8 The hottest and coldest places

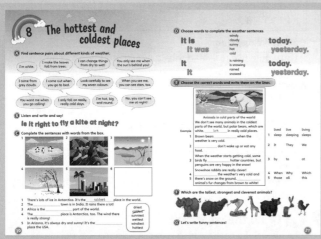

Pronunciation practice /aɪt/ in words ending in *-ite* or *-ight*. See B.

Flyers words: *fur, metres, a little* (adverb)

Not in YLE wordlists: *Africa, America, Antarctica, Arizona, India, snowshoe rabbit*

Equipment needed

o   Six different colouring pencils. See A, B and C.

o   A world map (optional) and three pictures of places that show increasingly sunny weather. See C.

Ⓐ Find sentence pairs about different kinds of weather.

o   Revise weather words. Draw simple pictures on the board of rain, snow, a rainbow, the wind (a tree blown sideways), the sun and the moon.

Point to each picture and ask different learners: *What's this?* Write their answers on the board under your pictures (*rain, snow, rainbow, wind, sun, moon*).

o   Point to the speech bubbles in **A** and ask: *How many speech bubbles are there?* (12) Say: *These sentences are about six different weather words.* Point to the first speech bubble (I'm white.) Look upwards and shiver to help mime 'snow' and point to the weather words on the board. Ask: *Which weather word is this?* (snow) Ask: *Can you find another 'snow' speech bubble?* Learners find *I only fall on really, really cold days.* Say: *Colour these two snow speech bubbles blue.* Learners colour in the two speech bubbles with a blue colouring pencil.

o   Learners work in pairs. Say: *Look at the weather words on the board. These can help you. Now find five more pairs and colour those in five different colours. You can choose your colours.* Learners find and colour the other weather pairs.

o   Check answers by asking different pairs to read out one same weather sentence pair. They could mime the weather type as they speak, for example by pretending to put up umbrellas to indicate 'rain'.

> **Check answers:**
>
> **Wind:** I make the leaves fall from trees. / You want me when you go sailing!
>
> **Rain:** I can change things from dry to wet! / I come from grey clouds.
>
> **Rainbow:** You only see me when the sun's behind you! / Look carefully to see my seven colours.
>
> **Moon:** I come out when you go to bed. / When you see me you can see stars too.
>
> **Sun:** I'm hot, big and round. / No, you can't see me at night!

o   Ask different learners: *Do you like looking at the moon at night? Do you like sunny days best? Do you enjoy being outside when it's windy?* Learners answer. If you feel they might enjoy this, ask learners to pretend they are trees in the wind for a moment. Learners stand and wave their arms and make the noise of the wind.

Ⓑ Listen and write and say!

o   Ask: *What can we do outside in windy weather? Something fun. We can … ?* (go sailing, fly a kite) *Do you fly kites sometimes?* (yes/no)

o   Say: *Draw a kite in your notebooks now.* Learners can find a picture of a kite to copy if necessary on page 52. Learners draw and colour their kites.

o   Tell learners they are going to write something under their kite pictures. Say slowly: *Listen and write.* Learners start writing. Say: *I have a kite. My kite is …* Give learners time to write the colour of their kite, then continue with the dictation. *I like flying my kite. I fly my kite in the day. I don't fly my kite at night! That's not right!* Repeat the whole text. Learners check their sentences and spelling.

o   Ask 2–3 learners to read out their sentences. Ask: *How do you spell write?* (mime writing) *And kite? And night? And right?* (draw a tick in the air) Write on the board: *write   kite   night   right*

Point to each and say the words clearly making sure their endings are all pronounced /aɪt/. Say: *These words look different, but they all sound the same at the end.* Under 'write' add *right* to the board. Point to each word in turn asking two different learners: *What's this word?* Make sure learners pronounce the words exactly the same.

o   Learners look at **B** in their books and chant in chorus or in a chain: *Is it right to fly a kite at night? No!* Check pronunciation of /aɪt/.

Ⓒ Complete the sentences with words from the box.

o   Teach/revise superlative adjective '-est' form.
Ask three tall learners to come to the front of the class.
Say: *(Andrés) is very tall.*
Point to the second tallest learner and say:
But (Javier) is taller than (Andrés).
Point to the tallest learner and say:
And (Pablo) is the tallest.
Write on the board: *tall taller the tallest*

o   Write (or draw) on the board: *chips   an apple   ice cream*
Point to the words/drawings in turn and say: *An apple is colder than chips! But an ice cream is colder than an apple!*
Write on the board: *This is the coldest.* Point in turn to the words/drawings and ask: *Is this the coldest?* Learners say *yes* when you point to the ice cream. Draw an arrow from 'This is the coldest.' to the ice cream.

o   Show learners your three 'sunny' pictures. Ask: *Which is the sunniest place?* Learners point to the sunniest picture. Write *sunny, sunnier, the sunniest* on the board showing learners that we replace 'y' with 'i' before we add '-est' to adjectives that end in 'y'. If you have more pictures, you could do the same with 'cloudy', 'cloudier', 'the cloudiest'.

o   Learners look at the pictures. Point to the first picture and ask: *What's the weather like here?* (It's cold and it's snowing.) Ask the same questions about the next three pictures. (2 It's raining. 3 It's hot and sunny. 4 It's cold and windy.) Point to picture 5 and say: *It's hot and sunny and it's never very wet here. It's always very … ?* (dry).

Complete the sentences.

o   Point to the words in the box. Ask: *How many words are there?* (six)
Point to sentences 1–5. Ask: *How many sentences are there?* (five)
Say: *These sentences are about different places in the world and their weather.*

o   Read sentence 1: *There's lots of ice in Antartica. It's the coldest place in the world.* Point to picture 1 and ask: *What's the weather like there?* (it's snowing and it's really cold) Say: *Antarctica is the coldest place in the world.* If you have a world map, show learners where Antarctica is.

○ In pairs, learners read sentences 2–5 and choose words from the box to write on the lines.

> **Check answers:**
> **2** wettest **3** hottest **4** windiest **5** driest

○ Ask learners to find (or show them) where India, Africa, America and Arizona are on your world map if possible.

○ Learners draw and colour a picture of their own in the sixth box, for example: a rainbow, the moon and stars, a sunny day in the mountains, and then write a weather word about it in their notebooks, for example: *Rainbows are beautiful. I love looking at the moon at night. This is a sunny day in the mountains.*

○ Say: *Look at sentences 4 and 5.*
Write on the board: *windy   dry   sunny* and show the rule. Remove 'y' and add '-ier' or '-iest'.

○ Write on the board: *difficult   the most difficult*
Point and say: *We don't add '-est' to long words. We say 'more' or 'the most'.*
Add *beautiful* to the board.
In their notebooks, learners write a sentence with 'the most beautiful', for example: *She's the most beautiful girl in the class. It's the most beautiful picture in the book.* Ask 2–3 learners to read out their sentences.

Ⓓ Choose words to complete the weather sentences.

○ Teach/revise 'am', 'is', 'are/was', 'were' and past simple '-ed'.
Mime an unhappy and then a happy face while saying: *Yesterday I was sad, but today I'm …?* (happy!)
Mime playing an enjoyable and then a boring game on a mobile while saying: *Today, my game is very funny. Yesterday, my game was really boring.*
Mime feeling hot and then cold while saying: *Today it's sunny and I'm too hot! But yesterday it snowed and I was really cold!*

○ Learners look at the choices in the weather sentences and decide how to complete them in their notebooks. Ask 2–3 learners to read out their sentences.
Note: They can tell the truth or invent answers!

Ⓔ Choose the correct words and write them on the lines.
Reading & Writing Part 4

> **Movers tip**
> Reading and Writing Part 4 tests understanding of grammatical structures. Make sure learners can accurately make verbs agree with subjects and use pronouns to refer back to names or nouns, for example. Both are likely to appear in this multiple choice task.

○ Ask: *What clothes do you wear when it's cold?* (a coat, a scarf, a sweater, a hat, trousers, etc)
Which animals live in cold places? (penguins, polar bears, etc)

○ Tell learners to read the text quickly and to tell you which animals are mentioned. (polar and brown bears, birds, penguins, snowshoe rabbits)
Write these animals on the board.

○ Learners look at the example. Ask: *Which is the correct word? Lived, live or living?* (live) Ask, explaining the answer if necessary: *Why isn't 'lived' the correct answer?* (Because we're talking about where bears live now, not about where they lived in the past.)

○ In pairs or on their own, learners read the rest of the text again and choose the correct word for each gap and write it on the line.

> **Check answers:**
> **1** sleep **2** They **3** to **4** When **5** this

○ Ask: *What do brown bears do in very cold weather?* (They sleep.)

Where do some birds fly to when the weather gets colder? (They fly to hotter countries.)
Do penguins enjoy living in cold countries? (Yes!)
Why do snowshoe rabbits change from brown to white when there's snow on the ground? What do you think? Is it because they get cold? (no) *Is it because white is their favourite colour?* (no) *Is it because they don't want bigger animals to see them?* (yes!)

Ⓕ Which are the tallest, strongest and cleverest animals?

○ Write on the board: *tall, strong, clever, quiet, funny, hungry, nice, dangerous, slow, frightening* and *beautiful.*
Learners tell you how to change these to the superlative forms.
For example: 'tall', 'strong', 'clever' and 'quiet': Put 'the' in front of the word. Put '-est' on the end of the word.
'funny' and 'hungry': Put 'the' in front of the word. Take away the 'y' and put 'i' then add '-est' to the word.
'nice': Put 'the' in front of the word. Only put '-st' at the end of the word because 'e' is already there!
Write on the board: *the tallest, the strongest, the cleverest, the quietest, the funniest, the hungriest, the nicest, the slowest*

○ Remind learners that it's too difficult to say dangerousest frighteningest and beautifulest. We put 'the most' in front of these words. Write on the board: *the most dangerous   the most frightening   the most beautiful*

○ Point to 'the tallest' and ask: *Which animal is the tallest in the world?* (a giraffe)

○ In pairs or small groups, learners decide which animal they think is described by the other words. They can choose an animal from the pictures or any other animal and then make a list of their answers.

○ Groups compare answers. If their answers are different they can say, for example: *I think a hippo is stronger than an elephant. I think a monkey is cleverer than a dolphin. I think a kitten is more beautiful than a puppy.*
Suggestions: strongest – elephant, cleverest – dolphin, quietest – fish, funniest – monkey, hungriest – lion, nicest – rabbit, slowest – snail, most dangerous – shark, most beautiful – puppy, most frightening – crocodile.

Ⓖ Let's write funny sentences!

○ Write on the board: .... *is hot.* Ask different learners to say things which are hot. For example: tea, my face, Dad's coffee, vegetable soup, the sun, our shower, the water in my bath.
Write on the board: *the sun, water in my bath, Dad's coffee.*

○ Write these sentences on the board, saying them as you write them:
The water in my bath is hot.
But Dad's coffee is hotter than the water in my bath!
And the sun is the hottest.

○ Ask learners to suggest things which are big. Write their suggestions on the board. Then as a class, write three funny sentences on the board using 'big', 'bigger', 'the biggest' this time.
Suggestion: *My eye is big. But an orange is bigger. And my football is the biggest!*

○ Write these adjectives on the board: *quiet black white small quick*
In pairs, learners choose one of the adjectives, think of three things which it can describe, and write three funny sentences in their notebooks.

○ Learners could copy their sentences onto big sheets of card or paper and then illustrate them. Display their work on classroom walls if possible.

9   Me and my family

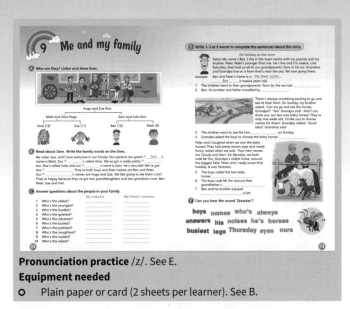

Equipment needed

o   Plain paper or card (2 sheets per learner). See B.

Ⓐ Who are they? Listen and draw lines.

o   Ask 2–3 different learners: *Have you got a grandmother? How old is she? Do you know?*

o   Point to the picture. Say: *Look at this family. It's this grandmother's birthday today!* Ask: *How many people are there in this picture?* (six)
What kind of pet can you see? (a cat)
Where's the cat? (behind the grandmother)
Five of the people in this family are holding things. What are they holding? (a camera, a plant, a box, a cake, a bag)

o   Point to the family tree. Say: *For six of the names, we can't see any faces. What are these six names?* (Hugo, Zoe, Matt, Alice, Sam, Julia). *Three of these people are men and three of these people are … ?* (women) *Listen! Someone's talking about them. Draw lines from the people who are outside the house to their names.*

o   Read the descriptions below twice. Pause between each description if necessary.
Say: *Listen and draw lines.*
Everyone's smiling in this picture but the grandmother is the happiest person here because it's her birthday today! Her name's Zoe. She's standing in front of her cat. Can you see her? She's wearing her favourite pink dress today.
Grandpa's got a present for Grandma in that box. Grandpa's name is Hugo. He's the oldest person in this family. Look! His beard and moustache are white now.
The woman who's wearing the green jacket is called Julia. Can you see her, too? She's got grey trousers on and she's holding a plant. It's another birthday present!
This grandmother has only got one daughter. Her name's Alice. She made the birthday cake this morning. She's holding it now. It looks great!
The man with the camera is the grandmother's son. His name's Sam and he likes taking photos. He's wearing a blue and white T-shirt this afternoon.
And can you see Matt? He's Jane and Sue's father. He's very strong. He's carrying a big bag. What's inside it? I think it's another present!

o   Learners check their answers in pairs.
Check answers by asking different learners to say sentences about the names and the people. For example: *Matt has got a bag.*

Check answers:
Zoe and the woman in the pink dress.
Hugo and the man with the white beard and moustache.
Julia and the woman in the green jacket with the plant.
Alice and the woman with the cake.
Sam and the man in the blue and white T-shirt with the camera.
Matt and the man with the brown beard and the bag.

---

o   Ask learners to suggest what presents could be in Hugo's box and Matt's bag. (clothes, chocolates, DVDs, another cat, a new phone, new shoes, a book etc.)

o   Learners find Sue in the family tree. Ask: *What's her sister's name?* (Jane)

o   Say: *Find Matt and Alice. How many daughters have they got?* (two) Ask: *Which of their daughters is older?* (Jane) *How old is she?* (13)

o   Ask: *Who's the youngest person in this family?* (Peter) *How old is he?* (five)

o   Learners draw their own family tree (using this one as a model) and write sentences about it. Display the family trees around the classroom.

Note: Stronger classes: Learners could write sentences like the ones in the audioscript and give them to another learner to answer.

Ⓑ Read about Jane. Write the family words on the lines.

o   Point to Jane in the family tree. Ask: *Who is Jane's sister?* (Sue) *Who is Jane's father?* (Matt) *Who is Jane's mother?* (Alice)

o   Continue with Jane's grandfather (Hugo), grandmother (Zoe), uncle (Sam), aunt (Julia), cousins (Ben and Peter).

o   Teach/revise '**grand**daughter' and '**grand**son'. Show learners how we add 'grand' to:
parents   >   grandparents
son and daughter   >   grandson and granddaughter
Ask: *Who are Hugo and Zoe's grandsons?* (Ben and Peter)
Who are Hugo and Zoe's granddaughters? (Jane and Sue)

o   Learners work in pairs. Give each pair eight A5 pieces of card or paper. In large letters, pairs write one word on each card: *mum, dad, sons, daughters, children, grandma, grandpa, grandparents.* Help with spellings if necessary.

o   Say: *Listen. When I ask a question, quickly choose and then hold up your answers.* Ask the following questions:

Which word can mean father?	(dad)
Which word can mean grandmother and grandfather?	(grandparents)
Which word can mean children that are boys?	(sons)
Which word can mean grandmother?	(grandma)
Which word can mean sons and daughters?	(children)
Which word can mean mother?	(mum)
Which word can mean grandfather?	(grandpa)

Note: If you would like this to be a competition, give the first pair to hold up the correct answer a point. The pair/pairs with the most points are the winners.

o   Say: *You didn't need one of your words. Which one?* (daughters) *Is a daughter a man or woman? A boy? A girl?* (a woman or a girl)

o   Read out the first three sentences of the text in **B**: *My sister, Sue, and I love everyone in our family! Our parents are great! Dad's name is Matt.* Point to the word 'Dad' in the third sentence. Say: *We know Matt is Jane's dad so this is the right answer.*
Give learners a minute to read the rest of the text then read it out pausing at the gaps. Learners call out the missing family words and then write them on the lines.

Check answers:
2 mother/mum   **3** aunt   **4** uncle   **5** cousins   **6** grandparents

---

- Teach/revise 'a lot'. Learners work in small groups. Say: *Sue and Jane like going to see their grandparents a lot!* Add something that you like doing a lot, for example: *I like going to the cinema a lot and I like eating chocolate a lot.*
  Ask: *What do you like doing a lot?*
- Groups talk and find three things that they all like doing, for example: *We like playing football a lot. We like eating ice cream a lot. We like listening to music a lot.* Each group then tells the class what they like doing. Write the three most popular activities on the board for learners to copy into their notebooks.

C Answer questions about the people in your family.

- Teach/revise the adjectives in this activity (old, young, loud, quiet, clever, busy, pretty, naughty, cool, silly) and then ask: *Is loud the opposite of quiet?* (yes)
  Ask different learners: *When do you make a lot of noise? When are you quiet?*
  Ask: *Is clever the opposite of busy?* (No. You can be clever and busy.)
  What's the opposite of pretty? (ugly)
  What's the opposite of naughty? (good)
- Remind learners that to make the superlative of 'busy', 'pretty', 'silly' and 'naughty' we must take off the 'y' and add 'i' before '-est'.
- Point at the first question and ask two or three different learners: *Who's the oldest person in your family?* Learners answer.
  Learners then work on their own, answering questions 1–10 by writing names of people in their family or their relationship to them, for example, *my grandma*, on the lines under 'My answers'.
- Learners work in A and B pairs, asking and answering questions, for example: *Who's the youngest person in your family?* They write the names of their classmate's family or the relationship to their classmates on the lines under 'My friend's answers'. If answers are names, learners may need to ask for spellings!

Optional extension:

- To practise writing superlative adjectives, in class or for homework, learners choose four of their answers in **C** and write sentences about their family in their notebooks. For example: *My father is the quietest person in our family. Mum is the busiest. My younger sister is the naughtiest. I'm the cleverest!*
- Learners could include a drawing of their four chosen family members and draw arrows to show which sentence describes each person in their picture.
- Continue in A and B pairs. Learner A looks at the questions on page 106 of their book and prepares to answer them. Learner B looks at the questions on page 108 of their book and prepares to answer them.
- Learner A asks Learner B the A questions.
  Learner B asks Learner A the B questions.
  Walk around and monitor this activity.

D Write 1, 2 or 3 words to complete the sentences about the story.
Reading & Writing Part 5

> **Movers tip**
> In Reading and Writing Part 5, candidates need to know family words. It is important that they recognise family synonyms, like *dad/father; mother and father / parents*. The less formal words (*Dad, Mum, Grandpa, Grandma*) are often used as names in the stories.

- Point to Ben in the family tree in **A**. Point to the text in **D**. Say: *This is a story about Ben and Peter and their grandparents.*
- Read out the first part of the text (or ask a confident learner to read it). Stop after ... *brother, Peter.*
- Point to the two examples and say: *Ben and Peter's home is in ... ?* (the town centre)
  Ask: *How old is Ben?* (12) Show learners where the answers to these two questions are in the story. Remind learners that all the missing words in questions 1–7 are in the story and should not be changed.
  Ask: *How many words are there in these two example answers?* (three, one)

- Point to the instruction in the task and ask: *How many words can you use in these answers?* (one, two or three)
- Give learners time to read through the whole story. Ask: *Who does Ben go and see?* (his grandparents) *Which animals does Ben see at the farm?* (horses) *Do Ben and his brother like going to the farm?* (yes)
- Learners complete sentences 1–7. Check answers by asking different learners to read out their completed sentence. Each time, ask: *How many words are there in this answer?*

> **Check answers:**
> **1** Saturday **2** car **3** (new) baby horses **4** names
> **5** Cloudy and Star **5** (biggest) field **7** that holiday

E Can you hear the sound 'Zzzzzzzz'?

- Ask: *What small thing that can fly makes the sound zzzzzz?* Learners should know 'fly' and 'bee' but are unlikely to know the word 'mosquito' so you might like to teach this word here if useful to your class.
  Say: *Be bees! Make that noise now!* (Learners say /z/.)
- Ask: *Can you think of a word that starts with this sound?* (zoo) Write 'z' on the board. Say: *When we see this letter, it always sounds like /z/.*
- Read out the first word: *boys* (/bɔɪz/). Ask: *Can you hear the /z/ sound at the end of this word?* (yes) *Can you see the letter 'z' at the end?* (no). *What letter can you see?* (s) Say: *Sometimes the letter 's' sounds like /s/. It's like the sound of a snake.* Pretend to be a snake and make a hissing noise. Say: *But sometimes, the letter 's' sounds like /z/.*
- Make sure learners have a red pencil. Point to the other words and say: *Listen to these words. Draw a red circle around the /z/ sounds in these words.* Read out the list slowly emphasising the double /z/ in 'noises' and the single /z/ in 'busiest'.
- Read out the list again asking learners to repeat the words after you.
- Learners find and circle the listed words in the story text. Ask different learners to read them out to you adding the word before and after each one.
- Ask: *How many /z/ sounds are in this sentence?* Read out slowly:
  Mrs Pen's cousin says she's got some funny new clothes and glasses! (seven)
  You could extend this activity by asking learners in small groups to make /z/ sentences. Write some words on the board for them to work with.

Suggestions:

animals, buses, clowns, clown's, colours, countries, daughter's, dresses, glasses, lions, names, sons, tigers, trousers, words, zoo
calls, changes, cries, dances, drives, finds, knows, moves, needs, phones, rains, sees, snows, travels, wears

Suggested sentences:

Zara knows the names of all the animals in the zoo.
Mrs Dances travels by helicopters and buses to different countries.
The clown's long trousers are really funny colours.
His daughter cries when she sees angry horses or tigers.
Mr Snow's son's wearing purple glasses.
She's putting dresses on her dolls. Look!

10 People in our street

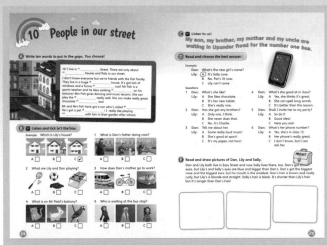

Pronunciation practice /ʌ/ for both 'o' and 'u' vowels (eg s**o**n, **o**ne, **u**ncle, **u**p). See C.

Equipment needed

- Movers Audio 10B and 10C.
- Colouring pencils or pens. See E.
- A photocopy of the questions on page 116 for each learner. See Project.

Ⓐ Write ten words to put in the gaps. You choose!

- Explain to learners that they are going to use their imaginations. They should not answer your questions out loud.
- Say, pausing between questions for learners to imagine their answers: *Close your eyes. Think about your dream home. What does it look like? Is it a house or a flat? Is it tall? Is it old or new? How many floors has it got? Has it got a lift? How many rooms are there in your dream home? Are there any rooms that are under the ground, too? Which is your favourite room? What can you see from the windows of your dream home? Is there a garden to play in?*
- Learners talk together in pairs or small groups about their imagined homes. Walk around and help with vocabulary if necessary.
- If you enjoy drawing, you could ask learners to give you ideas to help you draw a dream home on the board.
- Learners read the text in **A**. Ask: *Who's writing this text? Is it a boy, girl, woman or man?* Learners decide. Ask: *Which family is this person writing about?* (the Fish family) *How many people are there in the Fish family?* (three)
- Read the first sentence. Ask: *What kind of information do we need to put in the first gap?* (a name). Learners suggest names. Learners choose one that most of them like and read out the sentence again adding the name.
- Go through the other gaps in the same way asking what kind of information is needed in each case.
  Suggestions: 2 a number, 3 and 4 an adjective, 5 and 7 a kind of food, 6 a musical instrument, 8 a boy's name, 9 an animal, 10 a game or sport.
- In pairs, learners choose their own words and add them to the text. Encourage learners to use their dictionaries if necessary.
- Check answers by asking different pairs to read out one or two of their sentences to the rest of the class.

Ⓑ ▶ Listen and tick the box.

PartListening **4**

- Learners look at the example: *Which is Lily's house?*
- Say: *Look at the three pictures.* Ask: *What's different about these three houses?* (colour of roof and door, number of windows, tree/no trees)
- Play the example on the audio. Ask: *Which is Lily's house?* (C) Ask: *What does Lily's house look like?* (red roof, blue door and no garden) *Which house has got the most windows?* (Lily's house)
- Learners listen to questions 1–5 and tick the boxes. Play the audio twice.

> **Check answers:**
> **1** B **2** A **3** A **4** C **5** B

Audioscript

Look at the pictures. Listen and look. There is one example.
Which is Lily's house?
Boy: Which is your house, Lily? Is it the one with the grey roof?
Girl: No! Our house hasn't got a garden and its roof is red!
Boy: Oh! OK! And what colour is the door?
Girl: Blue. My favourite colour!
Can you see the tick?
Now you listen and tick the box.

One
What's Dan's father doing now?
Boy: What's Dad doing, Mum? Is he washing his car again?
Woman: No, Dan. Look! He's playing with the puppy.
Boy: Great! Can I go and see?
Woman: Yes, but put your coat on first.

Two
What are Lily and Dan playing?
Man: Are Lily and Dan playing table tennis?
Woman: Not today. And Dan didn't want to play football.
Man: Oh! … so they're playing badminton.
Woman: That's right. They like doing that.

Three
How does Dan's mother go to work?
Man: Hello, Dan! How does your mum travel to work? By bus?
Boy: She goes on the train. It's quicker.
Man: Does she ride her bike to work sometimes?
Boy: No. She never does that.

Four
What's on Mr Field's balcony?
Girl: Mr Field's got a new pet, Mum! It's on his balcony.
Woman: Is it a rabbit?
Girl: No, it's a parrot. Look!
Woman: Oh yes! What kind of pet would you like?
Girl: A kitten!

Five
Who's waiting at the bus stop?
Boy: Is that your mum at the bus stop?
Girl: No! It's my best friend's grandmother!
Boy: Oh! Which bus stops there?
Girl: The number one. It goes to the beach!

C ▶ Listen to us!

○ Say: *In B question 5, there were two family words. What were they?* (mum, grandmother). Write *mum* on the board and underline the 'u'. Ask: *In this word, how do we say this letter?* Say the sound yourself if necessary. Learners say /ʌ/.

○ Write 'grandmother' on the board. Underline the 'o' this time. Ask: *In this word, how do we say this letter?* If learners are unsure because 'o' is a different letter, say /ʌ/. Say: *Sometimes these two letters sound the same.*

○ Play the audio, telling learners to point to each word as they hear it. Say: *Listen for the /ʌ/ sound.* Ask: *How many /ʌ/ sounds are there in this sentence?* Play the audio again. Learners answer (nine).

○ Learners circle the 'o's in 'son', 'brother', 'mother' and the 'u's in 'uncle', 'Upunder', 'number' and 'bus'. Say: *Now let's look more carefully at 'one'.* Write 'wun' on the board. Say: *This is the wrong spelling, but does it sound like this?* (yes). Learners circle the 'o' in 'one'.

○ Repeat the sentence in chorus and then ask questions with everyone answering together. *Who's waiting?* (My son, my brother, my mother and my uncle!) *What are they waiting for?* (The number one bus!) *Where are they waiting?* (In Upunder Street!)

○ Draw learners' attention to other Starters and Movers words where 'o' is pronounced /ʌ/ as you discover them in the book, for example: another, come, love, Monday, monkey, nothing, some, someone, something.

   Note: For your own reference only, notice that in most cases, an 'o' that is pronounced /ʌ/ will have either an 'n' 'm' or 'l' or 'w' next to it.

Audioscript

My son, my brother, my mother and my uncle are waiting in Upunder Road for the number one bus.

D Read and choose the best answer. Reading & Writing Part **2**

> **Movers tip**
> In Reading and Writing Part 2, candidates should read the whole conversation before they choose the missing answers. This will help them understand the context more fully before they start choosing answers.

○ Say: *Dan and Lily are talking on the phone about a new person in their street.*

○ Learners read Dan's example question. Ask: *What does Paul want to know?* (the new girl's name) Point to the circle round A. *It's Sally Love.* Ask: *Can you hear the /ʌ/ sound in 'love'?* (yes!)

○ Choose how to continue this activity. If you want the test practice to be as authentic as possible, learners work on their own. If you would prefer learners to have more support, they should work together in pairs.

○ Learners read questions 1–6 and circle A, B or C to show Lily's correct answer. Check answers by asking different learners/pairs to read out a question and answer.

> **Check answers:**
> **1** C **2** A **3** B **4** B **5** B **6** C

Optional extension: Learners think of questions for wrong options 1A, 2C, 3A, 5C and 6A.

Suggestions: What does she like? Is his name Bill? What's she listening to? Can I have a sweet? Does she go to your school?

E Read and draw pictures of Dan, Lily and Sally.

○ Learners read the descriptions of Dan, Lily and Sally and draw their faces.

○ Encourage learners to show each other their drawings. To check understanding ask the following questions:
   What colour are Lily's eyes? (blue)
   Has Dan got a big nose or a small nose? (a big nose)
   Who's got the smallest mouth? (Dan)
   Is Lily's hair straight or curly? (straight)
   What colour hair has Sally got? (black)
   Who's got the longest hair? (Lily)

Opposites puzzle. Find the pairs.

○ Write on the board: *big, wrong, tall, short, hot, curly, ugly, difficult, beautiful, right, cold, sad, quiet, easy, dirty, small, clean, loud, straight, happy.*

○ Say: *After you wash your hands they are … ?* (clean) Point to 'clean' on the board. Ask: *Which word is the opposite of clean?* (dirty) Learners write *clean* and *dirty* in their notebooks. Say: *These two words are one opposite pair.* Point to the words on the board and say: *Now find some more!*

○ Learners work in pairs to find the other nine opposite adjective pairs and write them in their notebooks.

> **Check answers:**
> ugly/beautiful, tall/short, quiet/loud, happy/sad, difficult/easy, cold/hot, right/wrong, big/small, curly/straight

○ Divide learners into pairs. Give them five minutes to make as many sentences as they can. They should use any of these adjectives to describe something they can see in the classroom. For example: *Pat is happy. Our teacher is tall. This book is easy. I am right!*

○ Check answers by asking learners to read out their sentences.

🎒 My street

○ Give a photocopy of the questions on page 116 to each learner. Learners read the questions and copy and complete the answers in their notebooks or on a piece of paper to make an information sheet about their street.

   Note: Learners may find it more fun to write about an imagined street.

○ Learners draw a map of the immediate area where they live to illustrate their text.

○ Learners add their text and map to their project file. Alternatively, display these on a classroom wall if possible.

11 Things we eat and drink

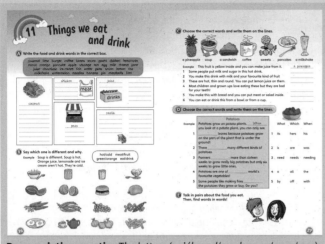

Pronunciation practice The letters 'ea' (bread/read, pear / pea / ear).
Flyers words: metre, use, other

Mime what you're eating.

- Tell learners to mime eating and drinking the following food and drink. Demonstrate first yourself. Mime and say:
  You're eating a very big apple.
  You're eating an ice cream.
  You're drinking a cup of hot coffee.
  You're drinking the milk from a coconut.

A Write the food and drink words in the correct box.

- Say: *Take some paper and cover the top half of page 26. I want you to look at the 16 pictures of food and drink in B, OK?*
  Say: *Look at the first four pictures. What can you see?* (soup, orange juice, lemonade, ice cream)
  Drill the pronunciation and ask different learners to come to the board to write the words.

- Do the same for the second row of pictures: *a watermelon, a lime, a burger, a mango.*

- Learners work in pairs. Say: *Write the words for the other two lines of pictures in your notebooks.*

- Check answers by asking two different learners to come to the board to write the four words.
  Third row: carrots, beans, grapes, peas
  Fourth row: eggs, tea, onions, pasta
  Note: Leave the words on the board for the activity in **B**.

- Say: *Now, look at the word boxes in A.*

- Point to the word 'coconut' in the box and to the different categories in **A**. Ask:
  Is 'coconut' a fruit, meat, a vegetable, a drink or a different food? (fruit) Point to the word 'coconut' under the fruit bowl.
  Point to the words 'chicken', 'peas', 'juice' and 'pasta' in the different categories. Check learners understand why these words are here and that they are also crossed out in the box.

- Learners look at the other words in the box, decide which group they belong to, and write them on the lines. Point out that some of the words are not shown in the 16 pictures.

Check answers:

fruit	meat	drinks	vegetables	other foods
lime	burger	coffee	beans	egg
mango	sausage	lemonade	carrot	cheese
kiwi	meatballs	tea	onion	chocolate
apple		milk		ice cream
pear		milkshake		fish
lemon		water		rice
watermelon				pancake
banana				noodles
				pie
				sauce

- Explain that we can make sauces from different foods, for example, vegetables, meat, fruit or cheese.
  Ask different learners: *What's in your favourite sauce?*
  And explain too that we can put lots of different things inside pancakes and pies.
  In pairs or small groups, learners talk about the kinds of pancakes and pies they like.

- Ask: *Which of the words in the orange box are not in the pictures?* (coconut, apple, pear, chicken, sausage, chocolate, lemon, milk, cheese, rice, bread, fish, coffee, kiwi, meatballs, milkshake, pancake, noodles, banana, pie, sauce)
  Note: If your learners like drawing, you could ask them to draw pictures for these words or to find pictures of them in magazines and to cut them out and make a wall poster or collage.

B Say which one is different and why.

- Point to the first row of four pictures and then to the four words for these pictures on the board ('soup', 'orange juice', 'lemonade', 'ice cream').
  Say: *Look at these four pictures. One is different. Soup is different. Soup is hot. Orange juice, lemonade and ice cream aren't hot. They're cold.*
  Point to the example sentences and to the words 'hot'/'cold' in the box in **B**.

- Point to the second row of pictures and to the words on the board: 'a watermelon', 'a lime', 'a burger', 'a mango'.
  Ask: *Which one is different?* (a burger)
  Point to the pictures of the watermelon, the lime and the mango.
  Ask: *Are these fruit?* (yes)
  Point to the burger.
  Ask: *Is this fruit?* (No, it's meat!)
  Point to the words 'meat'/'fruit' in the box in **B**.

- Point to the watermelon picture. Say: *A watermelon …*
  (point to the lime and the mango pictures) *a lime and a mango are … fruit.*
  Ask the whole class to say this sentence again:
  A watermelon, a lime and a mango are fruit.
  Point to the burger. Say: *A burger isn't … ?* (fruit) *It's … ?* (meat).
  Drill these sentences: *A watermelon, a lime and a mango are fruit. A burger isn't fruit. It's meat.*
  Learners write these sentences in their notebooks.

- In pairs, learners write sentences in their notebooks for the third and fourth row of pictures, using the words 'green'/'orange' and 'eat'/'drink' from the box.

C Choose the correct words and write them on the lines.

o Point to the picture of the pineapple. Write the following words on the board: *yellow red meat fruit vegetable eat*
Ask: *Which of these words could we choose to talk about a pineapple?* (yellow, fruit, eat) *Are pineapples meat?* (No, they're fruit!)

o Read out the example sentences: *This fruit is yellow inside and you can make juice from it.*
Say: *Which words tell us that this sentence is about a pineapple? Draw a circle round the words.* (fruit, yellow inside, make juice)

o Learners read sentences 1–6, putting circles round the key words. They then write the correct words next to the sentences and cross out the words they have used.

Say: *In America, people call sweets a different word. Do you know it?* (candy) *How do you spell 'candy'?* (C-A-N-D-Y) Learners write 'candy' above the sweets picture. Ask: *What's your favourite kind of candy? Which sweets do you like?*

o Write on the board: *a coconut: This fruit is .... inside. You can eat it and drink its ....·*
Ask questions to help learners complete the two sentences:
What colour is a coconut inside? (white)
What can we do with a coconut? We can eat it and drink its … ? (milk/juice)
What is inside a coconut? (juice/milk)

o Write on the board: *a watermelon: This is a kind of .... It's big and it's .... outside and .... inside.*
Learners copy and complete the two sentences about a watermelon.
One learner comes to the board and writes their two sentences. The other learners say if their sentences are the same or different.
Suggestion: This is a kind of fruit. It's big and it's green outside and pink inside.

o In pairs, learners choose one of the foods from **A** and complete two sentences about it: *This is a kind of…. It's … and it's … outside and … inside.* They do not write the word for what they are describing. Two pairs join together. One pair shows the other pair their sentences. The other pair guesses what they are writing about.

D Choose the correct words and write them on the lines.

Reading & Writing Part 4

o Write on the board: *potatoes*
Then, write these words on the board:
fries drink eat cook plant hockey vegetable like daughter

o Ask: *Which words could we use to talk about potatoes?* (fries, eat, cook, plant, vegetable, like) *Which words don't we use?* (drink, hockey, daughter)

o Say: *Read the text and look for words on the board which are in the text* (fries, plant, vegetable).
Note: at this point they should not try to complete the text.

o Ask: *What does the text say about potatoes? Say yes or no!*
Potatoes grow on trees. (no)
Potatoes grow below the ground. (yes)
You have to wait a year before you can get a potato from a plant. (no)
Lots of people like eating potatoes. (yes)

o Read: *Potatoes grow on potato plants. When you look at a potato plant …* Ask: *Can you see the word 'When' to the right? 'When' is the correct word for this sentence. Choose the correct word from the three words to the right of the box and write it on the lines in the text.*

o Learners write words on the lines.

o Say: *In the text, it says that people like making fries with potatoes. Can you tell me another word we use to talk about 'fries'?* (chips) Explain that people in Britain talk about 'chips', but that in other countries, like the USA, they use 'fries.'

E Talk in pairs about the food you eat. Then find words in words!

o Learners work in A and B pairs. Learner A looks at the questions on page 107 of their book and Learner B looks at the questions on page 108. Learner A asks Learner B the A questions.

o Say: *In pairs, write three foods you think most people in this class have for breakfast.* Give pairs time to write, then ask: *And which three fruits do you think most people in this class don't like?* Pairs write the fruits.
Write on the board: *breakfast food   fruit we don't like*
Ask two learners to come to the board. Under 'breakfast food', Learner A writes the different foods they think most children in the class eat for breakfast. Under 'fruit we don't like', Learner B writes the different fruits they think most children in the class don't like.
Learner A points to the first food on their list. Other learners in the class put their hands up if they wrote the same food word. Learner A counts the hands and writes the total next to that breakfast word. Learner A continues until they have a totals for each word on their list. Learner B then does the same for the fruits on their list. Pairs then check to see if they guessed the breakfast food and fruit people don't like.

o Say: *Watch me. Which word am I writing?* Write the word *watermelon* on the board, one letter at a time. Learners will probably think you are writing *water*, but add the letter *m* to the end. Continue until a learner says the whole word.
Say: *Point to the picture of a watermelon in A. Who likes watermelon?*

o Point out that the word 'watermelon' is a combination of two words – 'water' and 'melon'.

o Say: *Sometimes, we can find words inside words! Listen and write letters: b-r-e-a-d. What word did you write?* (bread) *Can you read the word 'read' in bread?* (Yes!) Ask: *Do 'read' and 'bread' sound the same?* (no!) Learners say *bread* and *read*.
Say: *Now, write another food word. p-e-a-r. Which word did you write?* (pear) *Which two words are inside the word pear?* (*pea* and *ear*) Say: *Listen: 'pear', 'pea'. Do these words sound the same?* (no) Say: *'Pear', 'ear' – the same or different?* (different) Say: *pear, pea, ear.* Learners repeat.

o Learners work in A and B pairs again. Learner A looks at page 107. Learner B looks at page 108. They take it in turns to spell out their three words and to find words inside the words.
Learner A: meatball: meat, me, at, ball, all; sandwich: sand, an, and; orange: or, ran, an
Learner B: mango: man, an, go; pancake: an, cake; candy: can, an, and

12   Party things

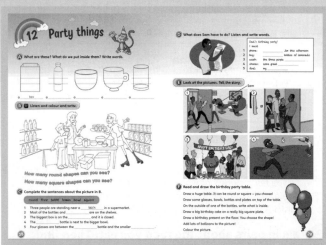

Flyers words: *shelf*

Equipment needed

o   Movers Audio 12B.

o   Colouring pencils or pens. See B.

Ⓐ What are these? What do we put inside them? Write words.

o   Point to the pictures in **A** and ask: *In which room can you find all of these things?* (in a kitchen) *Do we put things <u>outside</u> or <u>inside</u> them?* (inside)

Point to the picture of the box and ask: *What's this?* (a box) Point to the word 'box' on the line next to **a**.

o   Teach/revise the other words: bottle, bowl, cup, glass.

Learners write the words for these on the lines under the other pictures.

o   Ask: *What kinds of food do you buy in a box?* (tea, coffee, rice, pasta, etc.)

Write the suggestions on the board. Learners choose two words and write them on the lines inside the picture of the box.

o   In pairs, learners think of two things we put in the other containers and write the two words inside each picture.

Note: They can look at the food and drink words in Unit 11 for ideas.

o   Ask different learners to come to the board, draw the outline of the container, then say and write the two words they put inside the container.

Suggestions:

bottle: water, lemonade, juice   **bowl:** ice cream, soup, rice
cup: coffee, tea, soup   **glass:** lemonade, juice, water

o   Point to the picture of the box and say: *The box is square.* Point to the bowl and say: *The bowl is round.*

Say: *In pairs, write words for four more things that are square and four things which are round.* Tell learners to look for things in the classroom or in their *Fun for Movers* book.

When you check answers, ask learners to point to any of the things which are in the classroom or their book and say: *That/This (table/board) is square,* etc. Give them points for each word they have written.

Suggestions:

square: board, book, field, keyboard, map, mirror, room, sandwich, table, TV, window
round: ball, balloon, cake, CD, clock, DVD, face, hat, moon, orange, watch

Ⓑ ▶ Listen and colour and write.   Listening 5

> **Movers tip**
>
> In Listening Part 5, candidates are not judged on their colouring abilities. To get the marks, they need to show they understand and can follow the instructions. They either have to use the right colour to colour in the object, or write the correct word in the correct place. Candidates are not expected to colour in an object completely, so they shouldn't worry if they run out of time.

o   Learners look at the picture. Ask:

How many bottles are there? (12: 10 on the shelves and 2 on the table.)

How many boxes are there? (16: 14 on the shelves and 2 under the table.)

How many glasses are there? (11)

How many bowls are there? (two)

o   Draw a circle on the board and at the same time, ask: *What am I drawing?* (a circle) Say: *Yes! This is a circle. It's round.*

Draw a square on the board and ask: *What am I drawing?* (a square) *Is a square round?* (no!) You need four straight lines to make a square. Say: *A circle and a square are two different shapes.*

Say: *Now everyone! Take a pencil, crayon or pen! I want you to 'draw' some shapes. But don't draw on paper! Draw in the air!*

First, draw a little circle! Now, draw a huge box! Learners 'draw' the little circle and the huge box in the air.

Tell learners to 'draw' more shapes in the air: *a very tall bottle, a little star, a huge moon in the sky.*

Ask: *What did you 'draw'? Who can tell me?* Different learners describe their air pictures: a little circle, a huge box, a very tall bottle, a little star, a huge moon.

o   Point to the first question below the picture in **B** and then at the picture and ask: *How many round shapes can you see in this picture?* Learners count the things. (one bottle, the two bowls, the 11 glasses, the two cups, the four wheels = 20 round shapes)

Read out the second question: *How many square shapes can you see?* (one bottle, the two big boxes under the table, the 14 boxes on the shelves, the table, the six shelves, the board behind the boy = 25)

o   Say: *You are going to listen to two people talking about this picture.*

o   Play the audio. Learners listen to the example then listen and colour and write the five things in the picture.

> **Check answers:**
> 1   Colour round bottle on the table – green.
> 2   Colour juice in boy's glass – yellow.
> 3   Write APPLES on closed box.
> 4   Colour mother's hair – brown.
> 5   Colour small bowl – blue.

o   In pairs, learners choose what to write on the board behind the boy. Ask two or three pairs what their board in the supermarket says.

Optional extension: Learners could colour the rest of the picture.

Audioscript

Look at the picture. Listen and look. There is one example.
Man: Would you like to colour this picture of a supermarket?
Girl: Yes! Can I colour the woman's roller skates?
Man: OK. What colour?
Girl: I'd like to colour them pink, please.
Man: OK. That's fine!
Can you see the woman's pink roller skates? This is an example. Now you listen and colour and write.

One

Man:	Can you see the bottles on the table?
Girl:	There are two bottles. Which one shall I colour?
Man:	The round one. Make it green.
Girl:	All right. I can do that now.

Two

Man:	The boy's drinking something, I think.
Girl:	Yes, it's fruit juice. Shall I colour it orange?
Man:	No. Colour it yellow, please.
Girl:	OK. There!
Man:	That's great. Thank you.

Three

Girl:	The bigger box is closed. Look!
Man:	Oh yes. Let's write something on that.
Girl:	All right. I like writing. Can I write APPLES on that? They're my favourite fruit.
Man:	Yes. That's a very good idea.

Four

Girl:	Can I colour someone's hair now?
Man:	All right.
Girl:	That woman's? The one who's carrying the drinks?
Man:	Not hers. Colour that woman's. It's longer and curlier.
Girl:	OK. Shall I colour it brown?
Man:	Yes, please.

Five

Man:	Now, have you got a blue pencil?
Girl:	Yes, I have. I love that colour!
Man:	Me too. Colour the little bowl with that one.
Girl:	Brilliant! I enjoyed doing that.
Man:	Good! Well done!

C Complete the sentences about the picture in B.

o Read out sentence 1: *Three people are standing near a table in a supermarket.*
   Point to the people in the picture in **B** and to the word 'table' in the box in **C**.
   Say: *Cross out the word 'table' in the box.*

o Teach/revise: 'shelf'/'shelves'. Read sentence 2: *Most of the bottles and … are on the shelves.*
   Ask: *What can you see on the shelves? Bottles and … ?* (boxes)
   Learners write *boxes* on the line in sentence 2 and cross out this word in the box.

o Learners read sentences 3–5 and write words on the lines.

> **Check answers:**
> **3** floor   **4** square   **5** round … bowl

o Write on the board: *square   boxes   floor   table*
   Say: *Can you make another sentence about the picture in C with these four words?*
   Suggestion: Two square boxes are on the floor under the table.
   Do the same with these words:
   woman   roller skates   most   glasses
   Suggestion: A woman with roller skates is holding most of the glasses.

D What does Sam have to do? Listen and write words.

o Point to the boy in the picture and say: *This is Sam. It's his father's birthday today and there's a party for him this afternoon. Sam has to help his mum with things for the party.*
   Ask: *What things do people do before a birthday party?*
   (invite people to the party, buy food and drink, make or buy a cake, choose music, put the food and drink on the table, etc.)

o Say: *Look at the words and the lines in D. Which words could you write on the lines?*
   Suggestions: 1 cousin/uncle   **2** 2 / 3 / (a number)
   3 glasses / bowls / plates   **4** music / songs / photos
   5 phone / radio / football

o Say: *You are Sam. Listen and write what you have to do for the party.*
o Read the text below twice.

One

Sam, I need you to help me. We must ask Uncle Jim to come to the party this afternoon. Can you phone him? Uncle Jim's phone number is in my little red book.

Two

And we need some lemonade. Can you go to the supermarket for me? The lemonade there is very nice. But don't buy one bottle. Buy two. We need two bottles.

Three

We've got lots of party food! Oh! We can put it in our purple bowls. Right! I need three bowls, I think. They're in the kitchen cupboard. Wash three bowls for me, please. Thank you!

Four

And we need to play some great music at Dad's party. You choose the music, Sam. You're so good at that.

Five

Now, one more thing. I want to show a video. We need a laptop for that. Go and find yours. Right! That's everything, I think. Brilliant!

> **Check answers:**
> **1** Uncle   **2** two/2   **3** bowls   **4** music   **5** laptop

E Look at the pictures. Tell the story.   Speaking Part 2

o Ask: *Can any of you play baseball? What do you need to play baseball?* (a bat and a ball) *Have any of you got a baseball bat?*

o Point to the boy in **D** and in the first picture in **E** and say: *Look at Sam now. It's the afternoon.* Point to the man in the armchair in this picture and say: *And this is Sam's father. His name's Tom.*

o Say: *Look at these pictures. They show a story. It's called 'Tom loves his birthday presents.' Look at the pictures first.* (pause)
   Say: *Look at the first picture. Tom is watching baseball on TV. He really likes baseball. His son Sam is opening the front door. Uncle Jim and his family are outside. They have a birthday present for Tom.*

o Say: *Now you tell the story. Look at the other three pictures. In pairs, listen to my questions. Answer them and tell the story.*
   (point to picture 2)
   1 *Who's opening the door now?* (Tom's opening the door.)
   2 *How many people are outside the door?* (Three people are outside.)
   3 *What's the boy holding?* (The boy's holding a present.)
   (point to picture 3)
   1 *What's Tom doing now?* (Tom's holding a baseball.)
   2 *What are Tom's presents?* (Tom's got a baseball bat and a ball.)
   3 *Does Tom like his presents?* (Tom really likes his presents.)
   (point to picture 4)
   1 *Where are Tom and Sam now?* (Tom and Sam are in the park.)
   2 *What are Tom and Sam doing?* (They're playing baseball.)
   3 *Are they happy?* (Tom and Sam are really happy.)
   Note: Learners can say or write the story.

> **Movers tip**
> In Speaking Part 2, candidates can use the present tenses to tell the story. Short sentences like the ones above are fine and this kind of story would gain high marks.

F Read and draw the birthday party table.

o Learners read the instructions and draw the picture in their notebooks or on a piece of paper. They choose how many of each thing to draw and where exactly to put them. Tell learners to read all the sentences first before they start drawing their picture.

o When they have finished, learners compare their pictures in pairs. For example: *In my picture there are three glasses, but in your picture there are four.*

o Different pairs can then show their pictures to the rest of the class and describe the differences between them.

13 Different homes

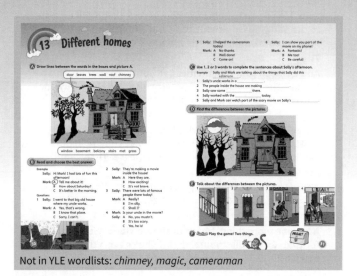

Not in YLE wordlists: *chimney, magic, cameraman*

A Draw lines between the words in the boxes and picture A.

○ Point to the house and ask:
Who lives here? Does this man live here? Is this a scary house? Do a lot of people live here? Which animals live here? (a cat, spiders, bats) *What's inside the house?* Encourage learners to use their imagination.

○ Point to the door in picture **A** and ask: *What's this?* (a door) Point to the word 'door' in the box above the picture and the line from it to the door in the picture. Teach/revise other words if necessary. Ask: *Does this line go to the correct place in the picture?* (yes)
Ask: *Are there any leaves in this picture?* (yes)
Where are the leaves? (on the trees)
Can you see the word 'leaves'? (yes – above the picture)
Learners draw a line between the word 'leaves' and the leaves on one of the trees.

○ Ask: *Is there a balcony in this picture?* (yes)
Where's the balcony? (outside / in front of the big window) Ask: *Can you see the word 'balcony'?* (It's in the box under the picture.)
Learners draw a line between the word 'balcony' and the balcony.

○ Learners draw lines between the other words and the things in the picture.

○ Ask: *Can you make a sentence about the leaves in picture A?*
For example: *There are lots of leaves on the two trees.*

○ Say: *Work in pairs. Take your notebooks and write three sentences about the house and garden in A. Use three different words from under the picture in each sentence, but don't use the word 'basement'!*
Ask different pairs to read out two of their sentences.

○ Say: *Now, I want you to write a sentence with the word 'basement'.* Explain that you will give points for the longest sentence and the best sentence. All pairs read out their sentence for 'basement'. Everyone counts the number of words in each sentence and you or the class decide on the best sentence.
Note: With bigger classes, you could do this in groups of eight. Four pairs write then read out their sentences to the group, who count the words and decide on the best sentence.

Listen and say what is speaking.

○ Say: *This is a magic house. The things inside it and outside it can speak!* Read out the sentences below. Learners look at picture **A** and say who/what is speaking. (All the words are above or below the picture.) Make it more interesting/fun by using different voices for the different sentences!

1 *We're on the trees.* (leaves)
2 *I'm on the first floor, outside the window.* (balcony)
3 *I'm under the ground, at the bottom of the house.* (basement)
4 *The cat's sleeping on me.* (mat)
5 *There are eleven of us in this house.* (windows)
6 *I've got a big spider on me.* (wall)
7 *I'm at the top of the house. Rain falls on me.* (roof)

B Read and choose the best answer.   Reading & Writing Part 2

○ Point to the girl in the picture in **B** and say: *This is Sally.* Point to the man in the picture in **A** and say: *And this is Sally's uncle. He works at the house. What does he do?* (**Suggestions:** He cleans the windows, gives the cat food, looks after the garden, etc.)
Say: *Sally and her friend Mark are talking on the phone. Read the example. What are they talking about?* (Sally's afternoon)
Point to the circle round the letter A before *Tell me about it!* Ask: *Why are B and C not good answers?* (Answer B is suggesting doing something on Saturday, we could say C if someone is asking when to do something.)

○ Read out Sally's sentence 1: *I went to that big old house where my uncle works.* Ask: *Would you like to visit that house? Why? Why not?*
Ask different learners to read out the things Sally and Mark say in 2–6 (not the answers). Ask: *Why was Sally's afternoon great?* (because some film people were there and she could help the cameraman).
Learners choose the best answers for 1–6.

> **Check answers:**
> 1 B   2 B   3 A   4 C   5 B   6 A

C Use 1, 2 or 3 words to complete the sentences about Sally's afternoon.

○ Ask: *Is Sally telling Mark about her weekend?* (no – about her afternoon) Point to the word 'afternoon' on the line in sentence 1.

○ Learners complete sentences 1–5 with 1, 2 or 3 words.

> **Check answers:**
> 1 (big)/(old) house   2 a movie   3 famous people
> 4 cameraman   5 phone

D Find the differences between the pictures.   Speaking Part 1

> **Movers tip**
> In Speaking Part 3, a simple and effective way for candidates to talk about the differences between the pictures is to make an affirmative statement about one picture and then make the same statement negative for the other picture. For example, *Here, there's a basement but in this picture there isn't (a basement).*

○ Write on the board: *basement, eleven, open, balcony, two trees, leaves, the stairs, on the mat, two bats, on the wall, flowers, clouds.*

○ Say: *There are twelve differences between picture A and picture D.* Learners draw a circle round the things in picture **D** which are different. In pairs, they talk about how to describe these differences.

o Say: *Listen to my sentences about picture A. Say how picture D is different.*

In picture A, there's a basement but in picture D …? (There isn't a basement/there's no basement.)

In picture A, there are eleven windows but in picture D … ? (there are seven windows.)

In picture A, the front door is open but in picture D … ? (the front door is closed.)

There's a balcony … (There **isn't** a balcony.)

There are two trees … (There are **three** trees.)

There are leaves on the trees (There are **no leaves**.)

The man's cleaning the stairs (He's cleaning a **window.**)

The cat's sleeping on the mat (It's **running in the garden.**)

There are two bats above the house (There's **one** bat.)

In picture A, the spider's on the wall (It's on the **door.**)

I can't see any flowers in picture A. (There **are some** flowers.)

There aren't any clouds…. (There's a **cloud in front of** the **moon.**)

E Talk about the differences between the pictures.

o Ask questions about the four pictures:

How many people can you see? (1 one woman 2 one man 3 two children 4 three girls)

Where are they? (1 in a hall 2 outside a house 3 outside a school 4 outside a library)

o Write on the board: *inside   outside*

Ask: *Which picture is different?* (Picture 1 because the woman is inside. In pictures 2, 3 and 4, the people are outside.)

o Write on the board: *open   closed*

Ask: *Which picture is different?* (Picture 4 because the door is open. In pictures 1, 2 and 3, the door is closed.)

o Do the same with: *upstairs/downstairs, purple/yellow, round/square.*

> **Check answers:**
>
> Picture 3 because the children are coming downstairs.
> In pictures 1, 2 and 4, the people are going upstairs.
>
> Picture 3 because the door is yellow. In pictures 1, 2 and 4, the doors are purple.
>
> Picture 2 because the windows in the house are round.
> In pictures 1, 3 and 4, the windows are square.

F Play the game! Two things.

o Divide the class into teams of 4–5 learners.

o Say: *Can you tell me two things you can find in a garden?*

Suggestions: flowers, trees, leaves, plants, grass

o Say: *Listen. For each sentence, your team has to write two things. Spelling must be correct.*

Read out the sentences. Allow time (for example, one minute) for them to think of their answers to each one and to write in their notebooks or on a piece of paper.

1 *Two things you sit on.* (chair, armchair, sofa, seat)

2 *Two things you watch.* (TV, videos, films, DVDs, movies)

3 *Two things you listen to.* (music, the radio, the TV, CDs, band, mp3s)

4 *Two things you find in a car, near the driver.* (radio, window, mirror, clock)

5 *Two places you can put things in at home.* (cupboard, bookcase, box)

6 *Two places to have a wash.* (bath, shower)

o Teams exchange their answers. Say the sentences again. Learners say the answers the other team has written. A point is given for each correctly spelt acceptable answer.

The winning team is the one with the most points.

Fun for Movers pictures

o Learners work in four groups. Give each group one of the questions to read and answer. Tell learners they only have two minutes to find their answers.

Say: *Look at all the pictures in your 'Fun for Movers' book. Read your question again and find the pictures. Write their page numbers under your question.*

1 Which pictures show people inside different places?

2 Which pictures show people outside?

3 Which pictures show no grown-ups or children?

4 Which pictures show things you can hold in your hand?

o You could then ask all groups to look at the pictures in *Fun for Movers* and decide:

Which picture do you like the most? What do you like about it?

Are there any pictures you don't like? Why not?

 A famous house

o Learners find out about a famous house. This could be where a famous person lives/lived or a house where a TV series or film was made.

o Learners research the house online or in the library, find pictures of it and prepare a few facts about the house for the class.

o They show the class their pictures (or even a video) of the house. The class guesses who they think lives in the house or the film/TV programme that was made there.

o Learners then tell the class the facts that they have found out about the house.

14 Our homes

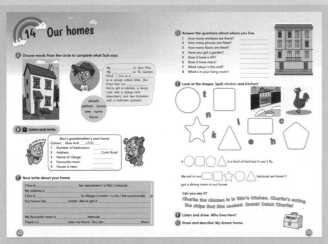

Flyers words: *light, dark, across, middle*

Not in YLE wordlists: *rectangle, triangle, pentagon*

Equipment needed

o   Movers Audio 14B.

o   A light blue and dark blue pen, crayon, or other objects. See E.

Ⓐ Choose words from the circle to complete what Jack says.

o   Write on the board: *big small new old nice noisy quiet*
Point to the house in **A** and say: *This is Jack's home.*
Learners choose one word each from the board to describe Jack's house and two words to describe their own homes and write sentences. In groups of 3–4, they compare their sentences.
Suggestion: *Jack's house is old and small, but mine is big and quiet.*

o   Learners read Jack's text and choose four words from the yellow circle to write in the gaps.

> **Check answers:**
> name, address, house, rooms

o   Ask different learners to read out one of the four sentences to check answers.

o   Ask: *What's Jack's family name?* (Fine)
What's the number of Jack's house? (78)
How do you spell the name of Jack's village? (W–E–L–L)
How many bedrooms are there in Jack's house? (two) *Where are they?* (upstairs)
Say: *When you go into a house from a street and you don't go upstairs or downstairs, where are you?* (on the ground floor)
Which rooms are on the ground floor in Jack's house? (the kitchen, living room and dining room).
Note: If you want, you could explain that in North America, people call the 'ground floor' the 'first floor'!

Ⓑ ▶ Listen and write. Listening Part 2

> **Movers tip**
> In Listening Part 2, candidates have to read prompts and complete a form. Make sure they are familiar with the format and know that sometimes parts of the answer are given. In this exercise, they only have to write a word or number.

o   Point to the boy in **B** and say: *This is Ben.* Point to the woman and say: *This is Ben's grandmother. They're talking on the phone.* Point to Ben's notes and ask: *What are they talking about?* (Ben's grandmother's new home)

Say: *Look at Ben's notes. How many questions must you answer?* (five) *Which answers are numbers?* (1 and 2) *In which question do you have part of the answer?* (2 – the name of the road)

o   Say: *Listen to Ben and his grandmother.*

o   Play the audio twice. Do not stop the audio between answers.

> **Check answers:**
> **1** 2   **2** 56   **3** Tyre   **4** kitchen   **5** (a) river

o   Ask:
Are the bedrooms upstairs or downstairs? (upstairs)
Are there chickens or kittens in her garden? (chickens)
When she can see the chickens, which room is she in? (the kitchen)
What do you think Ben sends his grandmother? I think it's something for her new house? Learners make suggestions.
Suggestions: some cups / flowers / pictures / photos / a plant / a clock

Audioscript

Listen and look. There is one example.
Boy: Hi Grandma! Are you happy in your new house?
Woman: Yes, Ben. It's great!
Boy: What colour is it?
Woman: It's blue and white.
Boy: Blue and white! That's nicer than ours!
Can you see the answer? Now you listen and write.
One
Boy: How many rooms have you got?
Woman: We've only got six rooms, but that's OK.
Boy: Wow! That's a lot! Six bedrooms?
Woman: No! We've only got two bedrooms upstairs.
Boy: Two … oh!
Two
Boy: And can you give me your new address? I want to send you something.
Woman: Oh! Is it something nice?
Boy: Yes!
Woman: OK. I live in Cook Road, at number 56.
Boy: Number 56, Cook Road. Brilliant! Thanks.
Three
Boy: And what's the name of the town, Grandma?
Woman: My new house isn't in a town, Ben. I live in a village called Tyre.
Boy: Tyre? Is that T–Y–R–E?
Woman: Yes, that's right.
Four
Boy: What's your favourite room in the new house?
Woman: My kitchen because it's got a big window and I can watch my chickens in the garden!
Boy: I love feeding your chickens, Grandma!
Woman: I know! And I love my kitchen!
Five
Boy: What's near your house?
Woman: There's a river near my house. You can go there and fish!
Boy: A river? Wow! That's so cool! See you next weekend, then!
Woman: Yes! Bye for now, Ben.

C Now write about your home.

○ Learners choose from the words: 'an apartment' / 'a flat' / 'a house' and write their answer on the first line.

  Note: Explain that 'flat' and 'apartment' are similar in meaning. 'Flat' is generally used in British English and 'apartment' is used more in American English, but 'apartment' is now often used instead of 'flat' in British English when describing new or more expensive homes.

○ Learners complete the other gaps. After 'We've got a …', they write all the rooms in their home. In the last two gaps, learners choose a place near their home and write what they do there.

○ In groups of 3–4, learners read out their sentences and compare their homes.

D Answer the questions about where you live.

○ Learners answer questions 1–7 by writing numbers for questions 1–3, yes/no for questions 4–6, a colour in 7 and the things that are in their living room (sofa, armchairs, tables, etc.) in 8.

○ Large classes: learners each choose one question to ask. Smaller classes: each learner chooses two or three questions to ask. Learners get up, walk around and ask each other their questions.

○ Ask different learners to tell the class who they talked to, which questions they asked and what the answers were.

E Look at the shapes! Spell *chicken* and *kitchen*!

  Note: Some learners find these two words very difficult to spell and say.

○ Say: *Look at the six different shapes. What do we call them?*
  Teach/revise: a circle, a star, a square, a triangle, a rectangle, a pentagon.

○ Teach/revise the words 'light' and 'dark'. Point to something light blue and then to something dark blue (or hold up light blue and dark blue pens or pencils).
  Say: *These are both blue. But they're different. One is light blue and the other is dark blue. In the day, it's light outside. At night, it's …* (dark).

○ Say: *Listen and colour the big shapes in E.*
  Colour the triangle pink, please.
  Can you see the rectangle? The rectangle is grey.
  Make the square yellow, please.
  The circle is light blue. The pentagon is light green.
  You don't have to colour the star because the star's white!

○ Say: *Look at the seven letters. Say the letters. In pairs, tell each other which letters these are* (c, h, t, e, n, i, k).

○ Say: *Listen and write one or two letters in the different shapes.*
  *Write **ch** in the circle.*
  *Write **t** in the star.*
  *Write **i** in the square.*
  *Write **en** in the triangle.*
  *Write **k** in the rectangle.*
  *Write **ck** in the pentagon.*

○ Learners look at the shapes in the two sentences and copy the letters into the same shapes.

○ Ask: *How many letters are in 'chicken' and 'kitchen'?* (seven)
  Which letter is not in 'chicken'? (t)
  Which letter is in 'chicken' twice? (c)

○ Learners work in A and B groups. Learners in group A spell 'chicken' with each learner saying the next letter to complete the word. Do the same with group B and 'kitchen'. Then, they swap over and group A spell 'kitchen' and group B spell 'chicken'.

○ In their notebooks, learners write two short sentences, one with chicken and another with kitchen. For example: *There's a chicken in my garden. / A chicken is brown and red. Our kitchen's small. / We eat in our kitchen.*

○ Point to the kitchen picture in **E** and say: *This is Kim's kitchen.* Point to the chicken and say: *This is Charlie the Chicken.*

○ Say: *Listen.* Point to 'Can you say it?' Read out: *Charlie the chicken is in Kim's kitchen. Charlie's eating the chips that Kim cooked. Quick! Catch Charlie!*

○ Learners practise saying the sentences in pairs or small groups.
  Ask: *What other birds do you know?* (penguin, duck)
  Stronger learners could work in groups to try to make up a tongue twister about penguins.
  Suggestion: *Pat pointed to a pink penguin in Paul the pop star's car park!*

F Listen and draw. Who lives here?

○ Say: *Here's a different house. Listen and draw it!* Read out the sentences, drawing the shapes with your hand to help learners.
  Draw a big, fat circle. Under the circle draw four short fat legs but don't draw any feet! At the bottom of the circle, draw a tall square – a rectangle. (This is the door.) Across the middle of the big, fat circle, draw six small circles. (These are the windows.) On top of the big circle, draw another tall square/rectangle. (This is the chimney.)
  Who lives in this house? A person? A robot? An alien? Draw him / her / it! Would you like to live there?

G 📦 My dream home

○ On the board, draw a simple plan of your own home (to show all the rooms if possible). Ask learners to guess what the different rooms in your home are, then label them.

○ Tell learners that they can have the home of their dreams. They can choose where it will be, what colour it is, how many floors and bedrooms it has got and what it is near.

○ Write on the board:
  Address:
  Colour of house:
  Number of floors:
  Number of bedrooms:
  House is near:

○ Learners draw their dream house, labelling the rooms. Then they copy and complete the notes from the board or write a short description under the picture. If possible, display their drawings around the classroom or make them into a class book. They could do this for homework.

15   At our school

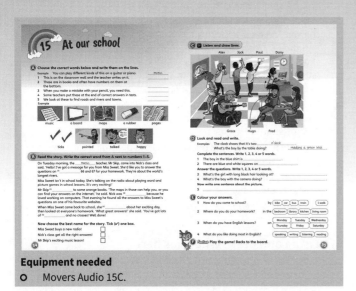

Equipment needed

o   Movers Audio 15C.

Ⓐ Choose the correct words below and write them on the lines.

o   Point to the example picture and word. Ask: *What's this?* (music) *Can you play music on a piano?* (yes) *And on a guitar?* (yes) Read out the example sentence and ask: *Does this sentence talk about a board or maps?* (No – music)

o   Learners read sentences 1–5 and write words on the lines.

> **Check answers:**
> **1** a board   **2** pages   **3** a rubber   **4** ticks   **5** maps

o   Write on the board: *A ruler. You can take this and …* . Ask learners to complete the sentence about a ruler.
Suggested answer: … draw (straight) lines.

o   Write on the board: *XX – crosses.*
Say: *Look at sentence four. Change words to make a sentence about crosses.*
Suggestion: Some teachers put these at the end of wrong answers in tests.

Ⓑ Read the story. Write the correct word from A next to numbers 1–5.

Reading & Writing Part **3**

o   Read out the first three sentences of the text in **B**.
Ask: *Which day of the week was it?* (Tuesday)
Who was Mr Skip? (the music teacher)
Where was Nick? (in his classroom)
Who was the message from? (Miss Sweet)

o   Learners read the rest of the text. They do not write anything.
Ask: *What were the homework questions about?* (the longest rivers in the world)
What did Miss Sweet talk about? (playing word and picture games in school lessons)
Where did Nick find the homework answers? (on the internet)
Were Nick's answers correct? (yes)

o   Learners read the text again and write words from the box in **A** in each gap.

> **Check answers:**
> **1** pages   **2** pointed   **3** happy   **4** talked   **5** ticks

---

o   Point to the three possible names for this story.
Ask: *What's the best name for this story?* (Nick's class get all the right answers!)
Point out that 'radio' is in the text but Miss Sweet didn't buy a radio and that Mr Skip is the music teacher but the story isn't about an exciting music lesson.

Tell me about …

o   Say and write on the board sentences about things you like doing at school.
Suggestions: I like teaching new things to my class. My favourite lesson is painting. I enjoy reading stories to my classes.

o   Underline the start of each of the three sentences on the board:
I like …
My favourite lesson …
I enjoy …
Point to these words. Ask different learners to suggest ways that they could complete these sentences. Then learners copy and complete the three sentences about the things they like doing at school.

Ⓒ ▶ Listen and draw lines.

Listening Part **1**

o   Learners look at the picture. Ask:
Where are the children? (in the classroom)
How many people are there in the picture? (eight)
How many names are there outside the picture? (seven)

o   Play the audio. Stop after the example. Ask: *Which two things did you hear about Hugo?* (He's wearing a red T-shirt and holding a book). Check learners can see the line between Hugo and the boy.

o   Play the rest of the conversation. Learners listen and draw lines between five names and five children.

> **Check answers:**
> Lines should be drawn between:
> **1** Jack and boy drawing a camera on board.
> **2** Alex and girl sitting at table wearing blue sweater.
> **3** Paul and boy in black trousers taking photos.
> **4** Daisy and girl playing guitar.
> **5** Fred and boy looking at train picture on wall.

Ask: *Which name did you not use?* (Grace) *Which children did you not draw lines to?* (The boy who's drawing the guitar and the girl who's looking at the computer).

> **Movers tip**
> In Listening Part 1, there is always an extra name and two people in the picture are not identified.

Audioscript

> *Look at the picture. Listen and look. There is one example.*
> Woman: Is this your class? Are these your classmates?
> Boy: Yes. That's my friend Hugo. He's wearing a red T-shirt today.
> Woman: He's holding a book. Is it an e-book?
> Boy: No, but he's got one of those too.
> *Can you see the line? This is an example. Now you listen and draw lines.*
> *One*
> Boy: Can you see Jack? He's drawing on the board.
> Woman: Which boy is he?
> Boy: He's drawing a camera and he's got jeans on!
> Woman: Oh yes! I can see him now.

Two
Boy: Look at Alex!
Woman: Where's she?
Boy: She's sitting at the table.
Woman: Is she wearing a blue sweater?
Boy: Yes, and a grey skirt. She's a really good friend.

Three
Woman: Who's that boy?
Boy: Which one?
Woman: The boy with the black trousers.
Boy: That's Paul. He's taking photos of the boys. Can you see?
Woman: Oh yes!

Four
Woman: And which kid do you sit next to in class?
Boy: Daisy.
Woman: Is she the one on the computer?
Boy: No, that's not her. She's playing the guitar.
Woman: Oh yes, I can see her. I love her glasses.

Five
Boy: Do you know Fred?
Woman: Is he the boy with brown hair at the back of the classroom?
Boy: No. He's looking at the train on the wall.
Woman: Oh, yes. I can see him now.

D Look and read and write.

> **Movers tip**
>
> In the first part of Reading and Writing Part 6, candidates have to write words to complete two sentences and answer two questions. They might find different ways to complete these sentences or answer these questions. Some candidates might write one word answers. Others might write two, three, four or five words.
>
> When practising this task, encourage learners to think of two ways to complete each sentence or answer each question, and then choose the one they think is best.

o   Point to the picture in **C** and say: *Let's talk about these classmates and their classroom.*
Point to the boy with the red hair and say: *The boy with red hair is looking at a* .... *?* (a train/poster)
Point to the table and ask: *What's on the table?* (a pair of glasses, an orange book)

o   Learners look at the two examples and work in pairs or on their own. Point to sentences 1–4. Say: *Now complete sentences 1 and 2 and then answer questions 3 and 4.* Remind learners they can write 1, 2, 3, 4 or 5 words.

> **Check answers:**
> (Suggestions) **1** drawing (a guitar)   **2** the (classroom) floor
> **3** a website (about trains)   **4** taking a photo/picture

o   Ask these questions, one at a time: *How many people can you see in this picture? What are they doing? Where are they? Who are they? Why are they here?*
Suggestions: There are eight people. They are in a classroom/school. They are drawing, playing, reading. They are classmates. They are enjoying the break.
Write on the board: 1 *These eight* .... *are* .... , ... *and* .... *in the classroom.*
2 *These eight* .... *are in the classroom because it's the* ....
Learners say words to complete the sentences.
Suggestions: 1 children / kids / classmates   drawing / reading / playing / taking photos
2 children / kids / classmates   break

o   Say: *Listen to the questions and write words! How many people are*

drawing? What are they drawing? Where are they drawing? Who are they? Why are they drawing? Learners write one or two word answers to each question. Then, in pairs, they write a sentence about the boys on the line next to 5.
Suggestion: The two boys/classmates are drawing a guitar and a camera on the board because they love drawing/they're bored.
You could continue like this, prompting learners to answer questions about the boy with the camera and/or the girl with the guitar.

E Colour your answers.

o   Point to question 1 in **E**. Tell a learner to ask you the question: *How do you come to school?* Answer the question: *I come to school by bike / car / bus / train. / I walk to school.*

o   Say: *Now, you answer the questions. Colour your answers. But don't show other people your answers!* Learners read and colour the circles that contain their answers.
Say: *Work in pairs! Which answer is correct for your partner? How does he or she come to school? Where does she or he do her homework? Draw another circle round your partner's answers to questions 1–4. Play the game! Try and find all your friend's answers before they find yours!*

o   In pairs, learners ask and answer questions 1–4.

o   Divide learners into three groups. Say: *Group 1, read and remember question 1. Group 2, read and remember question 2. Group 3, read and remember question 4.* Learners then get up and move around the class on their own and ask all the other learners their question and count the different answers. When they have asked everyone, they write sentences. (You could write the different sentences on the board for them to copy and complete).

1   *In our class, most people come to school by bus / bike / car / train.* .... *people walk / come here by* .... *. Only* .... *people walk to school. / come to school by* ....

2   *In our class, most people do their homework in their bedroom / kitchen / living room / the library. Only* .... *people do their homework in* ....

4   *In our class, most people like speaking / writing / reading / listening the most. Only* .... *people like* .... *the most.*

F Play the game! Backs to the board.

o   See page 7 for the instructions for this game. (The words here are all connected to school.)
Suggested words:
alphabet board bookcase break classmate
classroom crayon cross desk e-book eraser homework
keyboard lesson letter mistake mouse page paper
picture playground poster question rubber ruler
sentence teacher test text tick word

16 Let's do some sport!

Flyers word: *popular*

Not in YLE wordlists: *shuttlecock*

Equipment needed

○ Movers Audio 16B

A Who said what? Write the words in the sentences.

○ Point to the boy and girl's T-shirts and ask: *What are their names?* (Vicky and Fred)

Ask more questions about Vicky and Fred. For example:
Where do they live? How old are they? What are their favourite sports? Do they have any brothers and sisters? etc. Learners use their imaginations and answer the questions.

○ Point to the two speech bubbles and say: *Vicky and Fred are telling us about last weekend.* Point to the cloud and say: *There are ten words in this cloud. Which words can you see twice?* (played, shouted, jumped, watched) *You need to use some words in both texts! The word 'played' is in the first text and there is a line through it in the cloud. This is an example! Use the other words to complete the two texts.*

Learners choose and write a word in each gap.

> **Check answers:**
> Blue bubble: *watched, jumped, shouted, laughed*
> Green bubble: *played, watched, jumped, shouted, rained*

○ Ask: *Who looks happy – Vicky or Fred?* (Fred) *Which text talked about happier things?* (the blue bubble) *Fred enjoyed his Saturday!* Learners draw a line between the blue bubble and Fred.

Who doesn't look happy? (Vicky). *Which is Vicky's speech bubble?* (the green one) Learners draw a line between the green bubble and Vicky.

Say: *Don't worry! Vicky found her mouse on Monday! Where do you think Vicky found her mouse?* In pairs, learners write where they think the mouse was.

Different pairs ask you questions: *Was the mouse in the bath / under her bed / on her desk?* etc. (Vicky's mouse was inside the kitchen cupboard. It was eating some cake!)

Say *Well done!* to any learners who guessed correctly where Vicky's mouse was. You could also give them a sweet or a cake or another small prize!

B ▶ Listen and write a letter in each box.

Listening Part **3**

> **Movers tip**
> In Listening Part 3, candidates should listen carefully to all the information and not just choose a picture because they hear a word for something they see. For example, the woman's son loves his new ice skates (and we have ice skating in picture G) but his favourite hobby is walking in the mountains.

○ Revise words for family. Write on the board:
..........................*and* .... = *children*
the child of your .... *or aunt* = ...
Point to the lines and ask learners to tell you the missing words (son, daughter, uncle, cousin)

○ Point to the six people in the pictures in **B** and say: *These people are all Mrs Ship's family. Mrs Ship is 42 years old. Which picture shows Mrs Ship's mother? Which people are Mrs Ship's son and daughter? Who is Mrs Ship's uncle?* Learners look at the pictures and words and point to each of the family members.

○ Point to the pictures of the different sports and actions and say: *Six of these pictures show the hobbies that Mrs Ship's family like. Listen and write the letter of the person's hobby in the box next to the correct picture.*

○ Play the audio twice.

> **Check answers:**
> Daughter D   Son A   Sister H   Uncle E   Cousin B

○ Point to the pictures of the hobbies in **B** again and say: *What do you think? Are these hobbies exciting? Cool? Dangerous?*
Write on the board:
I love .... *It's really exciting!*
.... *is cool!*
I think .... *is dangerous and scary too!*
In pairs, learners choose different hobbies to complete the sentences.

Audioscript

Listen and look. There is one example.

Mrs Ship is talking to Alice about her family and their hobbies.

Which is each person's favourite hobby?

Girl:	Hi, Mrs Ship!
Woman:	Hello Alice!
Girl:	Where did you go today?
Woman:	I went to see my mother. She loves cooking! She made me a chocolate pancake!
Girl:	Oh! My favourite!

Can you see the letter C?

Now you listen and write a letter in each box.

Girl:	What does your daughter like doing, Mrs Ship? She's one of my classmates, but I don't know her very well.
Woman:	Oh, she loves going to the lake. She's learning to sail there. Can you do that?
Girl:	No, but I'd like to!
Woman:	I've got a son too.
Girl	Have you?
Woman	Yes. He's four years older than you. He loves his new ice skates but his favourite hobby is walking in the mountains.
Girl	Cool! I'd like to do that one day, too.
Woman:	My sister likes being outside too. She often goes to the lake. She's really good at fishing. That's her favourite hobby.

C Find the answers to the questions. Write numbers.

○ Say: *Now, Alice is telling Mrs Ship about the day that she played baseball.* Point to the three questions and say: *Mrs Ship is asking her these three questions about that day. Find the answer to questions 1, 2 and 3. Write the numbers in the circles in front of the answers.*

> **Check answers:**
> 1 Baseball   2 On Friday.   3 Yes, it was great!

○ Learners role play the dialogue in pairs.

○ Learners choose a different game/sport that they like and write about it, using the questions and answers in **C** to help them. Then, they role play the dialogue with a partner.

D Choose the correct words and write them on the lines.
Reading & Writing Part **4**

○ Ask: *Who likes football?* Learners put up their hands. Count how many children in the class like football. Ask: *Who plays football? Where do you play? Who likes watching football? Do you watch games on TV or do you go and see games?*

Say: *Read the text. Do not try to complete it.* Ask: *What's another name for football?* (soccer) *Which famous football player does the text talk about?* (Lionel Messi)

Where do people play this sport? (in a lot of countries)

○ Say: *Look at the example.* Explain that 'the' is the correct answer because we don't say 'a' world or 'this' world.

○ Learners look at the other gaps and choose the correct words.

> **Check answers:**
> 1 who   2 run   3 it   4 when   5 on

○ Ask: *Who's your favourite football player? Which tennis player do you like? Why do you think that some people call football 'the beautiful game'?*

○ Say: *The text says that some players run about eight kilometres. Do you run a lot when you do sport?* Ask: *Which sports do you play?* Learners say the names of the sports they do. Then ask: *Who likes swimming / table tennis / hockey / fishing / sailing?* etc. Learners count hands each time to find the most popular sport in the class.

E Write the sport. You can make all the words from the letters in the sport.

○ Point to the word 'basketball' and ask: *How many letters are there in 'basketball'?* (ten)

Read out the words on the right: *ball, table, ask.* Say: *The first letter of 'ball' is the first letter in 'basketball', right?* (yes) *Are all the letters in 'ball' in 'basketball'?* (yes) *And are the letters t-a-b-l-e in 'basketball' too?* (yes)

Say: *And can you see – 'basketball' also has the name for a different sport inside! Cross out k-t and you get …* (baseball)

○ Learners look at the words and write the letters on the lines for the sports for 1–5. Remind them that the first word on the right starts with the same letter as the sport.

> **Check answers:**
> 1 football   2 table tennis   3 badminton   4 ice skating
> 5 horse riding

○ In pairs, learners make words from the letters in 'sports centre'.
Suggestions: (Starters and Movers words) centre/center, net, no, nose, on, one, open, pen, pet, poster, present, score, see, so, son, sport, stop, store, ten, test, top, tree (Flyers words: corner, once, screen, secret, sent, spot, tent, toe)

F Choose your sport!

○ Say: *Choose a sport that you like. Listen and write the answers for your sport.* Learners listen to your questions and write their answers.
1   *What do you need to do this sport? A ball? A bat? Special clothes?*
2   *Where do you play? Inside? Outside? On grass? In water?*
3   *How many people do you need?*
4   *What do you do? Do you run? Throw a ball? Hit a ball? Kick it?*

○ In pairs, learners look at each other's answers. They do not say which sport they are talking about – their partner has to guess from their answers!
Note: You could continue this in groups – different pairs choose a sport. Two pairs work together. One pair asks questions and the other answers. They guess the sport. Then they swap – the other pair asks questions, etc.

🏆 A sports project

○ Learners choose a sport that they don't know very much about.
Note: Your learners might not be very familiar with some of the sports on the Movers wordlist. If possible, show them a film of the sport.

○ Tell them to find out about that sport, on the internet or from sports books.
They can find answers to the following questions: for example, badminton.
How many people do you need? (two or four)
What do you need to play the sport? (racket, shuttlecock, net)
What do you do in the sport? (hit the shuttlecock over the net)
Where is this sport popular? (everywhere, but especially in China)
Is it an Olympic sport? (yes)

○ Learners prepare a poster about the sport and/or give a one-minute talk on it to the rest of the class.

17　Our hobbies

Flyers words: *arrive, group, special*

Equipment needed:

o　Movers Audio 17F

Talk about your hobbies.

o　Tell learners about things you like doing, for example: *I love doing sport on Saturdays and Sundays. I enjoy going to the cinema one evening a week.*

　Ask different learners:
　What do you do with your family at the weekend?
　What do you do with your friends after school?
　What do you like doing on holiday?

Ⓐ Listen and draw lines.

o　Point to the picture in **A** and ask: *How many people can you see?* (eight) *Where are the people?* (at/on a/the beach)

　Say: *Let's write words for things in the picture starting with different letters of the alphabet! Tell me a part of the body that starts with 'a'!* (arm) Write the word *arm* on the board. Learners come to the board and write words beginning with other letters of the alphabet. To help them, say: *Write words for clothes, people, colours, things and things that people are doing.*

　Note: There are no words for i, k, q, u, v, z. The **bold words** are in the suggested spoken script.

　Suggestions: beach / **boat** / book / bag / boy / blue / brown; clothes / child / carrying; dolphin / **drawing**; eyes; face / **feet**; **girl** / grown-up / grey / green; **hat** / hair / hand; jeans / **jumping**; leg / line; **man** / music; neck / nose; orange; **people** / **picnic** / **picture** / pink / **plane** / **purple**; red / **rock**; **sand** / sea / **sun** / shoulder / **shorts**; towel / trousers / **T-shirt**; **water** / woman / white / **wave** / **writing**; yellow

o　Say: *Choose one word from the board. Listen to Lucy talking about the people in the picture. If you hear your word, stand up!*

　Read the script. Ask different learners who are standing up: *What's your word?* (for example, *T-shirt*) Ask: *Can you say a sentence with 'T-shirt' about the picture?* **Suggestion:** *The man on the boat is wearing a T-shirt.*

　Ask some of the learners who are <u>not</u> standing up: *What's your word?* (for example, *jeans*) The class says a sentence for these words. **Suggestion:** *The girl with jeans is sitting on a towel. / writing in a book. / wearing a yellow sweater.*

o　Ask: *How many names are above and below the picture in A?* (seven) *Which are names for girls or women?* (Sally, Mary, Julia)

o　Ask: *Can you see the line between the name Charlie and the man next to the boat? Listen to what Lucy says about Charlie.* Read the script as far as 'That's my cousin, Charlie.' Ask: *What do we hear about Charlie?* (He's got a boat and a purple T-shirt.)

Point out that there will be <u>two</u> things to help learners identify each person in the picture. Read the rest of the script twice.

Learners draw lines between the names and the people.

o　Girl:　*I took this picture when I was on holiday. Some of the people are my friends and family. Can you see the man with the boat? The one who's wearing a purple T-shirt? That's my cousin, Charlie.*

One
Girl:　*My friend Sally is very clever. She's writing a new song. She's sitting on the beach.*

Two
Girl:　*Look at my mum! Her name's Mary. She took a picnic to the beach that day. It was very sunny because there were no clouds in the sky. Mum wore her favourite sun hat.*

Three
Girl:　*And there's my friend Peter. Over there between the two rocks. He's drawing a plane in the sand.*

Four
Girl:　*The waves in the sea aren't big today. Julia's happy. Look! She's got her feet in the water and she's wearing her new yellow shorts.*

Five
Girl:　*Isn't my grandfather Pat great? He's waving to the people on the beach. He's seventy now but he loves jumping out of planes!*

> **Check answers:**
> There should be lines between:
> **1**　Sally and the girl sitting writing a song on the beach.
> **2**　Mary and the woman carrying the two bags with the sun hat.
> **3**　Peter and the boy between the rocks, drawing a plane.
> **4**　Julia and the girl standing in the water and wearing yellow shorts.
> **5**　Pat and the man waving to the people from the parachute.

o　Say: *There is one name which you haven't drawn a line from.* (Matt) *Which person in the picture is Matt?* (the boy on the boat because the other person is a woman painting)

o　Write on the board:
　Matt is the boy in the ...
　Matt is the boy who ...
　Say: *Complete the sentences for Matt.*
　Suggestions: Matt is the boy in the green and red T-shirt.
　Matt is the boy who is on the boat / sailing / waving to the girl in the water / wearing a green and red T-shirt.

o　Write on the board:
　A plane. A towel. A dolphin. The people on the beach. Two bags. Between two rocks. On a boat.
　Say: *Close your books! Answer my questions! The words on the board are there to help you with some of the answers!*

o　Point to the board and ask: *What's the woman in the red dress carrying?* (two bags) Point to your head and ask: *What's on her head?* (a hat)

o　Point to the board and ask: *Who's the grandfather waving to?* (the people on the beach) *What colour are his trousers?* (blue)

o　Erase the words 'two bags' and 'The people on the beach'.
　Say: *Now, I want you to write questions. Write questions that start with 'What' or 'Where'. Your questions must give two of the answers from the board.* In pairs, learners look at the picture in **A** and write two questions.

o　2–3 pairs of learners work together. Each pair asks their two questions. The other learners in the group answer them using words from the board.

Suggestions

What's the boy drawing in the sand? / What's flying? (a plane)
What's on the girl's shoulders? (a towel)
What's swimming in the sea? / What's the woman drawing? (a dolphin)
Where's the boy who's drawing a plane? (between two rocks)
Where's the boy who's waving? (on a boat)
Note: With stronger classes, you could ask them to write a second question about each thing or person. For example, *What's the boy drawing in the sand?* (a plane) *What colour is his T-shirt?* (purple)

B **Write the words under the pictures.**

○ Say: *Look at the example picture and word* (hockey). *Is the girl playing hockey?* (yes) *Now, write the words for pictures 2–8 on the lines under the pictures. The first letter of each word is there to help you.*
Learners write words for pictures 2–8.

> **Check answers:**
> 2 ice skating 3 comics / comic books (American English)
> 4 DVDs 5 piano 6 swimming 7 laptop 8 table tennis

C **Choose the correct words from B and write them on the lines.**

> **Movers tip**
>
> In Reading and Writing Parts 1, 3, 4 and 5, the words candidates have to write are given. They should make sure they copy them carefully because their answers must be correctly spelt. Candidates should check their answers to each part before moving on to the next part and also check their spelling again when they finish. They have plenty of time to do this.

○ Ask: *Which words in sentence 1 tell you that the answer is 'ice skating'?* (dancing, on ice)
○ Learners read the other sentences and write the words on the lines.

> **Check answers:**
> 2 swimming 3 comics / comic books 4 a piano 5 DVDs
> 6 table tennis 7 laptop

○ Learners underline the important words in sentences 5–7.

> **Check answers:**
> 5 films, watch, computer 6 hit, small ball, bounces, game
> 7 carry, kind of computer

○ Say: *Can you say a sentence about 'hockey'?*
Suggestion: People hit a small ball in this game. You can play it on ice or on grass.

D **Choose words from B. Write the correct words next to numbers 1–5.**

○ Point to the picture of the girl with the photo and say: *This is Alex. She's holding a picture of her brother and sister. Read the first two sentences of the text.*
Ask: *What's Alex's sister called?* (Clare)
○ Learners read the rest of the text.
Ask: *How are Alex's brother and sister different?* (They like different hobbies and different kinds of weather.)
○ Learners choose words from **B** to complete the text.

> **Check answers:**
> 1 ice skating 2 laptop 3 DVDs 4 table tennis
> 5 comics / comic books

E **Now choose the best name for the story about Clare and Dan.**

○ Learners choose the best name for the story. (My brother and sister)
○ Ask: *Does the text tell us about a day in the park?* (No. It says that Clare went skating in the park, but it talks about lots of different days and places too.) Ask: *Is the text about <u>my</u> favourite sport?* (No. It's about <u>Clare</u> and <u>Dan</u> and their favourite sports <u>and</u> hobbies.)

○ Write on the board: *Clare likes .... weather.*
Say: *Look at the text in D again and tell me 1, 2 or 3 words to complete this sentence.* (sunny)
○ Write three more sentences on the board (one sentence at a time). Ask learners to copy and complete the sentences with words from the text in **D**.
1 *Clare and .... went ice skating on the park lake.*
2 *On Saturday, ... and his friends watched DVDs.*
3 *Mark and Dan go down to the .... to play table tennis.*

> **Check answers:**
> 1 her friends 2 Dan 3 basement

F ▶ **Listen, then tell the three word story!**

○ Point to the words in **F**. Read out the first group of words and write them on the board: *home, cupboard, bags.* Ask: *How many words did I say?* (three)
Read out and write the second group on the board: *bags, car, beach.* Ask: *How many words are there?* (three) *Which word was in both sentences?* (bags) Circle 'bags' on the board.
Point to the other groups of words in **F** and explain that for lines 1–6, the first word in each group is the same word as the last word in the group before.
○ Say: *These words are from a story about Julia's day on the beach. Can you find Julia in the picture in A?* (The girl standing in the water) *Listen to Julia and read the words!*
Play the audio. Learners listen and read the words. Play the audio twice, then ask questions:
1 *Where were the beach bags?* (in the hall cupboard)
2 *Who went to the beach?* (Julia and her mum)
3 *Who carried the bags from the car?* (Julia's mum)
4 *Who did Julia want to see?* (Matt)
○ Using the words in **F**, the whole class tells the story again. They could also continue the story about Julia's beach day, starting with the words in line 7 (Julia, went to sleep, sun).

Audioscript

> Girl: At home this morning, I opened the hall cupboard to get out our beach bags. I put our things into the bags, then I put them in our car. My mum drove to our favourite beach. When we got to the beach, I got out of the car quickly. I put my hat on my head. Mum put her hat on too. I wore my towel round my shoulders. My mum carried both the bags. I didn't help her with the bags today. I wanted to say hello to Matt. Matt was in his boat in the sea.

G **Play the game! Draw your circle.**

○ Write the following list of categories on the board. Then beside the list, draw a circle with your answers inside it.

1 Your favourite sport or hobby.
2 A hobby you don't like.
3 Something you would like to learn to do.
4 A sport you watch on TV.
5 Something a person in your family can do, but you can't.
○ Ask learners to guess which sports/hobbies you might say for 1–5.
○ For example: *I'd like to learn to sail. I don't like running. My father can paint, but I can't. My favourite hobby is cooking. I watch tennis on television.*
○ Learners draw a circle and write their words inside it.
○ In pairs or groups of three, learners show each other their circles and guess which sports/hobbies they have written for each sentence.

18   At the hospital

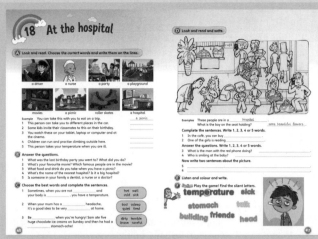

Pronunciation practice Silent letters. See F.

Flyers word: *jobs*

Not in YLE wordlists: *notice, silent*

Equipment needed

○ Colouring pencils or pens. See E.

A Look and read. Choose the correct words and write them on the lines.
Reading & Writing Part 1

○ Point to the pictures and ask:
Some pictures show people working. Which pictures? (a driver, a nurse)
Which places can you see? (a playground, a hospital)
Which things can you see? (movies, a picnic, roller skates)
Note: Explain that 'movie' and 'film' mean the same thing. 'Movie' is used more in American English and 'film' is used more in British English.

○ Say: *Now look carefully at the words under the pictures.* Read the example sentence: *You can take this with you to eat on a trip.*
Ask: *Is a driver food?* (No!) *Is a nurse food?* (No!) *Is a picnic food?* (Yes!)
'A picnic' is the correct answer for this sentence. Point to 'a picnic' on the line at the end of the example.

○ Ask: *How many pictures and words are there?* (eight)
Say: *There is one example and five sentences.* You do *not need to* write all the words. There are two words that you do not need to use.

○ Learners read the sentences and write the words.

○ When you check the answers, write them on the board, deliberately making the mistakes below. For each answer, ask: *What's wrong with this answer?*
  1 *driver* (you forgot the 'a')
  2 *parties* (you wrote the plural instead of the singular)
  3 *movie* (you wrote the singular)
  4 *a play ground* ('playground' is one word, not two)
  5 *a nerse* (it should be 'nurse' with a 'u').

> **Movers tip**
> If candidates make these kinds of mistakes in the Reading and Writing, they will not get a mark for the answer, even if they have matched the correct words to the sentences.

○ Write sentence 4 on the board. *Children can run and practise climbing outside here.* Point out that this sentence is about a place. Ask: *Which word in this sentence tells us that it is about a place?*

(here)
Write on the board, under 'here': *at this place.* Say: *We can say 'here' or 'at this place'.*
Point to the picture of the hospital in **A**. Ask: *What do doctors do here?* (help ill people) Say: *Doctors…?* (help ill people) *at this…?* (place).

B Answer the questions.

○ Ask three different learners to ask you questions 1, 2 and 3. Answer them.

○ Learners read questions 1–5 and prepare their answers. In groups of 3–4, learners ask and answer the five questions.

○ You could ask more questions:
Suggestions:
Is your hospital old or new / big or small?
Is your doctor/dentist a man or a woman?
What's your favourite picnic food?

C Choose the best words and complete the sentences.

○ Point to the picture in **F** of the boy with a temperature. Read out sentence 1, pausing at the gaps:
Sometimes, when you are not … and your body is …, you have a temperature.
Ask: *What's our normal body temperature?* (36° or 37°) *When you have a temperature of 40°, are you sick?* (yes) *Are you well?* (no)
Ask learners which of the words in the box to write in the gaps. (well, hot)
Write on the board: *not well   sick   ill*
Explain that these words all mean the same and that 'sick' is used more often in American English than in British English.

○ Learners read sentences 2 and 3 and choose and write words for each gap.

> **Check answers:**
> **2** bad   quiet   **3** careful   terrible

○ Ask: *What are the three wrong words?* (cold, sick, asleep, tired, dirty, brave)
*What can you do when you're **cold**?* (have a hot drink!)
*What's a good thing to do when you're **tired**?* (sleep!)
*What can you do when your hands are **dirty**?* (wash them!)

D Look and read and write.
Reading & Writing Part 6

○ Point to the picture in **D** and ask:
Where are these people? (in / inside / at a hospital)
Point to the first example and read: *These people are in a hospital.* Ask: *Is this sentence correct?* (yes)
Read the second example: *What is the boy on the seat holding?* Ask: *Where's the boy on the seat? What's he holding?* Learners point to the boy and answer (some flowers / a plant). Point to the words 'some beautiful flowers' on the line after the example question.
Learners read sentences 1 and 2 and questions 3 and 4 and write words.

> **Check answers:**
> (Suggestions) **1** (nice) cakes and fruit   **2** a (really funny) comic
> **3** phoning/calling his friend   **4** a/the nice doctor

> **Movers tip**
> In Reading and Writing Part 6, candidates may get more marks if they can write compound sentences. Train them to link ideas with *and*, *but*, *or* and *because*. Stronger learners could also use relative clauses (*who*, *that* and *which*).

o Write on the board: *who   which*

   The man ....is talking on the phone is sitting down.

   Point to the line between 'man' and 'is' and ask: *What do I write here? 'who' or 'which'?* (who)

   Add to the board:

   The seat ....is between the boy and the baby has a bag on it.

   Point to the line between 'seat' and 'is' and ask: *What do I write here? 'who' or 'which'?* (which)

   Ask learners to tell you why these words are used.

   the man is a person – we can only say **who**

   the seat is a thing – so we can't say **who** but we can say **which**

o Write on the board: *girl   comic   in her hands   listening to music*

   Ask learners to write a sentence with these words about the girl with the comic. Explain to learners they will need to add a few extra words.

   Say: *And think: do you need 'who' or 'which' here?*

   Suggestion: The girl who has got a comic in her hands is listening to music.

o Now write on the board: *comic   that   girl   in her hands   funny*

   Ask learners to write a sentence with these words about the comic and the girl.

   Suggestion: The comic which the girl has got in her hands is funny.

o If learners need more support, write sentences on the board. Learners complete them in pairs by choosing 'who' or 'which' and their own endings.

   Write on the board:

   The doctor who/which is looking at the baby .....

   The woman who/which is holding the baby ...

   The phone who/which the man is holding .....

   The nurse who/which is going out the door ...

   The plant who/which is by the window ...

   The girl who/which is listening to music ....

   Suggested sentences

   The doctor **who** is looking at the baby *is smiling*.

   The woman **who** is holding the baby *has got long curly hair*.

   The phone **which** the man is holding *is red*.

   The nurse **who** is going out of the door *is holding some paper*.

   The plant **which** is by the window *has got huge leaves*.

   The girl **who** is listening to music *is wearing boots*.

Ⓔ Listen and colour and write.

o Make sure that learners have colouring pencils or pens. Say: *This picture needs some colour. Let's colour it!*

   Read out the following instructions. Pause between each one to give learners time to colour.

   1 *Can you see the big plant in the picture? Colour that brown, please.*

   2 *Now find the bag – the one that's on the floor. Colour that pink.*

   3 *That nurse is helping the girl who hurt her leg. Find her hat and colour that blue.*

   4 *I'd like you to write something now. Look at the board under the cakes in the café. Write the word 'open' on it, please.*

   Check answers:
   1 big plant – brown   2 bag on the floor – pink
   3 nurse's hat – blue   4 the word 'open' on the board

o Say: *Complete my sentences about the things you coloured and wrote.*
   1 *The plant which is on the floor is ...* (brown)
   2 *The bag which is on the floor is ...* (pink)
   3 *The nurse's hat is ...* (blue)
   4 *The board says '...'* (open)

o If your learners enjoy colouring, they could colour the rest of the picture and compare their pictures at the end.

Ⓕ Play the game! Find the silent letters.

o Point to the word: 'temperature' and say: *There is one letter in this word which we write but we don't say. Which letter?* (the second 'e') Make sure that learners see the circle round the second 'e'.

   Point to the word: 'stomach' and ask: *Which letter don't we say?* (h) Do the same with 'head' (a), 'friends' (i), 'talk' (l), 'sick' (c) and 'building' (u). Learners circle the 'a', 'i', 'l', 'c' and 'u' in these words.

o Say: *Listen and write these words. Then, in pairs, find the letter in each word we write but we don't say.*

o **Suggested words** (the silent letters are underlined):

   k̲now   lis̲ten   came̲ra   jui̲ce   is̲land   vege̲table   sandwich
   choc̲olate   rac̲ket   cup̲bo̲ard (Tell learners that 'cupboard' has two silent letters.)

   Check answers:
   Learners from different pairs exchange notebooks. A learner from one pair comes to the board, says and writes the word and underlines the letter which we don't say. Learners check the words the other pair have written to see if they are correctly spelt and that they have underlined the correct letter. The pair who have written the most correct words and underlined the letter are the winners.

19 What is the matter?

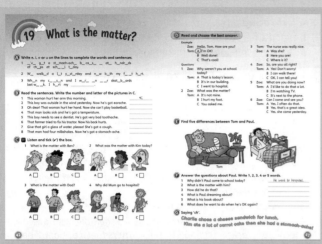

Pronunciation practice 'ch' spelling as /k/ or /tʃ/. See G.

Equipment needed

○ Movers Audio 19C.
○ Photocopies of page 117 (one per class/group) cut up into cards. See F.

A Write e, i, o or u on the lines to complete the words and sentences.

○ Point to sentence 1 and say: *The letters e, i, o and u are missing from this sentence. Where do I need to write 'i'? Where do the 'e's go? And the 'o's? How many 'u's do we need to write?*

Write on the board: _'v_ g_t

Point to the first line and ask: *Which letter do I write here?* (I). Write *I* on this line. Do the same with the second and third lines (e, o). Write the rest of sentence 1 on the board. Learners tell you which letter to write on each line.

Complete sentence 1 on the board, word by word.

○ In pairs, learners write *e, i, o, u* in 2 and 3. In sentence 3, they complete the sentence by also writing a part of the body.

> **Check answers:** (ask different learners to read out the sentences)
> 1 I've got a stomach-ache because I ate hundreds of chips at school today.
> 2 We walked a lot yesterday and now both my feet hurt.
> 3 When my cousin and I were on our skateboards last week, I hurt my hand (**Suggestions:** hand / foot / leg / arm).

Note: Make sure that learners use a capital 'I' to write the pronoun 'I'.

B Read the sentences. Write the number and letter of the pictures in C.

○ Ask: *Where's your nose?* Say: *Point to your nose.* Learners point. Do the same with 'ears' and 'stomach'.

Say: *Now do these things! Put your hands above your head! Wave your arms! Open and close your mouth, now your eyes! Can you move your nose?*

The first time, learners do the actions one by one. Then, say them again and they do them all at the same time!

○ Hold your shoulder and say: *Ouch! My shoulder hurts.*

Learners hold their shoulder and repeat this sentence. Do the same with 'foot', 'arm', 'hand' and 'leg'.

○ Put your hand on your stomach and say: *Ow! I've got a stomach-ache.* Do the same with 'toothache', 'headache', 'earache', and 'backache'.

○ Write on the board: *My stomach hurts. I've got a stomach-ache.* Repeat these two sentences. Learners say them after you. Make sure learners pronounce the long /ɜː/ in 'hurts'.

Point out that the 'ch' in 'stomach' and in 'ache' are both pronounced /k/.

○ Say: *In both sentences, part of your body hurts. We can use 'hurts' with any part of our body* (for example: eye, ear, foot), *but we use 'ache' with only a few parts of our body* (ear, tooth, head, stomach, back) *I've got backache. … (My back hurts.)*

On the board, under 'I've got a stomach-ache', write:

He's got toothache. She's got a headache. I've got earache and backache.

Say: *He's got toothache. His tooth hurts.*

She's got a headache. Her head … (Pause to elicit from learners: *hurts.*)

I've got earache. My ear … (hurts)

○ Point out that we write 'toothache', 'headache', 'backache' and 'earache' as one word, but we usually write 'stomach-ache' with a hyphen between the two words.

○ Write on the board: *She hurt her hand when she caught the ball.*

Explain that we also use 'hurt' to talk about a moment in the past when we did something to part of our body. (In this case, the woman's hand might or might not hurt now, but perhaps she can't use it.) This verb is irregular and doesn't add 'ed' to the end to form the past simple.

○ Ask one learner to read out the first sentence: *This woman hurt her arm this morning.*

Point to the 4C on the line at the end of this sentence and to the woman in picture 4C and ask: *Which part of her body did this woman hurt?* (her arm) *Is this the correct picture for this sentence?* (yes)

○ Learners read sentences 2–8 and write the number and letter of the picture in **C** where they can see this person on the lines.

> **Check answers:**
> 2 1B   3 4A   4 3C   5 1A   6 3B   7 2B   8 3A

C ▶ Listen and tick the box.

> **Movers tip**
> In Listening Part 4, intonation and key words like 'no', 'yes', 'I see', 'all right' and 'OK' can often help candidates to choose the right answer.

○ Learners listen to the four conversations and put a tick in the box under the right picture. Play the audio twice.

> **Check answers:**
> 1 B   2 B   3 C   4 A

Audioscript

> *Listen and tick the box.*
>
> *One*
> *What's the matter with Ben?*
> Woman: You don't look well, Ben.
> Boy: I know.
> Woman: Have you got toothache again?
> Boy: No. It isn't that.
> Woman: What then? Have you got a headache?
> Boy: No. It's my ear. I've got earache today.
> Woman: Let's phone the doctor.

Two
What was the matter with Kim today?

Girl: Kim didn't come to school today.
Man: Why not? Was she tired?
Girl: No.
Man: Did she have a cold, then?
Girl: No. She has a cough.

Three
What's the matter with Dad?

Girl: Dad, what's the matter? Have you got stomach-ache?
Man: No. Not today.
Girl: Does your back hurt?
Man: No. But I've got a temperature, I think.
Girl: Oh dear!

Four
Why did Mum go to hospital?

Boy: My mum had to go to hospital this morning.
Woman: Oh dear! Why? Did she hurt her leg?
Boy: No. It wasn't her leg or her arm.
Woman: What did she do?
Boy: She hurt her hand.
Woman: I see.

o Ask: *Can you say a sentence about picture 1C?* Do the same for 2A and 2B. Write learners' sentences on the board.
   Suggestions: 1C He's got a headache. / His head hurts. 2A She's got a cold. 2B She's got a cough.

o In pairs, learners take it in turns to say a sentence about one of the pictures in **C**. The other learner listens and says which picture the sentence is about.

D Read and choose the best answer.   Reading & Writing Part 2

o Point to the picture of the boy on the sofa in **E** and say: *This is Tom. He is talking to his classmate Zoe on the phone.* Say: *Read the example and question 1 and tell me: Who was not at school today?* (Tom)

o Read the example question and three answers (A, B, C) with learners and ask: *When someone asks 'How are you?', do you say 'Fine thanks!'?* (yes) *When you get all the answers right, do I say 'Well done!'?* (yes) *When you tell me you like learning English, I can say … ?* (That's cool!)

o Learners choose and circle the best answers for 1–6.

> **Check answers:**
> **1** C   **2** B   **3** A   **4** A   **5** B   **6** B

Complete the sentences about Tom. Use 1, 2 or 3 words.

o Write on the board (or read out the sentence): *Tom didn't go to … yesterday.* Learners tell you the missing word (school) Write/say three more sentences:
   Tom went to hospital because he … . (hurt his foot)
   The nurse that Tom saw was … . (really nice)
   Tom's not in … now. He's at home and he's OK. (hospital)

E Find five differences between Tom and Paul.

o Point to the picture of Tom and the picture of the boy in bed and say: *This is Paul.*
   Say: *Tom and Paul both hurt a part of their body but five things are different. For example, Tom is at home, but Paul is in hospital. What other different things can you see?*

o In pairs, learners make sentences about the other four differences.
   Suggestions:
   1 Tom's awake, but Paul's **asleep**.
   2 Tom has got fair/blond(e) hair, but Paul has got **black** hair.
   3 Tom hurt his leg, but Paul hurt his **arm**.
   4 Tom's on the sofa, but Paul is in **bed**.

F Answer the questions about Paul. Write 1, 2, 3, 4 or 5 words.

o Point to the picture of Paul. Ask: *Where is he?* (in hospital) *What's the matter with Paul?* (His arm hurts. / He hurt his arm.)
   Read out the first sentence and example answer: *He went to hospital.*

o Read question 2 and ask learners to suggest answers. Write their suggestions on the board.
   Read question 3. Give a card from the photocopy of page 117 to one learner and ask them to mime the situation. Encourage learners to use their imagination! Learners can choose their favourite story from the ones on the cards or they can imagine another story.
   Suggestions:
   2 He hurt his arm. / His arm hurts.
   3 See the cards on page 117.
   Accept any reasonable answers, for example:
   4 His new skateboard.
   5 A boy who climbed a mountain.
   6 Play badminton with his best friend.

o Learners copy the answers onto the lines in **F**.

o Learners could draw a picture of another person who has a different problem (The pictures in **C** show lots of possible problems) and, in pairs, write a similar question and answer conversation. Walk round and help if necessary.
   Ask 2–3 pairs to read out their conversation.
   For example:
   Learner A: *What's the matter with Anna?*
   Learner B: *She hurt her foot.*
   Learner A: *How did she do that?*
   Learner B: *She fell off her bike.*
   Learner A: *Oh dear! Where is she now?*
   Learner B: *She's lying on the sofa.*

o In pairs, learners write two sentences like the ones in **A**, with the letters 'e', 'i', 'o', or 'u' missing. Their sentences could be about Tom or Paul or about one of the people in the pictures in **C**. Pairs then exchange sentences and fill in the missing letters.

G Saying 'ch'.

o Say and write on the left of the board: *school.* Point to the letters 'ch' in this word and say: /k/. Learners say: *school.*

o Say and write on the right of the board: *chair, lunch.*
   Point to the letters 'ch' in these words and say: /tʃ/. Learners say the words, then all the words on the board.

o Say: *Listen to the words. Is it /k/ or /tʃ/?*
   Say: *cheese, sandwich, stomach, catch, ache, beach.*
   Learners point to the part of the board with the same sound.
   (With smaller classes, you could ask them to move and stand on the left or the right of the classroom.)
   Note: Flyers words that also have 'ch' as /k/ are: chemist, mechanic.

> **Check answers:**
> school /k/: stomach, ache
> chair, lunch /tʃ/: cheese, sandwich, catch, beach

o Say: *Listen! Can you say this sentence? Charlie chose a cheese sandwich for lunch.* Learners say the sentence a few times.
   Ask: *And can you say this sentence? Kim ate a lot of carrot cake then she had a stomach-ache!*
   Learners say the sentence a few times. Point to these sentences in **G**.
   Half of the class say the Charlie sentence and the other half say Kim's sentence. At first, take it in turns, then both groups say their sentence at the same time!

53

20 Where?

Flyers words: *hill, same, left, right*

Equipment needed
o Coloured pencils or pens. See D.

A Write the words under the pictures.

o Point to the pictures and ask: *Are these pictures of food?* (no) *Are they places?* (yes!)
Point to the first picture (1a) and ask: *What's this?* (a playground)
Point to the words 'a playground' under picture 1a.

o Point to picture 1b and ask: *What can you see here?* (a clothes shop)
Note: Remind learners that 'shop' and 'store' mean the same. 'Store' is used more in American English.
Point to picture 1c and say: *The woman is buying a ticket. She wants to see a film. What's this place?* (a cinema)
Point to picture 1d and say: *People who are ill sleep here. What's this place?* (a hospital)
Learners find the words 'a shop', 'a cinema' and 'a hospital' in the word box and write them under the pictures.

o Learners find the words in the box and write the words for the places under each of the other pictures.
Note: Some words will be needed more than once.

> **Check answers:**
> 1 **b** a shop   **c** a cinema   **d** a hospital
> 2 **a** a supermarket   **b** a market   **c** a shop   **d** a car park
> 3 **a** a farm   **b** a lake   **c** a river   **d** the sea
> 4 **a** a beach   **b** a beach   **c** a beach   **d** a funfair
> 5 **a** a mountain   **b** stairs   **c** a lift   **d** a mountain

Who's the quickest?

o In groups of four, learners practise saying the first four places (a playground, a shop, a cinema, a hospital). Each learner says one word.

o Each group then competes against the other groups. The group to say all four places correctly in the quickest time is the winner.

o You could continue this with the other groups of four words and with two or more learners from each group saying the words together.

o In pairs, learners write the words from the box in their notebook in alphabetical order (without the article). The first pair to finish says *Stop!* They read out the words. If they have ordered them correctly, they are the winners.

Check answers:
beach, car park, cinema, farm, funfair, hospital, lake, lift, market, mountain, playground, river, sea, shop, stairs, supermarket

B Which picture is different and why?

> **Movers tip**
> In Speaking Part 3, any reason for saying why one of the pictures is different is acceptable. Candidates just have to say why they chose that picture. For example, in **A4** in this unit learners can say that picture **d** is different because the people are not on the beach, or because they are wearing trousers, or because there isn't any water, etc.

o Ask learners questions about the pictures in **A**:
Where can you see water? (3b, c, d; 4a, b, c)
Which pictures haven't got any people in them? (1a, b, d; 3a)
Which pictures can you see trees in? (1a; 2d; 3a, c)

o Write on the board: *inside.*
Point to picture 1b and say: *These clothes are inside the shop.* Point to picture 1d and say: *These beds are inside the hospital.*
Point to picture 1a. Say: *The trees in the playground are … (outside). How do you spell 'outside'?* One learner comes to the board and writes *outside* on the board.

o Say: *Look at pictures 1a, b, c, d. One picture is different. Why?*
Ask a learner to say which one is different and why (using the words 'inside' and 'outside' from the board).
Suggested answer: The playground is different because it's outside. The shop, the cinema and the hospital aren't outside. They're inside.

o Write on the board: 2 *driving/buying*   3 *swimming/not swimming* 4 *beach/funfair*   5 *up/down.*
Learners look at the four pictures in 2–5 in small groups and write sentences to say which one is different and why, using the words on the board to help them. Check answers by asking different groups to read out their sentences.
Suggested answers:
2   The car park is different because that person is driving. In the supermarket, the market and the shop, the people are buying things.
3   The farm is different because people aren't swimming there. People are swimming in the lake, the river and the sea.
4   The funfair is different because the children are not on the beach. They're having fun at the funfair!
5   The lift is different because the people are going up in it, and the people on the mountain, on the stairs and on the hill are coming down.

C Read the story. Choose a word from the box. Write the correct word next to numbers 1–5.

Reading & Writing Part **3**

o Point to the word 'sunny' and its picture. Say: *I like sunny weather. Do you? Is the weather sunny today?* (yes/no)
Ask: *Can you make a sentence with sunny in it?* Learners make suggestions, for example: It's sunny today.
Ask: *Can you make a question with 'sunny' in it?* (Is it sunny today?)

o In pairs, learners choose another word from the word box and write a sentence and a question with their chosen word.
Ask different pairs to read out their sentence and question.

Note: With larger classes, you could do this in larger groups.

o If learners can't make sentences or questions with any of the words, teach/revise the words and help learners make sentences and questions with them.

o Say: *This is a story about a brother and a sister. What are their names?* (Fred and Grace)

o Point to the word 'afraid' in the box and ask: *Find a word in the story that means 'afraid'. The word begins with 'f'.* (frightened) Point to this word in the second paragraph.

Point to the word 'sunny' on the line in the example and to this word and the picture of the sun in the box.

o Learners read the story, choose words and write them on the lines next to 1–5.

> **Check answers:**
> **1** lake **2** afraid **3** sandwiches **4** give **5** doctor

o Write on the board: 1 *The children went to the forest on … morning.*
Ask: *When did Grace and Fred go to the lake?* (Saturday)
Write *Saturday* on the line on the board.

o Write five more sentences on the board. Learners copy the sentences and then, in pairs, they complete them about the story.
> **2** They went there on their … .
> **3** The children saw three ducks on a … .
> **4** The children put a … on the grass and sat down.
> **5** Fred and Grace drank some … and ate their … .
> **6** The children gave the ducks some … .

> **Check answers:**
> **2** bikes **3** small island **4** rug
> **5** (apple) juice, (cheese) sandwiches **6** (of their) bread

o Point to the three names for this story. Ask learners: *What's the best name for this story? Grace's new bike?* (no) Explain: *We read that Grace and Fred ride their bikes to the lake, but the whole text is not about this.*
Mum has a picnic? (no) *(Grace and Fred had a picnic, not their mum.)*
Fred's duck friends? (yes) *The story is about Fred and Grace making friends with the ducks.*

D Make your pictures the same!

o Teach/revise: 'left' and 'right'. As most children are right-handed, it may help to say: *You write with your right hand!* Check that learners have coloured pencils or pens.
Learners work in A and B pairs. Learner A looks at the picture on page 109. Learner B looks at page 110. Say: *You both have a picture of Grace and Fred. Which part of the story can you see in your pictures?* (eating sandwiches by the lake)
Say: *Read the sentences under your pictures. Colour the things in your picture.* When learners have finished colouring their pictures, ask:
Where did Grace and Fred sit that day? (on a rug) *Can you see a rug?* (no) *Take a pencil and draw their rug, please! Draw a rug under Grace and Fred! Brilliant!*
What did Grace and Fred drink that day? (apple juice) *Can you see any apple juice in your picture?* (no) *Take a pencil and draw two glasses of apple juice on the rug near Grace and Fred! Thank you.*
Say: *Your pictures are different. You have different colours in different places. Learners with picture A, tell learners with picture B what things to colour. Then, learners with picture B, tell your partner what to colour in their picture.*
When they finish, learners compare their pictures.

o Learners can colour the rest of the picture in colours of their choice.

E Find the 'k's!

o Say: *Look at the words above the picture in A and at the words in C. How many 'k's can you find? Draw a line under all the 'k's! When you find them all, put both hands in the air and shout: OK!*

> **Check answers:**
> **in A:** market, supermarket, car park, lake
> **in C:** walk, lake (in the pictures), bike, lake, rocks, ducks, drink, asked, took, look, like, sick, think
> Note: 'duck' is in the text seven times.

Write on the board: *think*. Point to the letters 'nk' and ask: *Can you find another word in the text that has 'nk' at the end?* (drink) Add the word *drink* to the board.

Write on the board: *lake*. Point to the letters 'ke' and ask: *Can you find another word in the text that has 'ke' at the end?* (bike, like) Add the words *bike* and *like* to the board.

Write on the board: *rock* Point to the letters 'ck' and ask: *Can you find another word in the text that has 'ck' at the end?* (duck, sick) Add the words *duck* and *sick* to the board.

Write on the board: *took*. Point to the letters 'ook' and ask: *Can you find another word in the text that has 'ook' at the end?* (look) Add the word *look* to the board.

Write on the board: *desk*. Point to the letters 'sk' and ask: *Can you find another word in the text that has 'sk'?* (asked) Add the word *asked* to the board.

Say: *There is another word in the box above the text in C which has the letter 'k'. Which word?* (walk) *Can you tell me another word like 'walk' with a different first letter?* (talk)

Explain: *At the end of words (and syllables too), the letter 'k' likes to have some letters in front of or behind it. The letters 'k' likes are: 'oo', 'c', 'n', 'l' and 's'. And it also likes 'e' to come after it. Some words like 'skate', 'skirt', 'skip' start with 'sk' too.*

Other Starters and Movers words: book, cook; clock, pick up; think, thank; like, make, wake; basketball.

> **K words**
>
> In pairs or small groups, learners make a word cloud with words that have 'k' in their spellings. They could use an online programme like *tagxedo* or *wordle* to do this, or they could make their own with colouring pens and add pictures. They could do this for homework and add it to their project files.

Play the game! Where am I hiding?

o Hide yourself somewhere in the classroom, for example behind your desk or a cupboard. Ask learners:
What am I doing? (hiding)

o Use the 20 pictures in **A**. Tell learners you are hiding in picture 1a, b, c or d. They ask you questions to find out where you are.

o Write examples of good questions to ask on the board:
Are you outside?
Are you inside?
Are you on holiday?
Are you in water?
Are you moving?
Are you buying something?
Is it cold?
Is it sunny?

o Learners choose one of the 20 pictures and 'hide' themselves in it. In small groups, they take it in turns to guess where each of them has hidden.

21 Here and there in town

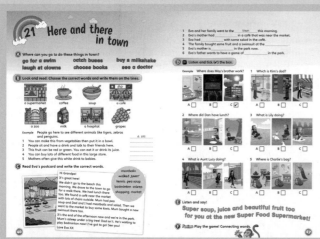

Pronunciation practice /uː/ for vowel spellings in words such as *juice, soup, you, food*. See E.

Flyers word: *postcard*

Not in YLE wordlists: *super*

Equipment needed

- Movers Audio 21D.

Which place is this?

- Write the following sentences on the board, underlining as suggested:

  You can go and see a film <u>here</u>.

  You go to <u>this place</u> to see a film.

  <u>Where</u> are you going? I'm going to see a film!

  Say: *These sentences are about a place that you can find in most towns.* Ask: *What's this place?* (a cinema)

- Ask: *How many of you like going to the cinema to see a film? Put up your hands!*

  Learners count the number of hands. Write on the board (including the number): *… children in this class like going to the cinema to see a film*

- Ask: *Do you know another word for 'film'?* (movie) Add to the sentence on the board: *… or a movie.*

  Say: *Can you see the word 'move' in 'movies'? People in America used this word to talk about films because the pictures they saw in a cinema weren't like photos. The people they saw in a movie 'moved'!*

A Where can you go to do these things in town?

- Ask learners to think about their town / the nearest town. In pairs, learners write a list of different places that people can go to in a town. Encourage them to use dictionaries if necessary. Ask: *Can you think of ten different places in a town?*

- Check answers by asking a pair for one of their answers. Ask: *How many of you wrote that answer, too?* Pairs check their lists and put up their hands if they have the same answer. Continue in the same way with different pairs. If a pair gives an answer that no-one else has thought of, congratulate them!

  Suggestions from Movers wordlist: cinema, park, bookshop, library, bus station, train station, car park, hospital, café, market, supermarket, pool, sports centre, shops, shopping centre, zoo (and sweet / shoe / cake / clothes shop / store etc.)

  Ask: *Which building in your town do you like most? Are any buildings in your town ugly?*

  Encourage learners to share ideas when they are answering these questions.

- To give learners practice in using infinitive for purpose, say: *Look at the six things you can do in A.* Ask: *Where can you go to go for a swim?* (to a [swimming] pool). *Where can you go to choose books?* (to a bookshop / library)

  In pairs, learners ask and answer the other four questions. Check answers by asking different pairs: *Where do you go to catch buses / see a doctor / buy a milkshake / laugh at clowns?*

  Suggestions: at a bus station / bus stop, in/at a hospital, in/at a supermarket / a café / a circus

  Ask different learners: *What's your favourite milkshake? Do you like going to the circus? What makes you laugh the most?*

- Ask: *Why do people go to a station?* (to catch a train) *Why do people go to a shopping centre?* (to buy clothes / shoes / toys / games / bags / books) *Why do people go to a zoo?* (to see animals)

B Look and read. Choose the correct words and write them on the lines.

Reading & Writing Part 1

> **Movers tip**
>
> For Reading and Writing Part 1, candidates should know that one picture will not be needed for an answer. Encourage them to underline the key words in each definition. These words will help them find the correct answers.

- Learners look at the pictures. Say: *Four of these pictures are places and four of these pictures are things you …?* (eat or drink) Learners draw red circles around the place words, and blue circles around the food and drink words.

- Say: *Look at the words coffee and café. Listen! Stand up when I say the drink. Sit down when I say the place.*

  Say (pausing between words): *Coffee, café, café, coffee, café, coffee, coffee, café!*

- Read out the example: *People go here to see different animals like tigers, zebras and penguins.* Ask: *Which place is the answer?* (a zoo) *Which words help us choose the right answer?* (go, see, animals, tigers, zebras, penguins)

- Say: *Look at questions 1–5.* Learners decide if each sentence is about a place or about food and drink. They underline the key words that help them decide.

  Say: *Look at the pictures and words, choose your answers and write them on the lines.*

> **Check answers:**
> **1** soup **2** a café **3** grapes **4** a supermarket **5** milk

- In pairs, learners talk together and then write in their notebooks:

  – three things they can see in a hospital (For example: bed, doctor, nurse, medicine, people, windows, cupboards, doors)

  – three things they can drink in a café (For example: milk, tea, coffee, lemonade, water, orange juice, cola)

  – three kinds of fruit they can buy in a supermarket (For example: apples, bananas, pears, pineapples, oranges, mangoes, watermelons) Walk around and check spellings.

- Ask pairs: *How many letters are there in your nine words?* Each pair tells you what their total is. Ask the pair with the highest number of letters to read out their list of nine words, one at a time.

C Read Eva's postcard and write the correct words.

- Learners look at the picture on the front of the postcard.

  Ask: *Where's Eva now? On a beach? In a park? In the mountains?*

  Without looking at the text, learners guess.

  Ask: *Who thinks Eva's on a beach / in a park / in the mountains?*

  Learners put up their hands. Count the answers, then write on the board (insert the number of learners):

... *children think Eva's on a beach.*
... *children think she's in a park.*
... *children think she's in the mountains.*

o   Learners read the postcard. Ask: *Who's Eva writing to?* (her grandpa)
Does Eva like this place? (yes)
Did Eva have lunch on the beach? (no)
Who is Eva on holiday with? (her mum and dad)
Where's Eva now? (in a park)
Point to and read out the sentence on the board, including the number you wrote in it: (...) *children think she's in a park.* Say: *Well done! You were right! Eva is in the park!*

o   Read out 1: *Eva and her family went to the town this morning.* Point to the crossed-out word 'town' in the yellow word circle.

o   Learners find and write words for 2–6. Remind them that three words will not be used.

> **Check answers:**
> 2 pea soup   3 meatballs   4 market   5 asleep   6 badminton

Let's talk about holidays.   Speaking **4** Part

o   Ask different learners the following questions.
Where do you go in the holidays? To the park? To the beach? To the mountains? To the countryside?
Who is with you in the holidays? Your family? Your friends?
What do you do in the holidays? Do you swim? Do you eat ice cream? Do you go to the cinema? Do you play computer games?

o   Ask a volunteer to come and sit with you. Say: *Now let's talk about holidays.*
Where do you go in the holidays?
Who is with you in the holidays?
What do you do in the holidays?
Tell me about your favourite holiday.

o   Repeat this with another learner.
Note: In the Movers Speaking Test, learners are not asked to say two different things when they answer the 'Tell me about ...' question, but it is good if they do that.

D ▶ Listen and tick the box.   Listening **4** Part

o   Learners look at the example: *Where does May's brother work?*
Ask: *Which places can you see in the three pictures?* (a shop, a cinema, a sports centre)

o   Play the first part of the audio. Learners listen. Point to the answer (C) and ask: *Does he work in a sports centre?* (yes)

o   Play the rest of the audio. Learners listen to questions 1–5 and tick the boxes.

> **Check answers:**
> 1 B   2 C   3 A   4 B   5 A

Audioscript

> *Listen and tick the box.*
>
> *Example*   *Where does May's brother work?*
> Boy: Where does your brother work, May? Does he work in a shop?
> Girl: Not now. He works at the sport centre.
> Boy: Which one?
> Girl: The one opposite the cinema.
> *One*   *Which is Kim's dad?*
> Woman: Is your dad in town today, Kim?
> Boy: Yes, but he isn't at the supermarket.
> Woman: Oh! Is he at the market then? It's market day today.
> Boy: I know. But Dad's at the library this morning.
> *Two*   *Where did Dan have lunch?*
> Woman: Did you have lunch at home, Dan?
> Boy: No, Grandma. We had a picnic on the grass at the zoo.
> Woman: You didn't eat in the café there then?
> Boy: No!

> *Three*   *What is Lily doing?*
> Woman: What's Lily doing? Is she having a swimming lesson?
> Boy: No, she's fishing with her friend.
> Woman: Oh! And where's her sister?
> Boy: She's helping at the farm today.
> *Four*   *What is Aunt Lucy doing?*
> Girl: Hello Aunt Lucy! Are you at the hospital?
> Woman: No! I'm waiting to buy my ticket.
> Girl: At the train station?
> Woman: No. At the bus stop. I'm coming to see you!
> *Five*   *Where is Charlie's bag?*
> Woman: Where's your bag, Charlie? Why haven't you got it?
> Boy: It's OK, Mum. It's in our classroom.
> Woman: Not in the sweet shop or in the playground again?
> Boy: No, Mum. Don't worry!

Ask and answer questions

Divide learners into different A and B pairs. A learners look at the questions on page 109. B learners look at the questions on page 110. Pairs take turns to ask and answer their questions.

E Listen and say! Super soup!

o   Teach/revise 'Super!' Walk around the classroom. Point at someone's shoes/boots and say: *Super shoes! Super boots!*

o   Write on the board: *juice   you   new   clock   food*
Point to the five words and say: *Four of these words sound the same. But one of them sounds different. Which one? Listen!* Say the words slowly and carefully making sure you use the /uː/ for the vowel sound in 'juice', 'you', 'new' and 'food'. ('clock' (/klɒk/) is different).

o   Tell learners to imagine they are working at a street market and want to shout about what they are selling! Make sure they are pronouncing the underlined vowels correctly (/uː/). In chorus they call out:
Super soup, juice and beautiful fruit too for you at the new Super Food Supermarket!

F Play the game! Connecting words.

o   Write the word *café* on the board, vertically, then write words connected with 'café' around the letters. For example:
c a k e
w **a** t e r
c o **f** f e e
t **e** a

o   Write other places on the board, for example: *park, farm, shop, town, city, road, circus, funfair.* Learners work in groups. Point to the café example on the board and say: *Choose one place and write words round it.*

> **Suggested connecting words:**
> **park**   **p**layground, foot**b**all, wate**r**, duc**k**s
> **farm**   **f**ield, t**r**actor, work, far**m**er
> **shop**   **s**upermarket, **h**ungry, d**o**or, sho**p**ping,
> **town**   s**t**reets, r**o**ads, flo**w**ers, statio**n**
> **city**   **c**entre, fam**i**ly, hospi**t**al, lorr**y**
> **road**   moto**r**bike, sh**o**p, c**a**rs, **d**rive
> **circus** **c**lown, k**i**ds, tiger, dan**c**e, laugh, hor**s**e
> **funfair** **f**un, b**u**sy, ca**n**dy, **f**antastic, **g**ames, **t**icket, **r**ide

22   A trip to the city

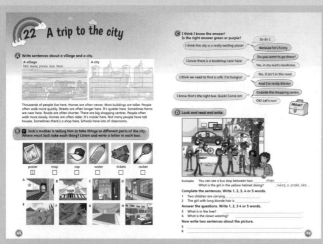

Pronunciation practice sounding 'qu' /kw/. See 'Questions! What's really quiet? What moves quickly?'

Equipment needed

- ○ Movers Audio 22B.
- ○ Colouring pencils or pens. See D.

Ⓐ Write sentences about a village and a city.

- ○ Point to the picture behind the lines in the first box. Ask: *What's this?* (a village) *How many homes are there in a village? What do you think?*

- ○ Read out the sentence that is already written in the 'village' picture: *Not many people live here.* Ask: *Is this right or wrong?* (It's right.)

  Ask: *What's good about living in a village?*

  Suggestions: It's quiet. There are pretty gardens. You can play and ride bikes. You can climb trees.

  Ask: *What's not good about living in a village?*

  Suggestions: It's not exciting. You can't go to the cinema. There are no shops. The houses are old. You don't have lots and lots of friends.

- ○ Point to the picture in the second box. Ask: *What's this?* (a city)

  How many houses and flats are there in a city? Do you know the answer?

  How many people live in our city / town / village? Guess!

  Learners answer.

  Read out the first sentence below the pictures. *Thousands of people live here.* Ask: *Is this sentence about a city or a village?* (a city)

  Learners write this sentence on the first line in the 'city' picture.

  Learners read the other sentences and write them in the 'village' or 'city' picture.

  > **Check answers:**
  > **In a village:** It's quieter here. Sometimes farms are near here. Roads are often shorter. People often walk more slowly. Homes are often older. Not many people have tall houses. Sometimes, there's a shop here.
  > **In a city:** Thousands of people live here. Homes are often newer. Most buildings are taller. People often walk more quickly. Streets are often longer here. There are big shopping centres. It's noisier here. Schools have lots of classrooms.

- ○ Read out the following sentences. Working in pairs, learners listen and find words in the city or village texts which match the definition. Ask different pairs to give an answer.

  Children go here to have lessons. (school classrooms)

  There are often cows and sheep in these places. (farms)

  You can buy all kinds of things here. (a shop / shopping centre)

  These have lots of rooms in them and sometimes stairs or lifts too.

(buildings)

Cars, buses and lorries drive on these. (roads/streets)

Note: If anyone questions the difference between 'roads' and 'streets', one explanation is that roads don't always have buildings in them, but streets always do.

Ⓑ ▶ Listen and write a letter in each box

- ○ Point to the eight pictures of places in **B** and say: *These places are all in a city. Which places can you see?* (a station, a circus, a sports shop, a library, a river, a park, a (swimming) pool, a computer shop)

- ○ Say: *Listen. Jack and his dad have to go to this city.* Point to the pictures of the objects in **B** and say: *Jack's mother is telling them to take these things to different places in the city. Listen! What's the first thing that Jack has to take? Where does he have to take it?* Learners listen to the example on the audio. Check that learners understand that Jack has to take the poster to the library (D) and that they can see the letter D in the box next to the poster.

- ○ Play the rest of the audio. Learners compare answers in pairs. Play the audio a second time before checking answers.

  > **Check answers:**
  > tennis racket G   cap C   tickets B   water E   map A

- ○ Ask different learners questions: *The man at the swimming pool is really good at fixing things. In your family, who is good at fixing things?*

  Jack and his family have three tickets for the circus. Do you like going to the circus? Why / why not?

  Jack and his dad are taking a map of the city. Do you take a map with you when you go to the city?

Audioscript

> *Listen and look. There is one example.*
> *Jack's mother is telling him to take things to different parts of the city. Where must Jack take each thing?*
>
> | | |
> |---|---|
> | Woman: | Right, Jack. I'd like you and Dad to take some things to the city with you. |
> | Boy: | OK! |
> | Woman: | Can you take this poster to the library, please? It's about piano lessons. Ask them to put it up on the wall. |
> | Boy: | All right, Mum. |
>
> *Can you see the letter D?*
> *Now you listen and write a letter in each box.*
>
> | | |
> |---|---|
> | Woman: | Take this tennis racket, too. You can put it in your bag. |
> | Boy: | Where should I take that? |
> | Woman: | Take it to the swimming pool. The man there is really good at fixing things. I phoned him this morning about it. |
> | Boy: | Oh! OK. |
> | | |
> | Woman: | And take your new baseball cap. The one that's too small. |
> | Boy: | Should I take it back to the sports shop? |
> | Woman: | Yes, and choose a bigger one, OK? |
> | Boy: | All right. |
> | | |
> | Boy: | Do you want me to take these tickets, too? |
> | Woman: | Yes. We can't go on that day now. Take them to the circus. Get three tickets for Tuesday. OK! |
> | Boy: | All right. |
> | | |
> | Woman: | And here's a bottle of water. |
> | Boy: | What's that for, Mum? To take to the park? |
> | Woman: | No, to take on your walk by the river. You always get thirsty in the city. |

Boy:	You're right… Good idea!
Woman:	Oh! And here's the city map that I got from the computer shop.
Boy:	OK.
Woman:	It's got a mistake on it! Show it to the man at the station, please. We don't want people to catch the wrong train!
Boy:	*(laughing)* All right! Don't worry, Mum.

Questions! What's really quiet? What moves quickly?

o Say: *Listen! Question. Quiet. Quickly. Which are the first two letters of 'question', 'quiet' and 'quickly'?* (qu)

o Divide learners into small groups. Ask them to write the answers to these questions: *What makes a loud noise when it moves in a city?* (a plane, a train, a motorbike, a lorry, a bus, a car) *What makes quieter noises in a city?* (TVs, radios, phones, people, the wind) *What's really quiet?* (snow, bikes, computers, birds, mice, spiders)

o *What moves really quickly in a city?* (planes, trains, cars, etc.) *What moves more slowly in a city?* (bikes, people, cats, etc.) *What moves really slowly?*

o Write on the board: *Which is quieter? A car or a computer? Please answer our question quickly and quietly!*

o Two groups join together. They put the words both groups have written in order from the loudest to the quietest and from the quickest to the slowest.

  Ask the class the question, pointing to each word as you speak. Then, groups take turns to ask and answer the question quickly and quietly.

C I think I know the answer! Is the right answer green or purple?

> **Movers tip**
>
> In Reading and Writing Part 2, candidates have to choose a correct response to something that someone has said. The options are right or wrong depending on context and function. For example, if the first speaker is making a suggestion, the correct answer is likely to be something beginning with 'Yes', 'No' or 'OK' or expressions like 'Good idea!' Help learners prepare for this task by asking them to reply to suggestions in class.

o Ask three confident learners to come to the front of the class with their books and stand side by side. Ask the one in the middle (eg Maria) to read out the first speech bubble in **C**: *I think this city is a really exciting place!* Say to the class: *Listen! Which person is really listening to what (Maria) said?*

  One learner reads out the green answer and the other learner reads out the purple answer. Learners point at the student who gave the green answer.

o Learners role play their conversation again. When she hears the green answer, Maria turns to that classmate and nods/smiles. When she hears the purple answer, Maria turns to that classmate / shakes her head / frowns because 'Because he's funny.' can't be a correct reply.

o Ask three other groups to act out the other mini conversations in the same way showing which response is correct by nodding/ shaking their heads.

  Correct responses: Do you want to go there?
  And I'm really thirsty!
  OK! Let's run!

D Look and read and write.

Reading & Writing **6** Part

o Point to the picture and say: *Ben lives in the city. Some people are laughing in Ben's street because they're watching Ben's uncle. Ben's uncle is a clown.*

o Look at the two examples. Ask: *Where's the bus stop?* Learners point to the bus stop. Point to the two shop windows and ask: *What are these?* (shops) Point to the words two shops on the line in the first example.

  Ask: *Where's the girl in the yellow helmet? What's she doing?* (a riding a bike) *What colour is her bike?* (purple). Point to the words *riding a purple bike* on the line in the second example.

  Say: *There are two more people in this picture with helmets on their heads. Where are they?* (on the motorbike) *What colour are their helmets?* (purple and blue)

o Explain to learners that they can write between one and five words for their answers to 1–4. Learners read 1–4 and write words on the lines.

> **Check answers:**
>
> (Suggestions) **1** a (big) TV/television / (computer) screen   **2** playing a (red) / the guitar   **3** a (little black / grey / gray) cat/kitten   **4** funny clothes and blue boots

o Write the first example on the board and say: *The bus stop is between two shops …..* Ask: *Can you make this sentence longer? Can you add words to the end?*

  Learners suggest words to add.

  Suggestions: an old man is waiting there. / but I can't see a bus.

  Say: *Now, write two more sentences about the people and the things in the picture in D. Write them on the lines next to 5 and 6. You can write a short sentence like 'I can see a bus stop.' or a longer sentence like, 'The bus stop is between two shops.' or you can write a very long sentence like 'The bus stop is between two shops and an old man is waiting there.'*

o Learners write sentences in 5 and 6.

  Suggestions:

  These people look happy.
  Two people are riding a motorbike.
  An old man is waiting at the bus stop.
  The red car is bigger than the white car.
  The clown is throwing and catching three balls.
  The girl in the red jacket is laughing because the clown is funny.
  You can see some handbags, shoes and boots in one of the shops.

Colour that car!

o Learners look at the picture again. Say: *Listen and colour.* Read out each instruction allowing time for learners to colour each object.

  1 *Can you see the car – the small one that's in front of the bigger one? Colour that car red, please.*

  2 *Now find the man with the beard. Can you see him? Colour one of his bags. Colour the bag that is in his hand. Make it blue.*

  3 *There are three televisions in the picture. Colour the one that the boys are carrying. Can you see it? Colour it yellow.*

  4 *And now, colour the coat, the one that the clown is wearing. Colour it purple for me, please. Great! Thanks.*

o Learners look at each other's pictures and see if they are the same.

> **Check answers:**
>
> **1** small car – red   **2** bag in man's hand – blue   **3** television in boys' hands – yellow   **4** clown's coat – purple

🧳 City project

o Learners choose a famous city and find out about it on the internet to create a fact sheet. They can glue a picture onto a piece of card and write answers to the following questions: Where is this city? How many people live in this city? Why is this city famous? What's the weather like in this city? How do people travel in this city?

o Learners can then complete two sentences:
  I'd like to go to this city because …   In this city I'd like to …

o Learners can add their city fact sheets to their project file. Alternatively display them on the classroom walls if possible.

23   The world around us

Pronunciation practice /dʒ/ /g/. See E.

Flyers words: *engineer*

Equipment needed

- ○ Movers Audio 23C.
- ○ Colouring pencils or pens. See C.
- ○ Photocopies (one for each group of 3–4 learners) of the quiz on page 118. See F.

Ⓐ Draw circles round the things that you can see in the picture.

- ○ Point to the picture in **A** and say: *Look at this picture. The weather is great and the children are enjoying their day.* Learners read the words and then draw circles round any of these things that they can see in the picture.

> **Check answers:**
> grass, plants, rocks, a waterfall, mountains, clouds, a path

- ○ Ask seven different learners to come and each write one of the seven words that they have circled on the board.

  Say: *Help me clean the board. Make a sentence about the picture with each of these words.*

  Different learners say a sentence about the picture containing one of the words on the board. For example: *There is grass round the lake.*

  Ask all learners to repeat the sentence, then rub the word 'grass' off the board. Continue till there are no words left on the board.

  Suggested sentences:

  The plants are near the lake.

  There is one really big rock and one smaller rock.

  The beautiful waterfall is behind the children.

  There are three mountains.

Ⓑ Look at the picture and read. What are these sentences about?

- ○ Point to the picture and ask: *Where are the children?* (in the countryside)
- ○ Point to the sentences in **B** and say: *These sentences are about things you can see in the picture.*

  Read out sentence 1: *People like walking or climbing up these when they are on holiday.* Ask: *Do you know what this sentence is about?* (mountains) *Is the answer 'mountain' or 'mountains'?* (mountains because 'these' is a word to talk about more than one thing.) *Can you see the mountains in the picture in B? How many mountains are there?* (three) Learners write *mountains* on the line in 1.

- ○ Ask a learner to read out sentence 2. Ask: *You can go sailing on the sea, on a river and on …?* (a lake) *Do we write 'lakes' or 'a lake'?* (a lake) *Which word tells us to write this?* (it) *Is the lake in the picture big or small?* (small) Learners write *a lake* on the line in 2.

- ○ Say: *Read sentences 3–6 and write words on the lines. You can find all of them in the picture in A. Remember to look for words like 'these' or 'it'!*

  In pairs, learners look at the picture and write words on the lines.

> **Check answers:**
> **3** a forest   **4** leaves   **5** a village   **6** the sun

- ○ Point to sentence 6 and say: *Let's change this sentence and make it about the moon! Which words do we need to change?* Write on the board: *Go outside*

  Ask: *Do you see the moon in the day or at night?* (at night) Write: *at night* on the board after 'Go outside'. Continue writing sentence 6 on the board until you come to 'hot' and 'yellow'. Ask: *Is the moon hot?* (no – cold) *Is the moon yellow?* (no – white) Ask: *Is the moon always round?* (no – sometimes) The sentence on the board should read:

  Go outside at night, look up and see this! It's big, cold, white, and sometimes round.

Ⓒ ▶ Listen and colour and write.

> **Movers tip**
>
> In Listening Part 5, candidates have to colour parts of the picture and write a word. The words that they have to write are from the Movers wordlist. The word isn't spelt for them, but other information will help learners recognise the word. Candidates must spell the word correctly.

- ○ Read out these sentences about the picture. Learners stand up if the sentence is correct and sit down if it is wrong.

  There's a waterfall in the picture. (yes)

  The girl is fishing. (no)

  There are some flowers at the bottom of the mountain. (no)

  One of the boys is sleeping. (yes)

  The weather is sunny. (yes)

- ○ Say: *Listen to a man and a girl talking about the picture. First, there's an example.*

  Play the example. Then, play the rest of the audio twice.

> **Check answers:**
> **1** Colour the biggest rock - purple.
> **2** Colour the waterfall - blue.
> **3** Write 'swim' on the board after 'Do not'.
> **4** Colour the smallest fish - orange.
> **5** Colour the nearest roof - red.

- ○ Say: *Now, draw one more thing in the picture and colour another thing.* Give them two minutes to do this.

- ○ Write on the board: *Draw a .... (behind / between / in / in front of / inside / near / next to / on / under) the ...., please!*

  Colour the .... black / blue / brown / green / grey / orange / pink / purple / red / yellow, please!

  Note: You could ask learners to tell you prepostions of place and colours and/or write them on the board.

  Say: *Your pictures are different now. Work in pairs. Learner A, tell B which thing to draw and which thing to colour in their picture. Learner B, listen and draw and colour! Then, Learner B, you tell A.* When they finish, their pictures should look the same!

Audioscript

Look at the picture. Listen and look. There is one example.

Man: Hello. Would you like to colour this picture?

Girl: Yes, please!

Man: Can you see the boy fishing?

Girl: Yes. Can I colour his hat?

Man: OK. Make the boy's hat yellow.

Girl: Right. I'm doing that now.

Can you see the yellow hat? This is an example. Now you listen and colour and write.

One

Man: Now, find the rocks in the picture.

Girl: Right. I can see them on the ground.

Man: Colour the biggest rock purple.

Girl: OK.

Two

Man: Can you see the waterfall?

Girl: Yes. Shall I colour it?

Man: Yes, please. Make it blue.

Girl: OK. There!

Man: Thank you.

Three

Girl: What can I do now?

Man: Can you see the board in the lake?

Girl: Yes! Can I write something on it?

Man: Yes. Write 'swim' on it after 'do not'.

Girl: Oh! You mean people shouldn't go swimming here?

Man: That's right. It's too dangerous.

Four

Man: There are three fish in the water.

Girl: Yes. I can see them. They can swim really fast!

Man: I know! Colour the smallest one.

Girl: What colour?

Man: How about orange? That's a good colour for a fish!

Girl: Good idea!

Five

Girl: Right! What now? More colouring?

Man: Yes! Can you see the houses?

Girl: There are two. Which one shall I colour?

Man: The nearest one, but only colour its roof. Make it red.

Girl: OK. I'm colouring that roof now.

Man: Brilliant! Thanks.

D Read and cross out the wrong words.

o Say: *Look at the words in A. Which words could you find in a text about jungles?*

Suggestions: flowers, rocks, grass, a waterfall, plants

Ask: *What do you know about jungles?*

(There are jungles in different parts of the world. Lots of animals and plants live in them, the trees are very tall, etc.)

o Read out the first sentence: *Jungles are cold/hot and dry/wet places.* Ask: *Are jungles cold or hot?* (hot) *Are jungles dry or wet?* (wet) Learners cross out 'cold' and 'dry' in this sentence.

o Learners read the rest of the text and cross out the wrong words, leaving the correct words to complete the text.

> **Check answers (words remaining):**
> **3** green **4** often **5** animals **6** rivers **7** crocodiles **8** water
> **9** boat

o Ask questions about the text:

Why are jungles green? (Because it often rains and there are lots of plants.)

Where do people live in jungles? (next to rivers and waterfalls because they need water)

How do people travel along the river? (by boat)

E Write *g* or *j* to complete the words, then say the sentences!

o Write on the board: *game   glass   goat*

Point to each word and say it at the same time. Learners repeat the words.

o Point to the first sentence in **E**. Ask: *Which letter do we need to complete these words?* (g) Say: *Write the 'g's in the sentence!*

Sentence: There are some **g**reat **g**reen **g**rapes in **G**race's **g**randma's **g**arden.

Ask: *Did you write a capital (big) letter for Grace's name? Check!*

Ask a learner to say the sentence. Then, ask a pair of learners to say the sentence, then a group of 3, then 4, then 5 learners. Do this a few times till all the learners in the class say the sentence.

o Write on the board (below *game, glass, goat*): *jump giraffe*

Ask: *Do 'jump' and 'giraffe' start with the same sound?* (yes).

Add to the board: *cage, engineer*. Point to the 'ge' and 'gi' in these two words and say /dʒ/, *cage, engineer*.

o Say: *Write the letter 'j' or 'g' in the second sentence in E.*

Sentence: **J**ill's hu**g**e **g**iraffe en**j**oys ve**g**etables and **j**ungle **j**uice!

Practise saying both sentences, then half of the class says the grapes sentence and the other 'answers' with the giraffe sentence.

o Learners can write their own words with 'g' or 'j' missing. They can use the wordlists on pages 116–123 of their books to find these. Then, they give their words with no 'g's or 'j's to another learner, who writes the 'g's and 'j's.

They could also write their own sentences with 'g's and 'j's.

F Do the *World Around Us* quiz!

o Give one photocopy of the quiz on page 118 to each group of 3–4 learners.

o Each group discusses the answers to the questions and/or looks for the answers in encyclopedias or on the internet.

> **Check answers:**
> **1** Russia **2** the Vatican City **3** Mount Everest **4** the Nile
> **5** South China Sea **6** Caspian Sea **7** Shanghai **8** Australia
> **9** Angel Falls **10** the Taiga

o Learners answer the questions about their country. You could ask them to do this as a research project for homework.

24 Travelling, texting, phoning

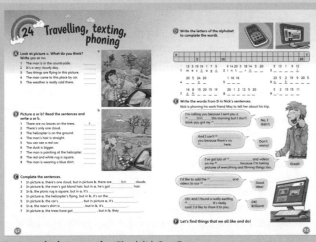

Pronunciation practice Final /t/. See E.

Flyers words: *sound*

Equipment needed

o Photocopies (one for each learner) of the activity on page 119. See F.

o Magazines with pictures of people, places, etc. See F.

A What do you think? Write *yes* or *no*.

o Learners keep their books closed. Say: *Close your eyes and listen to these sentences.* Say the sentences twice.

1 *The man in this picture is in the countryside.*
2 *It's a very cloudy day.*
3 *Two things are flying in this picture.*
4 *The man came to this place by car.*
5 *The weather is really cold.*

Say: *Write down five things that you saw in the picture in your head. For example, a man.*

Allow learners time to write five things, then they compare their lists in pairs or small groups.

Suggestions: trees, a river, clouds, a bird, a plane, a car, snow.

o Say: *Open your books. Look at picture a on page 52. Is the picture like the one that you saw in your head?* Make sure learners understand that all of their imagined pictures will be very different. That is a good thing!

Now, read the sentences next to the picture. If you think the sentence is correct for the picture, write 'yes'. If the sentence is not correct write 'no'.

Ask learners to suggest why each sentence is right or wrong.

Suggestions

1 *Yes. We can see trees, a river and grass.*
2 *No. There's only one cloud.*
3 *Yes. A helicopter and a kite are flying.*
4 *Yes, probably, because he is next to a red car.*
5 *No. The man is only wearing a shirt; no coat or sweater.*

Close your books. Answer the questions.

o Say: *Look at the picture in A for one minute and try to remember as much about it as possible.*

After a minute, say: *Close your books, please.*

o Ask the following questions. In pairs, learners discuss the answers to the questions and write their answers in their notebooks.

1 *What colour's the man's shirt?*
2 *What animal can you see?*
3 *What colour's the car?*
4 *How many trees are there in the picture?*
5 *What kind of hair has the man got?*
6 *What's blue and in front of the trees?*

o Learners swap notebooks with another pair. Check answers by asking different learners to write an answer on the board. They correct each other's answers and give marks for correct answers which are also correctly spelled.

> **Check answers:**
> **1** pink **2** a duck **3** red **4** two **5** curly/brown **6** a/the river

B Picture a or b? Read the sentences and write *a* or *b*.

o Say: *Look at pictures 'a' and 'b'.* Ask: *Which things can you see in both pictures?*

Suggestions: a man, a helicopter, a duck, a car, clouds, a river, a picnic, two trees

o Learners read sentences 1–9 and write 'a' after the sentences which correctly describe that picture and 'b' after the sentences which describe picture 'b'.

> **Check answers:**
> **picture a**: 2, 5, 6, 7
> **picture b**: 3, 4, 8, 9

C Complete the sentences.

> **Movers tip**
>
> For Speaking Part 1 and Part 3, candidates need practice in linking ideas using 'and' and 'but'. For example: 'In this picture, the man's hair is straight and blond, but in this picture, the man's hair is brown and curly'. Practise comparing pictures and objects in class.

o Ask: *How many differences can you see between the two pictures?* In pairs, learners find the differences. (There are ten.)

Note: In Speaking Part 1 there will only be five differences.

o Ask: *Can you see clouds in picture 'a'?* (yes) *How many clouds are there?* (one) *And in picture 'b', are there any clouds?* (yes) *How many clouds are there?* (two)

Say: *This is one of the differences. Now, complete sentences 2–7 to talk about more differences.*

o Learners complete sentences.

> **Check answers:**
> **2** brown **3** round **4** ground **5** blue ... red **6** pink ... blue
> **7** leaves ... don't have / have no leaves

o Ask: *Which differences did you not complete sentences about?* (the kite, the man pointing/phoning)

Ask learners to say or write sentences to talk about these differences.

D Write the letters of the alphabet to complete the words.

○ Ask: *How many letters are there in the English alphabet?* (26) Point to the letters 'a' and 'z' in **D** and say: *Write the 24 missing letters, please.*

Point to the letter 'e' and the number 5 and say: *'E' is the fifth letter of the alphabet. Write the numbers for the other letters in the boxes!*

Point to the word *message* in **D** and explain: *The numbers above the letters and/or lines are the number of that letter in the alphabet.*

Say: *Let's complete the word in 2! Which letter is 5?* (e) *There are two number 5s, so write two 'e's! Letter number 20 is at the end of this word and it's also the third letter. Which letter is it?* (t) *Which word can you read now?* (internet)

○ Learners write letters to complete words 3–9.

> **Check answers:**
> **3** email **4** text **5** app **6** website **7** photos
> **8** tablet **9** e-book

○ Ask: *Do any of you read e-books? What's more fun to read an e-book or a book with paper pages?* Learners answer. If learners are interested, take some time to chat about the differences between these two ways of reading books.

E Write the words from D in Nick's sentences.

○ Point to the man in the picture and say: *This is the man in picture 'b'. His name's . ..?* (Nick). *He's phoning May. Nick and May work in the city.*

Point to the computer screen and say: *May and Nick have a travel website. Nick's here in the countryside to take photos for their website.*

○ Point to 4 **'text'** in the first part of the sentence in the first bubble. Point to this word in **D** (number 4). Say: *Complete Nick's part of the conversation. Find the words for the numbers in D and write them on the lines in the green speech bubbles.*

○ Learners copy and write the missing words in Nick's speech bubbles.

> **Check answers:**
> **1** message **3** email **2** internet **7** photos **8** tablet
> **7** photos **6** website **5** app

○ Ask: *Yes, no or we don't know!? Did Nick text May?* (yes) *Did May get the message?* (no) *Did Nick use his phone camera?* (no – his tablet) *Did he use his phone to send emails?* (no) *Why not?* (because there was no internet in the countryside). *Is May excited about seeing the photos and video?* (Yes!) *What did Nick find?* (an exciting app)

○ Write on the board: *internet.* Say: *Listen: There was no internet in the countryside. What's the sound at the end of 'internet'?* (/t/)

Can you find two more words in D that end with the sound /t/? (text, website) Add these two words to the board.

Say: *Nick can't get onto the internet in the countryside. Can you say that sentence?* (Make sure that learners pronounce the /t/ sound at the end of 'can't', 'get' and 'internet'.)

Do the same with these three sentences, making sure they say the final /t/ in 'text', 'wrote', 'want', 'put', 'website', 'bought' and 'brilliant':

Nick wrote May a text in the morning.

Nick and May want to put a video on their website on Monday.

Nick bought a brilliant app.

Note: The vowel sounds at the start of the next word will help learners say the final /t/ at the end of 'text' 'put' and 'website'.

○ Learners role play the telephone conversation between Nick and May.

○ Form pairs of learners. Say: *Work in pairs! Write a message to your partner! Don't write more than 25 words.* Learners write their message in their notebooks. Allow learners four minutes to write their message.

Say: *Right, now write your message in numbers. Find the correct numbers for your letters in D.* Learners write their coded message on a different piece of paper.

Working in pairs, learners exchange their coded messages. Using the number code in **D** again, they change the numbers back into words. Pairs check that the sent and received messages are the same!

Optional extension:

After they read the message, learners could write a number coded answer and give that back to their partner to decipher!

F Let's find things that we all like and do!

○ Give out photocopies of the activity on page 119, one to each learner.

○ Each learner writes their answers to the questions.

○ Learners work in groups of 4–5. They read out a question and compare their answers.

Say: *Find things that you all like or do; things that only two or three of you do or like; and one thing that only one person in the group does or likes.*

○ When groups find all these things, they complete the sentences in the bottom box about their group.

○ Ask different groups to read out their sentences to the rest of the class.

Find and compare.

○ Learners work in pairs or groups of 3–4. They take a magazine and choose two pictures which are similar (for example, they both show a person), but different in some way.

○ Learners write five sentences that describe their two pictures' similarities and differences. For example:

In both pictures, a woman is standing up.

In both pictures, a woman is wearing a skirt.

In only one picture, a woman is wearing a hat.

In the first picture, the woman is tall but in the second picture, the woman is short.

○ Learners then pass on their sentences and magazines to another group, who have to decide which two pictures the group wrote about.

25 Which one is different?

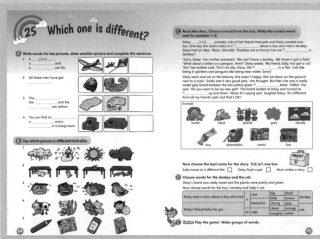

Equipment needed

- Colouring pencils or pens. See A.
- Photocopies (one for each pair of learners) of the 'Make groups' activity on page 120. See E.

A Write words for the pictures, draw another picture and complete the sentence.

- Say: *Look at the pictures in 1. What can you see?* (a plane and a kite) Point to the word 'plane' on the line in the sentence. Point to the second line in this sentence and say: *Write the word for the second picture (kite) here.*

- Ask: *Do you know another word for something that can fly?* (for example: a bird). Learners draw and colour another thing that can fly in the third box and write the word for the picture they drew on the last line in 1.

- Say: *Look at the other three groups of pictures. Tell me what you have to draw.* (another man with a beard, another yellow thing and another thing you can find in a living room).

- Learners draw and colour the pictures and complete the sentences.

> **Check answers:**
> **2** beards/a beard   **3** towel, toothpaste, (suggestion: T-shirt)
> **4** armchair, sofa, (suggestion: TV)

Complete the sentences about you and the people you know.

- Ask: *Who can draw very well in this class?*
  Learners say the names of learners who can draw well. These learners stand up.
  Say: (Names of the learners who are standing up now) *can draw very well.*

- Say: *Tell me other things which some of the people in this class can do.* Ask: *Who can sing? Who can run fast? Who can ride a horse? Who can play the guitar?* etc.
  Learners who do these things well stand up. The other learners say sentences about what these learners can do.

- Choose one of these activities (one you can't do well) and say a sentence comparing your ability to do this with learners who can do it.
  For example: *(Jennifer and Michael) can play the guitar but I can't.*

- Ask different learners to say similar sentences about other activities. Write two of these sentences on the board.
  Underline the words 'and' and 'but'. Explain that 'and' means that two people or things are the same or alike but when we use 'but', this tells us that what comes next is not the same.

- Write these sentences on the board:
  1 *... and ... have got ..., but I haven't.*
  2 *I like ..., but I don't like ....*
  3 *My ... and my ... are blue, but my ... isn't.*
  4 *In my house, there's a ... and a ..., but there isn't a ....*
  Say: *Write these sentences in your notebooks and complete them about you.*

- Collect learners' notebooks and give them to different learners to read out the completed sentences. The other learners say the name of the learner who wrote the sentences.
  Note: With bigger classes, do this in groups.

B Say which picture is different and why.   Speaking Part **3**

> **Movers tip**
> In Speaking Part 3 candidates can use both positive and negative sentences to talk about differences. For example: *The bird's on the table but these animals are under the table. These animals are under the table but the bird isn't under the table.*

- Point to the first line of pictures and say: *Look at these pictures. One is different.* Ask: *Which one is different?* (the hippo)
  Why? (Rain, snow and the sun are kinds of weather, but a hippo is an animal.)

- Say: *In pairs, look at the other pictures. Talk about which picture is different and why.*
  Learners look at the other sets of pictures and talk about the differences.

Suggested answers:

2 The bird is different because it's on the table. The rabbit, mouse and lizard are under the table.

3 The boy is different because he's crying/sad. The two men and the woman are laughing/happy.

4 The baby is different in the fourth picture because she has a ball. In pictures 1, 2 and 3, the baby has a toy animal.

5 The pencil is different because you write with a pencil. You read a comic, text and a book.

What can you remember?

- Give learners a minute to look at the pictures on page 54. They close their books.

- In pairs or small groups of 3–4, they write down all the things that they remember from the pictures in **A** and **B** in their notebooks.

- Learners call out the words they have written. Ask them to spell the words and to write them on the board. They receive a point for every correctly spelt word.

Suggestions:

armchair, baby, ball, bear, beard, bird, book, boy, cat, cloud, comic, hippo, kangaroo, kite, lizard, man, mouse, panda, pencil, phone, plane, rabbit, snow, snowman, sofa, sun, table, teddy bear, toothpaste, towel, woman (and the things that learners drew in their third pictures in **A**!)

C Read the story. Choose a word from the box. Write the correct word next to numbers 1–5.

○ Ask: *Who's got a pet at home?*
Learners with pets put up their hands.
Ask one of these learners: *What pet have you got?* (a cat)
What does your (cat) eat? What does it drink?

○ Ask other learners the same questions about their pets (dogs, rabbits, hamsters, fish, etc.).
Ask: *Has anyone got an elephant or a lion at home?* (No!) *Why not?*
(They're too big, dangerous, dirty, etc.)

○ Learners read the text and tell you which animals are mentioned. (a donkey, a kitten, a penguin, a cat, a snail, a lizard)

○ Learners read the text again and write the correct words from the word box on the lines.

> **Check answers:**
> **1** comic   **2** buy   **3** live   **4** plants   **5** head

○ Learners choose the best name for the story. (Daisy finds a pet)

○ Say: *Which one is different? A lizard, a donkey, a kitten, a penguin? Why?* Learners suggest differences. Accept any reasonable answers.
Suggestions: A donkey is different because it's bigger / you can ride it. A lizard is different because it eats insects. A kitten is different because it's a word to talk about a baby, the others aren't / it often lives inside a house. A penguin is different because it lives in the sea / it can swim.

○ Ask: *Would you like to have a lizard as a pet?* (yes/no). Say: *In pairs, talk about different animals and choose the best pet and say why!*
When pairs have chosen the best pet, ask: *Which animals did you choose for pets?* Different pairs call out their animals. Pairs who chose the same animal get together and tell each other why they chose that animal. Learners who chose a different animal from anyone else tell each other what they like about their animals and compare them.

🧳 **All about pets**

○ Learners find out about a pet – what it eats and drinks, how many hours a day it sleeps, what's the best temperature for it, what different names people often choose for that animal, etc. Learners then prepare a poster or a short book about the pet or write an entry for a class blog, which can be added to their project file.

D Choose words for the donkey and the cat.

○ Point to and read out the sentence about Daisy's lizard and the plants on the balcony: *Daisy's lizard was really sweet and the plants were pretty and green.*
Say: *Daisy read a story in a comic. What was the story about?* (a donkey).
Ask: *Do you think the donkey was nice, beautiful or ugly?* Learners choose and draw a line between 'had a/an' and the word they choose.
Ask: *Was the donkey big, little, strong, clever or naughty?* Learners choose and draw another line to add the word they choose to the sentence.
Ask: *What colour was the donkey?* Learners choose a colour and draw a line to add it to the sentence and then to the last word in the sentence (donkey).
In pairs, learners compare their donkey sentences.

○ Point to and say the words: *black, brown, grey, orange, white.*
Ask: *What do these words tell us about?* (colour) Say: *We often put words for colour in front of the thing we are talking about* (for example, *brown hair, blue eyes*).
Point to and say the words: *big, little.* Explain that we put words like these and others like 'long', 'short' near the word they describe, but in front of words for colour (for example: long, brown hair; big, blue eyes).
Point to and say the words: *nice, beautiful, ugly.* Explain to learners that these words give our opinion about a person or a thing. We put them further away from the thing or person we are talking about. (For example: beautiful, big, blue eyes)

○ Write on the board: *The snail on Daisy's balcony was*
Say: *Now, choose words from the box in D to complete this sentence about the snail on Daisy's balcony!* In pairs, learners copy the start of the sentence from the board and complete it using words from **D**. They could also draw a picture of the snail. Different pairs compare their snail sentences (and pictures if they drew them).

○ Say: *Now, choose words for Sally's cat. Draw lines between the words.*
Ask different learners to read out their cat sentences.

○ Say: *Now, choose another animal you know – a pet or an animal from a movie or TV. Write a sentence about that animal.*
Learners tell each other about their animals. They could also draw or find a picture of the animal and write their sentence under it.

E Play the game! Make groups of words.

○ Write on the board: *neck   shoulder   back*
Ask: *What are all these words?* (parts of the body) *Can you tell me another word for a part of your body?* (arm, ear, eye, face, foot, hand, head, leg, mouth, nose) *Now, tell me a word for something that isn't a part of your body. For example, something that's inside this room!* (table, board, chair …)

○ Divide the class into two teams: A and B. Copy and cut up the activity on page 120. Give all learners in team A a copy of A and all learners in team B a copy of B.

○ Learners make five groups of three words which are connected. They add another word to each group. They then add another word to each group which is not connected.

○ Divide team A and team B into A and B pairs. In their A and B pair, learners then take turns to read out their own five-word groups whilst their partner decides which four words are connected (and why) and which word is different.

Suggested connected words:
A **1** things we need to do sport with: *tennis racket, skateboard, swimsuit*
   2 jobs: *pop star, cook, nurse*
   3 where we live: *town, village, city*
   4 water: *lake, wave, waterfall*
   5 things we write: *word, letter, sentence*
B **1** things in the sky: *rainbow, cloud, star*
   2 food: *noodles, pie, fries*
   3 health: *earache, toothache, cough*
   4 family: *aunt, son, daughter*
   5 things in the bathroom: *bath, toothbrush, shower*

26 Guess who lives here?

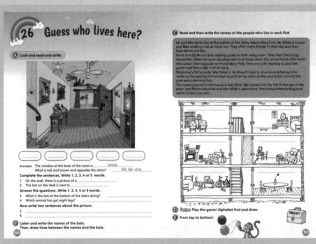

Equipment needed

- Colouring pencils or pens. See A and D.
- Photocopies (one for each group of 4 or pair of learners) of the sentences on page 121, cut in half. See E.

A Look and read and write.

Reading & Writing Part 6

> **Movers tip**
>
> There are lots of pictures in the book that you could use to prompt learners' imaginations. This will help them prepare not only for Reading and Writing Part 6 where they have to think of ways to complete sentences, answer questions and write about the picture, but also for Speaking Part 2.
>
> Ask learners to use their imaginations to tell you more about the picture. Everyone will be right of course! See below for how you might use the picture in A in an activity like that.

- Ask: *Where are we? Inside or outside school?* (inside)
  Is the sun above us or below us? (above us)
  Does it snow more often at the top or at the bottom of a mountain? (at the top)

- Say: *Look at the picture.* Ask: *How many bats are there?* (seven) *Are there any people inside this room?* (no)
  Write on the board:
  Who do you think lives in this house?
  Do they feed these bats? What do they feed them with?
  Do they have any other pets?
  What's outside their house?
  What's upstairs?
  What's downstairs in the basement?
  Learners work in groups to choose answers. Ask two or three groups to share their answers. Have fun with this.

- Say: *You have one minute to look at the picture. Try to remember where the bats are.*

- Learners close their books. They write the numbers 1–8 in their notebooks. Read out the sentences below twice. Learners listen and write *yes* next to the numbers of the right sentences and *no* next to the numbers of the wrong sentences.
  1 The biggest bat in the picture is flying below the fan.
  2 There's a green bat at the bottom of the stairs and it's sleeping
  3 Two bats are outside the house.
  4 You can see a bat in front of the window.
  5 The smallest bat in the picture is on top of the phone.
  6 In this picture, we can only see one spider.
  7 The bat which is above the hall table is brown.
  8 Most of the bats are inside the house.

- Learners open their books. Read out the sentences again. Learners check their answers by looking at the picture.

> **Check answers:**
> **Yes:** 1, 4, 6, 8
> **No:** 2, 3, 5, 7

- Say: *Let's correct the mistakes in sentences 2, 3, 5 and 7 now.* Write on the board:
  2 *The bat .... is sleeping at the bottom of the stairs isn't green. It's .... Point to the gaps and ask: Which words do I write here?* (which/that, purple)
  Do the same with 3, 5 and 7:
  3 *Only one bat .... outside the .... (is, house)*
  5 *The smallest bat in the picture is on the .... between the two .... (wall, pictures)*
  7 *The bat which is above the .... table is .... (hall, pink)*

- Say: *Read the two examples in A. Are they correct about this picture?* (yes)
  Learners read sentences 1 and 2 and questions 3 and 4 and write words on the lines.

> **Check answers:**
> (Suggestions) **1** a (white) horse **2** the (grey) phone
> **3** (It's) sleeping **4** the spider (on the wall)

- Say: *Now, write two more sentences about the picture, please! You can write about the bats or the room or anything else.* Learners write sentences on the lines in 5 and 6.
  Suggested answers:
  Simple sentences
  The sky is blue.
  The big grey door is open.
  There are seven bats here.
  Compound sentences
  The people are upstairs because they are afraid of the bats.
  I don't like black spiders because they look scary.
  Someone opened the door and then all the bats flew in.

Draw the bats in the picture.

- Learners look at the picture in A again and try to remember where the bats are and what colour they are. Give them about 30 seconds.

- Learners turn to page 107 of their books. They draw and colour the bats in the picture – without looking back at the original picture!

- Learners sit in pairs. They take it in turns to compare their partner's picture with the original picture on page 56.
  For example: *In both pictures, the big black bat is flying.*
  In my picture, the purple bat is at the bottom of the stairs, but in your picture, the bat is nearer the table.

B Listen and write the names of the bats. Then, draw lines between the names and the bats.

- Point to the boxes below the picture of the bats in A and say: *I want you to write the bats' names in these boxes.*
  In the first box, write the name, 'Quick'. You spell that Q-U-I-C-K. Did you write the first letter with a big 'Q'? The first letter of a name is big!
  In the next box, write the name, 'Cloud'. You spell that C-L-O-U-D. What's that name? (Cloud)
  In box three, write the name 'Dream'. That's D-R-E-A-M. Those letters spell the name ...? (Dream)
  Put the letters T-E-E-T-H in box four. Yes, write 'Teeth'!
  And in the last box, the name is longer. It's 'Sandwich'. You spell that S-A-N-D-W-I-C-H. What did you write in the last box? (Sandwich)

- Which bat do you think is Quick / Cloud / Dream / Teeth / Sandwich?

  In pairs, learners draw a line from each name below the picture to the bat they think is Quick, Cloud, Dream, Teeth and Sandwich in the picture. Pairs then tell another pair about their bats. Suggestion: *This is Quick. Quick can fly very quickly.*

C Read and then write the names of the people who live in each flat.

- Ask: *Do more people in your country live in houses or flats?*

  Do people live near you? Is your home in a house or an apartment? Does anyone live above/below you?
- Point to the picture and say: *This house is in the centre of a city called Talltown. There are six flats in this house.*
- Point to the sentences above the picture. Say: *Read about the people who live in these flats.* When they have finished, ask: *Do you think they like living there?* (Anna and Bill Brown don't!) *Would you like to live there?*

  Learners read the sentences again and write the names of the people on each line.
- On the board, draw a table (see below) to show the six flats. Point to the table and say: *These are the flats.* Point to the middle column and say: *Here are the stairs.* Check answers by asking different learners to say sentences about where the people live. Write the correct name(s) in each flat.

Anna and Bill Brown		Julia Blue
Miss Green		Mary Pink
Mark Grey		Mr and Mrs White

Rooms and what we do in them.

- Say (or write on the board):

  People cook in this room and they sometimes eat there. Which room is this? (a kitchen)

  We have a shower and a wash then dry our bodies here. Which room is this? (a bathroom)
- Ask learners to suggest sentences like these about the different rooms in the picture in **C**.

  Suggestions:

  living room: *People sit and watch TV in this room.*

  dining room: *People sit at the table and have lunch or dinner in this room.*

  bedroom: *People sleep in this room and they sometimes get dressed there.*

  hall: *When you go into a home, this is often the first room you stand in.*
- Ask: *Which is your favourite room? Where do you have dinner?*

D Play the game! Alphabet find and draw.

- Ask learners to say the alphabet in English. Tell one learner to write the letters on the board as the other learners say them.

  Ask: *Which of the letters are vowels?* (a, e, i, o, u)

  Rub these letters off the board. Rub the letters q, v, x, y, z off too.
- Say: *Let's find things in the picture in C that begin with the letter C.*

  Different learners name one thing in the picture in **C** that begins with the letter 'C'.

  Suggestions: chair / computer / CDs
- Point to the other letters on the board. Say: *Find one thing in the picture in C starting with each of these letters.*

  In pairs, learners try and find and write words for all the letters as quickly as possible.

  Ask different pairs to tell you words. Write them on the board.

  Suggestions: bike / bed / book / bookcase / bottle, door/desk, flower/floor, guitar, keyboard, lamp, mirror/mat, names, poster, radio / roller skates, skateboard / sofa / stairs, table, water

  Note: For any letters (except 'h' and 'j') that learners haven't written words for, prompt them by pointing to the things in the picture or describe them, eg. *You play this on a piano.* (music)

- Point to the letters 'h' and 'j'.

  Say: *We haven't got words for these letters. Let's draw things in the picture with these letters.*

  First, the letter 'h'. Draw a hat on Julia's bed. You can colour it too. Draw and colour a hat for Julia.

  Now 'j'. Draw a jacket on the back of the chair in Mary Pink's apartment. Then, colour the jacket pink.

  One more thing, please! Can you draw a big, tall green plant? Let's put the plant in Anna and Bill's apartment, between the armchair and the door.
- Say: *The people who live in these apartments all have a different favourite colour.* Ask: *Can you guess what colour each person likes?* (Their family name is their favourite colour!)

  Say: *Colour the walls of each apartment the right colour for each family.* Learners can colour the rest of the picture too if they want.
- Learners show each other their pictures.

E From top to bottom!

- Copy and cut up the sentences on page 121 into two halves (A and B). Learners work in groups of four (Pair A and Pair B). Give pair A the A sentences and pair B the B sentences. Explain that Pair A has the answers to B's sentences and pair B has the answers to A's sentences.

  Read out the example sentence: *The leaves on carrot plants are .... the ground.* Ask: *Can you see the leaves on a carrot plant?* (yes) *Why?* (because they're above the ground) All learners write *above* on the line in the Example sentence.

  Ask: *And can you see the carrot on a carrot plant?* (no) *Why not?* (because the carrot is under/below the ground)
- Pair A start. They read sentence 1 and say which word completes the sentence. Pair B listens and says: *That's right!* or: *Sorry, that's wrong!* If the word is correct, Pair A writes it on the line in the sentence. If it's wrong, they don't write anything.

  Repeat this with Pair B and their sentence 1. Each pair tries to complete all their sentences as quickly as possible.

  For the wrong sentences, they can choose to try and complete them with another word or they can move on to the next sentence. The winners are the pair who complete all the sentences first or the pair who have completed the most sentences when you say: *Stop!*

  Teach/revise any words that learners didn't know or remember.

Answers to B's sentences		Answers to A's sentences	
1	below/under	1	end
2	inside/in	2	outside/at
3	up	3	between
4	top	4	down
5	between / after / before	5	on
6	above	6	inside/in
7	bottom	7	between / in / inside
8	out	8	around / round / on

Find out about bats

- Learners choose a kind of bat and find out about it.
- They do research on the internet to learn where the bat lives, what it eats, how many years it lives, what colour it is, how big/small it is.
- With their information, learners make a poster or give a presentation to the class about their bat.

27 Seeing differences

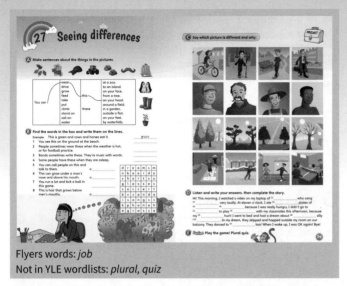

Flyers words: *job*
Not in YLE wordlists: *plural, quiz*

A Make sentences about the things in the pictures.

> **Movers tip**
>
> In Reading and Writing Part 1, candidates should underline key words in the definitions like *this, these, it, they*. These words help them to understand what type of word (singular/plural/ uncountable) they are looking for.

o Learners look at the pictures and tell you the words for each thing, looking carefully to see if the pictures show one thing or more than one thing. Different learners come to the board and write the words for the pictures. Remind them to write 'a' in front of the singular words.

> **Check answers:**
>
> 1 leaves   2 a balcony   3 a cap   4 a tractor   5 rocks
> 6 a moustache   7 a boat   8 penguins   9 boots   10 a plant

o Read out the first sentence in the table in **A**: *You can wear this on your head.* Point to the pictures in **A** and ask: *Which of these things can you wear?* (a cap and boots) Say: *You can wear this on your head. Can you wear a cap on your head?* (yes) *Can you wear boots on your head?* (no!)
Say: *This sentence is about a cap! Can you make a sentence about boots from the words in the boxes in A?* (You can wear these on your feet.) Point to the cap and say: *We say 'this' because there is <u>one</u> cap.* Point to the boots in **A** and say: *We say 'these' because …* (there are <u>two</u> boots.)

o Point to the four boxes in the table and say: *Now you make sentences about the other pictures. Write them in your notebooks.*

> **Check answers:**
>
> | You can drive this around a field. | a tractor |
> |---|---|
> | You can grow this on your face. | a moustache |
> | You can feed these at a zoo. | penguins |
> | You can take these from a tree. | leaves |
> | You can put these on your feet. | boots |
> | You can climb these by waterfalls. | rocks |
> | You can stand on this outside a flat. | a balcony |
> | You can sail on this to an island. | a boat |
> | You can water this in a garden. | a plant |

o Ask: *Are there any balconies outside your home?*
When you look out of your bedroom window, can you see any leaves?
Would you like to go on a trip to an island?

How good is your memory?

o Divide the class into teams of 5–6. Learners look at the sentences they wrote for 1–2 minutes, then close their books.

o Say one of the words from **A** (for example: *shell*). One team says the sentence. If it is the same as the original sentence in **A** (see **Check answers**), give them a point. If not, the next team says the sentence.
Note: Ask different teams in turn so that each team answers first at least once.

B Find the words in the box and write them on the lines.

o Tell learners to cover the sentences in **B** with a piece of paper. Say: *You have one minute to find as many words as possible in the wordbox.* After a minute, ask: *How many words did you find?* (There are ten going across – dream(s), bear, beard, shorts, glass(es), soccer, sand, song(s), phone, grass and two going down – bike, moustache.)

o Learners uncover the sentences. Read out the example: *This is green and cows and horses eat it.*
Ask: *What do cows and horses eat?* (grass) *Did anyone find the word 'grass' in the box?* Point to the word 'grass' on the last line of the box and on the line in the example.

o Learners read sentences 1–8 and find and underline the words *this* or *these*. Ask: *Which sentences are about plural words?* (2, 3 and 4)

o Learners read the sentences again, find the words in the box and write them on the lines next to the sentences.

> **Check answers:**
>
> 1 sand   2 shorts   3 songs   4 dreams   5 phone   6 moustache
> 7 soccer   8 beard

o Point to the picture of the girl in **B** and say: *This is Grace.* Ask: *What's Grace doing?* (dreaming) *Which animals can Grace see in her dream?* (cows and horses) *What are the cows and horses eating?* (sweets) *Are cows blue?* (no) *Are horses pink?* (no) *Do cows and horses eat sweets?* (no) Say: *In Grace's dream, cows are blue, horses are pink and they both eat sweets!*

o Say: *Find words in the box for:*
1 two words for things which are under your feet when you are standing. (grass, sand)
2 two words for hair which some men have on their face. (beard, moustache)
3 two words for things we can wear. (shorts, glasses)

o Ask: *To talk about glasses, do we need 'this' or 'these'?* (these)
Write on the board: *You wear these …*
Ask: *Where do you wear glasses? On your feet?* (No! On your nose)
Write: *on your nose.* to complete the sentence on the board.
Write on the board: *They help you … better.*
Ask: *What do glasses help you do?* (see) Write *see* in the gap in the sentence on the board.

o Write on the board:
a bike
You have to move your .... and .... in a circle to ride this.
Learners say words to complete the sentence. (Answer: legs, feet)
Ask: *Did you come to school by bike this morning?*
What parts of your body do you have to move to drive a car? (Your hands and feet)

C Say which picture is different and why. Speaking Part 3

o   Point to the first set of four pictures.
    Say: *Look at these four pictures. One is different*
    Ask: *Which one is different?* (The woman riding the bike.)
    Why is it different? (The woman is riding a **bike**, but the other people are **walking**.)

o   In pairs, learners look at the other three sets of pictures and discuss which picture is different and why.

o   Check answers by asking one pair of learners to say which picture is different and why. If the other learners in the class agree, they say: *Yes, you're right!* If they don't agree, they say: *Sorry! I think you're wrong!*

Suggested answers:

Set 2: The man in the second picture is different because he has got a moustache. The other men haven't got a moustache.

Set 3: The tree in picture 4 is different because it hasn't got any leaves. There are leaves on the trees in the other pictures.

Set 4: The girl who's skating is different because there's only one person in this picture. There are two people hopping, skipping and playing table tennis in the other.

o   Learners work in A and B pairs. Learner A has their book open at this page. Learner B looks at the pictures on page 111. In pairs, they look at the two sets of pictures and discuss the differences between each of them.

Check answers:

Set 1:

one person / two people riding bikes

girl walking / looking at a map

boy walking/running

man walking / riding a motorbike

Set 2:

no glasses / glasses

no hat / hat

sun hat / nurse's hat

no ice cream / eating an ice cream

Set 3:

day/night

sun/rainbow

no clothes / clothes between trees

sunny/snowing

Set 4:

hopping / watching TV

skating outside / inside

skipping / kicking a ball

boy and girl / boy and robot

Note: Learners may give other possible reasons for differences.

o   Learners work in groups of 3–4. They talk about the questions on page 111.
    Give groups time to think of and exchange their answers and then ask the class about question 5: *Which people have to wear a hat at work?* Learners answer, for example: a person who works in a supermarket. Ask: *Why do people who work there have to wear a hat?* Learners answer, for example: *We don't want their hair in our food!*

Note: You could do this in learners' first language if necessary.

Ask different groups to tell the class about their other answers, for example: what their favourite playground game is or which games they play at home.

A game

o   Learners plan and present a game they play at home or in the playground.

o   They describe what you need to play it, how many people are needed to play and the rules.

o   They can use pictures from the internet or photos of themselves playing it.

o   If practical you could then play some of the games in the classroom.

D Listen and write your answers, then complete the story.

o   Say: *I want you to take some paper and write ten answers. Write the numbers 1 to 10 going down the page. Ready?* Tell learners they can invent answers if they need to.
    Read out the questions below. Say the number before each question and pause between each question.

    1 *Write the name of someone you know who has a moustache.*
    2 *Now, write the name of the last place you walked to.*
    3 *What game do you like playing?*
    4 *What colour are your favourite shoes?*
    5 *How many people are wearing glasses in this room?*
    6 *Think about the food you ate yesterday. Write the word for something you ate.*
    7 *What's the name of your favourite song?*
    8 *How many people are in this room?*
    9 *Choose a part of your face. Write the word for it.*
    10 *I like lions. What are your favourite animals?*

    Note: Repeat any of the questions as necessary, giving learners time to write their answers.

o   Say: *Look at the story in D. Can you see the numbers? Write the answer you wrote for that number on the line after it. For example, on the first line after the number 1, write the name of the person you know who has a moustache. On the second line, after 7, write the name of your favourite song.*

o   Learners write their words for each number on the lines. When they finish, they read out their 'stories' to the people sitting next to them.

E Play the game! Plural quiz.

o   Divide learners into teams of 4–6 players. Each team will need a notebook and a pen. They write numbers 1–15.
    Say a word, for example: foot (See below for suggested words.)

o   Each team writes the plural of that word beside each number, for example: 1 feet.

o   When you finish saying the words, teams exchange notebooks and check each other's answers. Ask different learners to spell the words to you so you can write them on the board.

Suggested words:

1	foot (feet)	**2**	dress (dresses)	**3**	man (men)
4	tooth (teeth)	**5**	box (boxes)	**6**	hobby (hobbies)
7	photo (photos)	**8**	sausage (sausages)	**9**	toothbrush (toothbrushes)
10	scarf (scarves)	**11**	puppy (puppies)	**12**	idea (ideas)
13	leaf (leaves)	**14**	person (people)	**15**	child (children)

Optional extension: Teams write sentences to describe five of the words on the board. They read out their sentences. Erase words from the board as they are described. If there are still words on the board, ask them to say sentences so you can clean the board completely.

28 Our busy holidays

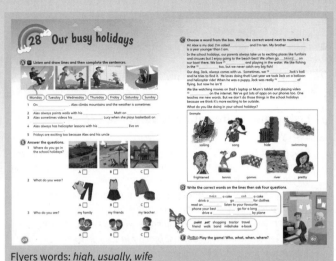

Flyers words: *high, usually, wife*
Equipment needed
- Movers Audio 28A.

A ▶ Listen and draw lines and then complete the sentences.

- Ask: *What day is it today? (*for example: Tuesday*)* Ask one learner: *(Francisco), what do you do on Tuesdays?*

  Ask different learners the same question about other days of the week.

- Point to the man in the pictures in **A** and say: *This is Alex Smile. He's a famous film star. When he's not making films, his weeks are exciting too. What does he do?* (He climbs mountains, paints, flies a helicopter, films a girl playing basketball.)

- Ask: *What does Alex do on Mondays? What is the weather like sometimes? Listen and tell me the answers to these questions!*

  Play the example on the audio. Learners answer the questions. (He climbs mountains. The weather is very cold.)

- Learners listen to the rest of the audio and draw lines between the other three days of the week and the pictures.

> **Check answers:**
> There should be lines between:
> 1 The boy and man painting the wall and Saturday.
> 2 The man filming the girl playing basketball and Tuesday.
> 3 The woman and man in the helicopter and Wednesday.

Audioscript

> *Look at the pictures. What does Alex Smile do every week? Listen and look. There is one example.*
>
> | | |
> |---|---|
> | Woman: | On Mondays, Alex climbs mountains. |
> | Man: | What, every week? |
> | Woman: | Yes. And sometimes, the mountains are very high and the weather is very cold. |
> | Man: | Oh, OK. |
>
> *Can you see the line from the word Monday? On Mondays, Alex climbs mountains. Now you listen and draw lines.*
>
> *One*
> | | |
> |---|---|
> | Woman: | Alex has lots of fun with his son, Matt, on Saturdays. |
> | Man: | Do they do sport? |
> | Woman: | No. They always go to painting school. |
> | Man: | Really? They paint pictures? |
> | Woman: | No. They're learning to paint walls. |

Two
Man:	Does Alex have any more children?
Woman:	Yes. His daughter's called Lucy. She plays basketball very well.
Man:	What, at school?
Woman:	Yes, every Tuesday. She's fantasic. Alex often films the games she plays in.

Three
Woman:	Alex is learning to fly. Did you know that?
Man:	No! Is he learning to fly planes?
Woman:	No, helicopters. His wife, Eva, is teaching him.
Man:	Brilliant! When does he have lessons?
Woman:	On Wednesdays.

- Learners complete sentences 1–4. They do not complete sentence 5 yet.

> **Check answers:**
> 1 Monday(s), (very) cold
> 2 son, Saturday(s)
> 3 daughter, Tuesday(s)
> 4 wife, Wednesday(s)

- Point out that 'on Monday/Wednesday' etc, can be at the beginning of the sentence (1) or at the end (sentences 2, 3 and 4).

- Ask: *Can you guess what Alex does on Fridays?* Learners suggest different things.

  Say: *Look at the picture on page 112. This is Alex on a Friday. He's with Charlie. Charlie's his uncle. What do they do?* (they fly in a balloon) Learners write 'fly in a balloon' on the line in sentence 5. *Where does the balloon go?* (above the clouds) *What does Alex take photos of?* (birds)

- Learners work in A and B pairs. Learner A looks at the picture of Alex in the helicopter in A in this unit. Learner B looks at the Alex in the balloon on page 112.

  Say: *Can you find three things that are the same in both pictures and three things that are different?* When one pair has found these, say: *Stop!* Ask them to tell you the things they found.
  Suggestions:
  same: two people, flying, clouds
  different: a man and a woman / a man and a boy
  flying in a helicopter / balloon
  clouds are white / blue
  no birds / birds

B Answer the questions.

- Say: *Today is (Monday). It's a school day.*
  Ask different questions:
  Where do you go on (Mondays)? (to school)
  What clothes do you wear? (a uniform, a skirt, trousers, jeans, etc)
  Who do you see? (my friends, my teachers, etc)
  What do you do? (learn English, read, write, listen, talk, play in the playground, etc)

- Say: *Imagine that it is the first day of the school holidays. Great! You don't have to go to school today! Read the questions in B and tick the boxes under the pictures or words.*
  Ask different learners to share their answers: *Where do you go in the holidays? What do you wear? Who do you see?*

- Write on the board:
  I always …
  I sometimes …
  I never …

Learners copy the words on the board and complete the three sentences about the things they do in the holidays in their notebooks.

o Ask learners: *Do you like being inside or outside in the school holidays*? *Stand up if you like being outside!*

Ask one learner to stand up and read out one of their three sentences. For example: *I always play football in the park.*

Ask: *Who plays football in the park in the holidays? Stand up!*

All learners who play football in the park in the holidays stand up and say: *Me too!*

Do the same with the other sentences and different activities.

C Choose a word from the box. Write the correct word next to numbers 1–5.

o Point to the girl in the third picture in **A** and ask: *What's Alex's daughter called?* (Lucy) Point to the boy in the second picture in **A** and ask: *What's Alex's son's name?* (Matt)

Point to the text in **C** and say: *Lucy is writing about her school holidays. Write her name in the first gap and her brother's name in the second gap.*

o Say: *Read the text and tell me: Are Lucy and Matt usually inside or outside in the school holidays?* Learners read the text quickly and answer. (outside)

o Learners look at the example: *We often go sailing on our boat there.* Point to the picture and word 'sailing' in the box below the text.

Write on the board: *go sailing*

Point out that we say: 'go sailing'. Point to the word 'go' in this expression. Say: *When we are talking about sports or hobbies, we often use words like go sailing, go swimming, go running.*

> **Movers tip**
>
> In Reading and Writing Part 3, most of the words needed to complete the gaps in the text are nouns or verbs (as they are here), but there may be an adjective or an adverb too (like 'frightened' here). Words like 'very' and 'really' often appear in front of an adjective or adverb. Looking at the words before and after each gap can help candidates to decide what kind of word is missing. When it is a verb, they should check that the form they've chosen (for example, past simple) fits in the gap too.

o Learners read the other sentences and choose words from the box to complete them. Check answers by asking learners which words around the gaps helped them.

> **Check answers:**
>
> **1** swimming (love + ing, in the water) **2** river (you fish in a river, the + noun) **3** hide (tries to find) **4** frightened (really, of)
> **5** games (playing)

o Ask: *Who takes Lucy and Matt to exciting places – Jack, their dog, or their parents, Alex and Eva?* (Alex and Eva) *What do the family hide from Jack?* (his ball) *Do they take their laptop or computer with them on holiday?* (no)

D Write the correct words on the lines then ask four questions.

o Point to the picture in **D** and ask: *What's Matt doing here?* (making a cake) *What's Lucy doing?* (eating a cake). Point to the words 'make a cake' and 'eat a cake' in the smaller box and on the lines in the bigger box in **D** and say: *You can make a cake and you can eat a cake. What other things can you make and eat?* (**Suggestions:** *pies, sauces, pancakes, etc.*)

Point to the line after 'drink a' and ask: *What can you drink? Find the word in the smaller box.* (a milkshake)

o Learners write words on the other lines. They can only use each word once.

> **Check answers:**
>
> go shopping for clothes, read an e-book, listen to your favourite band, phone your best friend, go for a long walk, drive a tractor, travel by plane

o Write on the board:
How often do you … ?
What days do you … ?
Ask learners to make and say questions with different expressions from the box.
Suggestions: How often do you drink a milkshake? What days do you phone your best friend?
Ask different learners these questions.

o Learners choose four different activities from the box in **D**. They make four questions (two with 'How often?' and two with 'What days?').

o In pairs, learners ask and answer their four questions.

E Play the game! Who, what, when, where?

o Draw the shapes below on the board (make them big). Write number 1 inside the square, at the top, number 2 inside the circle, at the top, number 3 in the top of the triangle and number 4 in the rectangle.

o Say: *Tell me the name of a famous person or a cartoon character.* A learner says a name and comes to the board and writes the name in the square. Repeat this till you have five famous people's names in the square.

o Say: *Tell me something you do at the weekend.* Six different learners say things they do and write them in the circle.

o Say: *Can you tell me where you were yesterday?* Write four places (with prepositions) in the triangle.

o Write the four time expressions below in rectangle 4.

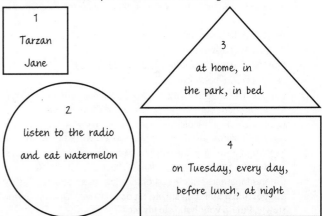

o Divide the class into teams of 4–5. On a piece of paper, each group writes as many different sentences as possible in five minutes, using words from each shape in each sentence. Tell learners to write the sentences starting with a name from the square (1), then an action from the circle (2), a place from the triangle (3) and a time from the rectangle (4). Encourage them to make funny sentences.

For example: Tarzan eats watermelon in bed at night.

o Collect the pieces of paper. Read the sentences and give each team a mark for each correct sentence.

29 About us

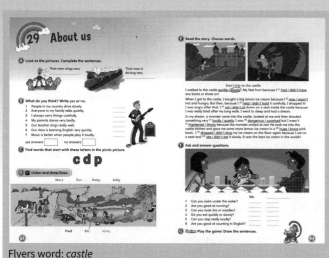

Flyers word: *castle*

Equipment needed

○ Movers Audio 29D.

○ Photocopies (one for each group of 8–10 learners) of the sentences on page 122. See G.

Ⓐ Look at the pictures. Complete the sentences.

○ Ask different learners questions about singing:

Do you like music? Do you like singing? When do you sing? Where do you sing? Are you good at singing?

Point to the picture of the man singing. Ask: *Is this man good at singing?* (no)

Write and draw on the board: *well* ☺ *badly* ☹

Do his friends like his singing? (no)

Does he sing well? (no) *Does he sing badly?* (yes)

Learners write *badly* on the line.

○ Write on the board: *slowly, quickly.* Say: *Move your heads slowly! Move your hands quickly!* to teach/revise these words.

Learners look at the picture of the man driving. Ask: *Is the man driving slowly or quickly?* (slowly) Learners write *slowly* on the line.

○ Explain that *slowly* is the word that tells us <u>how</u> someone does something. Say: *Pick up your books <u>slowly!</u> Say 'hello' <u>slowly!</u>*

Different learners tell the rest of the class to do other things slowly.

Suggestions: Stand up slowly. Sit down slowly. Open your book slowly. Put up your hand slowly etc.

Continue this, using the word 'quickly'.

Ⓑ What do you think? Write *yes* or *no*.

○ In pairs, learners read sentences 1–7. They decide which word in each sentence says *how* we do something and draw a red circle around it.

> **Check answers:**
> slowly, quietly, carefully, badly, well, quickly, loudly

Point out that most words that tell us how people do things end in '-ly'.

Write on the board: *My dad is a careful driver.* Put a circle round 'careful'. Add a second sentence: *My dad drives careful _ _ .* Ask: *Which two letters do I add to 'careful'?* (ly)

Say: *There is one word in B that tells us how someone does something, but it doesn't have 'ly' at the end. Which word?* (well)

Write on the board: *My favourite band make good music. They play music very* .... Point to the line at the end of the second sentence and ask: *Which word do I write here?* (well) *We don't say 'goodly' – we say 'well'!* Explain: *'good' doesn't follow the rule. It's irregular.*

Make comparisons with the learners' own language if possible.

○ Say: *Look at the words that you drew circles round. There are three pairs of opposites here.* Write on the board: *slowly.* Say: *Find the word that means the opposite of 'slowly'.* ('quickly' in sentence 6) Ask: *Can you find two more pairs?* (2 quietly – 7 loudly, 4 badly – 5 well).

○ Learners read the sentences again and write *yes* if they think each statement is right, or *no* if they think it is wrong.

Optional extension:

○ Ask: *How many sentences did you read?* (seven)

How many people are there in this class? Count! (eg 20)

Then how many times did you all write 'yes' or 'no'?

Write on the board: *7 X 20 =* .... *(140)* Write the total number of answers that your class gave on the board.

Ask: *Of (140) answers, how many answers do you think were 'yes'?* Each learner writes the number of answers they think were 'yes' in the box at the bottom of **B** next to the word 'yes'. Do the same for 'no'.

Different learners read out the seven sentences, one by one. Learners who answered 'yes' stand up and learners who answered 'no' remain sitting down. Count how many learners are sitting or standing each time and ask different learners to write the numbers of each answer on the board. At the end, total the 'yes' and the 'no' answers. Put a circle round the two numbers.

Say: *There were (eg) 100 yes answers. Did anyone write one hundred? That means that there were … (40) no answers. Did anyone write that number?* Say: *Well done!* to any learner who wrote the correct number. If no one did, see who wrote the nearest number to the total.

Suggestion: Learners could produce a bar chart or pictogram to show their answers.

Ⓒ Find words that start with these letters in the picnic picture.

○ Learners look at the picnic picture in **D**. Say:

I can see something in this picture that begins with 'g'. You can play music on it. What is it? (guitar) *And something that you can take to the park and fly that begins with 'k'?* (kite) *I can see something at the back of the picture. It's big and old. It begins with 'c'. What is it?* (castle)

○ In pairs, learners find two more things in the picture that begin with 'c', three things that begin with 'd' and three things that begin with 'p'.

Suggested answers: C: cow, car, cup, camera, comic, castle. D: doll, door, dress, dog, duck. P: picnic, people, panda, pineapple, plant.

○ Say: *Close your books! Answer my questions carefully!*

How many animals were in the picture? (4) *Which animals did you see?* (a cow, a dog, a duck and a panda) *Which animal was hiding?* (a panda)

How many kites were in the picture? (one)

How many red cars were there? (one)

Ⓓ ▶ Listen and draw lines. Listening **1** Part

○ Ask: *How many people are in the picture?* (nine) *How many names are there?* (seven)

Note: Make sure that learners remember that they won't hear all the names of the people in the picture or have to use all the names above or below the picture for their answers.

○ Say: *Listen to May talking to her teacher.* Play the example. Ask: *How do we know that this boy is called Bill?* (He's got a camera. He's got a pineapple on his T-shirt.)

○ Play the rest of the audio. Learners draw lines from five names to five other people in the picture. Let learners listen twice.

o   Ask: *Where are the father's shoes? Can you see them?* (in the plants)

Audioscript

Look at the picture. Listen and look. There is one example.

Man: Everyone's having fun here, May.
Girl: Yes, Mr Fly, they are! We all went for a picnic by the lake. Can you see Bill, the boy with the camera? He takes hundreds of photos!
Man: Oh! And what's that on his T-shirt?
Girl: It's a pineapple. He likes wearing really cool clothes like that.

Can you see the line? This is an example. Now you listen and draw lines.

One
Man: And who's that – the man with the guitar?
Girl: Oh, that's Fred. He's a friend of my dad's.
Man: Is he good at playing the guitar?
Girl: No, he isn't! And he plays very loudly! He gives me a headache!

Two
Girl: And there's my Aunt Mary.
Man: Which woman is she?
Girl: She's there! The woman who's eating the sandwich.
Man: And sitting on the ground?
Girl: Yes. She's really good at cooking and making fantastic picnics.

Three
Girl: And can you see that girl – the one next to the cow?
Man: Which one? There are two girls there.
Girl: The taller one. That's my cousin, Vicky. She's carrying her new radio very carefully!
Man: Oh yes. Do cows like music?
Girl: I don't know but I do!

Four
Man: And who's that? The girl with the comic?
Girl: That's Sally. She's one of my cousins.
Man: What's she doing on that rock?
Girl: She's looking for fish. It's difficult because they swim very quickly!

Five
Girl: And there's my dad in the orange T-shirt. His name's Dan. He wants an ice cream.
Man: Do they have ice creams at that castle?
Girl: Yes. But he had to walk very slowly.
Man: Why?
Girl: Because we hid his shoes! Ha ha!

E Read the story. Choose words.

o   Point to the man walking to the castle in the picture in **D**. Ask: *Who's this man?* (Dan) *Where's he going?* (to the castle)

o   Say: *These pictures show part of a story called 'Dan's trip to the castle'. Let's read the story.* Begin reading the story aloud. Stop at the example. *I walked to the castle slowly.* Ask: *Is this right? Did Dan walk slowly?* (Yes)

Ask: *Why did he walk slowly?* (because he didn't have any boots or shoes on)

Continue reading: *My feet hurt because I ....* Point to **(1)** 'had/didn't have' and ask: *Which one is correct – 'had' or 'didn't have' any boots or shoes on?* (didn't have) *Draw a circle round 'didn't have'.*

o   Learners read the sentences and put a circle around the correct word for 2–10.

Movers tip
Adding adjectives like 'tired', 'hungry', 'angry' and adverbs like 'quickly', 'slowly' to stories makes them a lot more exciting and interesting. Encourage learners to use them when they tell stories, for example in Speaking Part 2.

o   Ask: *What do you think? Was the monster big or small? Did the monster come into the room quickly or slowly? Was the monster's kitchen clean or dirty? Was it cold inside the castle? Did the monster have an ice cream too?* Encourage learners to use their imagination! Ask learners: *Do you think that Dan really had this dream? Or is it a story?*

o   Learners could read and act out the story in groups. Or, they could be the monster and write its story about meeting Dan at the castle.
Suggested story: I went inside the castle and saw a man. He was sleeping. I ran into the room and shouted loudly. The man woke up. I smiled at him and he smiled at me! I took him to the kitchen. I put some lemon ice cream into a huge pink bowl and gave it to him. He was hungry because he ate it all!

F Ask and answer questions.

o   Ask one learner to ask you the first question.
Learner: *Can you swim under the water?*
Teacher: *Yes. I can swim under the water very well.*
Write on the board: *Can you swim under the water? Yes. I can swim under the water very well.*

o   Learners read the questions and write *yes* or *no* in the column under 'Me'.

o   Learners work in pairs. Tell them to write their partner's name at the top of the other column. Learners then take turns at asking and answering the six questions and writing down their partner's answers on the lines in the second column. While they are doing that, write on the board: *well badly loudly quietly quickly slowly*

o   Three pairs ask and answer the five questions.

o   Ask the class to choose one of the words on the board to extend each answer. For example: *Can you run? Yes. I can run very quickly. Can you cook rice or noodles? No. I cook very badly.*

G Play the game! Draw the sentences.

o   Divide the class into an equal number of teams (4–5 learners in each). There are two teams in each group.

o   Cut up and give out one photocopy of the sentences on page 122 to each group of two teams. Learners put their sentences face down. Say: *The sentences are all about an animal that is doing something.*

o   The two teams in each group take it in turns. A learner from one team takes a piece of paper with a sentence on it. That learner has to draw a picture of (or mime) their sentence. For example: *An elephant is skating slowly.*
The learner cannot speak, except to say the number of words.

o   Teams get points for each sentence they guess. They have a maximum of three minutes to guess each sentence. The team with the most points is the winner in each group. You could also give a prize for the best picture for one of the sentences.

30 About me

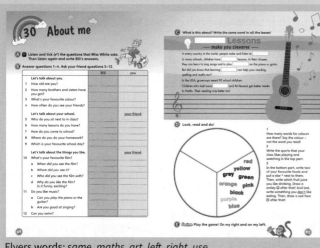

Flyers words: *same, maths, art, left, right, use*

Not in YLE wordlists: *brain, mark*

Equipment needed

- Movers Audio 30A.
- Photocopies (one for each group of six learners, cut up into cards) of the questionnaire on page 123. See C.

Answer your teacher's questions.

- Point to the boy in **A** and say: *This is Bill. Answer my questions about him.*

  Ask: *How old is Bill? How tall is he? Where does he live? How does he go to school?* Encourage learners to use their imagination.

A ▶ Listen and tick the questions that Miss White asks. Then listen again and write Bill's answers.

- Ask learners to read the questions in **B**. Learners listen to the interview with Bill and tick the five questions (next to the numbers) he is asked (2, 3, 8, 10, 12).
- Learners listen again and write Bill's answers in the column under 'Bill'. Pause the audio after each question and answer to give learners time to write.

Check answers:

2 (three/3 or two/2 sisters, one/1 brother)   **4** purple
8 (at the) library   **10** *Terrible Monsters*   **12** Yes.

Audioscript

Listen and write.	
Woman:	Hello. My name's Miss White. I work here at the library.
Boy:	Hello. My name's Bill.
Woman:	Well, Bill, can I ask you some questions about your home and hobbies, please?
Boy:	All right.
Woman:	First, how many brothers and sisters have you got?
Boy:	Three.
Woman:	Three?
Boy:	Yes. I've got two sisters and one brother.
Woman:	Thank you.
Woman:	Now, where do you do your homework?
Boy:	I come here to the library with my cousin after school.
Woman:	Do you come here often?
Boy:	Yes. We try and do all our homework at the library.
Woman:	That's good!
Woman:	Now two questions about the things you like.
Boy:	OK. What do you want to know?
Woman:	What's your favourite colour?

Boy:	That's easy! I love purple.
Woman:	Purple. OK. Another question about things you like. What's your favourite film?
Boy:	My favourite film … Oh, I know. 'Terrible Monsters!'
Woman:	'Terrible Monsters!' I don't know that one.
Boy:	It's great!
Woman:	Now for one last question. What about swimming? Can you swim?
Boy:	Oh yes! I'm good at swimming.
Woman:	Are you?
Boy:	Yes! I go to the swimming pool every Friday.
Woman:	Well, thank you for answering my questions. Goodbye, Bill.
Boy:	Bye.

B Answer questions 1–4. Ask your friend questions 5–12.

> **Movers tip**
>
> In the Speaking, candidates who can produce more than one-word answers will get more marks. Give learners lots of practice at answering questions. Encourage them and show them how to include more than one piece of information in their answers (see below). This will help develop their fluency and give them more confidence.

- Learners read questions 1–3 and write their answers in the third column under 'you'. Ask different learners one of the three questions.
- Tell a learner to ask you question 4: *How often do you see your friends?* Answer the question with one or a few words. For example: *every week.* Then extend your answer, saying who you see, where and when. For example: *I see my best friend Mary once a week at a café or we go to the cinema.*

  Learners write their short answer to 4 under 'you', then they talk about who they see, when and where in pairs.
- Say: *Let's listen again to Bill's answer to question 8.*

  Write on the board: *where   who   when*

  Ask: *Where does Bill do his homework?* (in the library)

  Write *in the library* under 'where' on the board.

  Ask: *Who does Bill do his homework with?* (his cousin)

  Write *with his cousin* under 'who' on the board.

  Ask: *When does Bill do his homework?* (after school)

  Write *after school* under 'when' on the board.
- Play Bill's answer to question 12 again. Learners listen and tell you when and where Bill swims. (*every Friday, in the swimming pool*)

  Write *in the swimming pool* under 'where', and 'every Friday' under *when* on the board.

  Ask: *Who does Bill go swimming with: his cousin / his dad / his mum / his friends from school?* Learners vote for the answer to this question.

  Note: Leave the three question words on the board for later.
- Say: *Read questions 5–9. What are all the questions about?* (school)

  In pairs, learners ask and answer these questions and write their partner's short answers in the third column.
- Say: *Now, talk to a different person!* Learners change seats to work with a different person. Say: *Everyone – think! What's your favourite film? Is it a new film? When did you see it? Where did you see it? At the cinema? At home? Who did you watch the film with? Was the film funny? Was the story good?*

  Say: *Now, talk in pairs about your favourite films! Ask and answer the questions in 10. Write your friend's answers.*
- Give pairs time to ask and answer the questions, then ask:

  Do you and your friend like the same film? (yes/no)

  How many people saw their favourite film at home? How many people watched their film last week? Who likes a funny film? Learners whose answer is 'yes' say *me!*

○ Learners read the questions in 11–12 and write the answers they think their partner would give.

Learners ask and answer the questions in 11–12. Ask them if they guessed their partner's answers correctly.

C What is this about? Write the same word in all the boxes!

○ Say: *Read the text in C. What is it about? What can you 'listen to', 'play', 'make', 'have lessons in' ?*(Music) *Write the word 'Music' in all the boxes, please!*

Read the text again and tell me: What does learning Music help you with? (reading, spelling, Maths) *In the test, whose Maths and reading was better?* (children who had more Music and Art lessons)

○ Ask: *How do you think that Music can help you learn Maths? Can it help you read better? Do you listen to music when you do your homework?*

○ Point to the lines below the text. Say: *Write the sentence in the box above the text on the first line.* Learners write: *Music lessons make you cleverer!* on the top line.

Say: *Now, I want you to write four more sentences about Music. Use the ideas in the text to help you!*

Suggestions: Music helps your reading and spelling! Music gets you better marks in Maths! Learn to sing in Music lessons! Read better with Music! Music is good for you!

Complete your questions then ask them.

○ Point to the words 'where', 'when' and 'who' on the board and say: *These words are question words. Can you find them in the questions in B?* (Yes – in 8, 10a, b, c)

Ask: *How many more question words can you find in B?* (four words – How, Which, What, Why) Add these question words to the board.

Say: *I come to school in the morning on the number 22 bus because it stops outside my house and the school.*

Say: *How do I come to school? Do I drive here?* (No – you come by bus).

Say the whole sentence again and ask: *When do I come to school by bus?* (in the morning).

Say the whole sentence again and ask: *Which bus do I come on?* (the number 22)

Say the whole sentence again and ask: *Why do I come to school on the number 22 bus?* (Because it stops outside your house and the school.)

○ In pairs, learners ask each other about how and when they come to school and why they come that way.

○ Say: *Find the question word 'How' in the questions in B. Which words come after the word 'How'?* Write the combinations on the board:

1 *How old*   **4** *How often*   **2,6** *How many*

Say: '*I'm eleven years old*' *is the answer to…* (How old)

'*Every day*'. '*Never*'. *are answers to …* (How often)

'*Six*'. '*A hundred*'. *are answers to …* (How many)

○ Give a set of six cards from page 123 to each group of six learners. Each learner takes a different card.

Say: *You have four questions. First, choose the correct words for the two questions and write them on the lines.*

○ Say: *Now, ask all the people in your group your four questions. Write their answers in your notebook.*

D Look, read and do!

○ Ask: *How many words for colours are there in the circle in D?* (nine) Point to the word 'red' and ask: *What colour is this word?* (blue) Say: *Everyone! Say the nine colours you can <u>see</u> – not the word you read! Say them quickly and quietly!* Learners practise this. In groups of 4–5, learners time each other saying the colours they can see – in the order they appear – from top to bottom! (blue, red, black, purple, green, brown, grey, yellow, orange)

○ Say: *You did a Test! You did the Stroop Test! In the Stroop Test, you don't **read** the **words**. You **say** the **colour** of the words. They're different! This test tests your reading and your brain! You can read more about the Stroop Test on the internet!* Learners can look on the internet for homework.

○ Say: *What's your favourite colour? Is it yellow? People who like yellow, put your hands up and say:'Yellow!' Do you love blue? Put your hands up and say 'Blue!' What's this class's favourite colour?* Say the nine colours in the circle. Each time, learners put up both hands and say the colour when it's their favourite. Count the number of learners each time and find the class's favourite.

○ Say: *And do you know what the favourite colour of most people in the world is? It's blue! Is that your favourite colour too? Tell me things that are blue!*

Suggestions: rivers, the sea, jeans, eyes, the sky

○ Ask: *What's the world's favourite car colour? It's not blue!* Learners say colours. (White is the world's favourite car colour).

Ask: *And what's the best colour to paint the walls of your house?* (Yellow is the most popular colour for walls in the world).

○ Ask: *Who asked questions about sport? Which sports do people in this class like playing?* (Learners who asked this question tell the other learners). Say: *Everyone, write the sports in the top part of the circle in D!* Learners write the words. Ask: *Which sports do people here like watching? Are they different from the ones they like playing?* Ask: *And which sport do most people in the world like playing? Soccer! That's what most people in the world like playing! Tennis, basketball, table tennis and baseball are favourite sports too!*

○ Say: *Who asked questions about food and drink? Which foods do people in this class love? What kind of fruit juice do people drink? What food don't people here like?* (Learners who asked these questions tell the other learners). Say: *Everyone, write the food and drink you hear in the bottom part of the circle that's on the left.*

Say: *Find a person in the class who likes (or doesn't like) the food and drink that you like (or don't like)!* Learners move around the classroom asking and answering about which foods they like.

○ In their groups, learners draw a circle like the one in **D** in their notebooks. They divide it into four parts (1, 2, 3, 4).

Say: *In part 1, write the places you like going to on holiday and what you do on holiday.*

In part 2 of the circle, write the addresses of your favourite websites and the names of your favourite apps and computer games.

In part 3, write how you come to school and what you like doing in the school break.

In part 4, write the words for your favourite room and the room where you watch television.

○ Groups could then show their circles and talk about them to the rest of the class.

E Play the game! On my right and on my left.

Note: You could ask learners to stand up if their answer is 'yes' and sit down if their answer is 'no'.

○ Stand up in the middle of the room and say a sentence.
For example: *On my right: I've got curly hair.*

Anyone in the class who has curly hair stands on your right. Anyone with straight hair stands on your left.

This continues with learners moving from side to side depending on the sentence.

Suggested sentences:

I've got long hair.

I like vegetables.

My favourite kind of sauce is tomato sauce.

I'm afraid of snakes.

I'm taller than 1 metre 20.

I'm a boy.

I read e-books.

I live in a house, not a flat.

I have milk for breakfast.

I like skateboarding.

I'm in this class.

I can ice skate.

I've got five cousins.

31 Why is Sally crying?

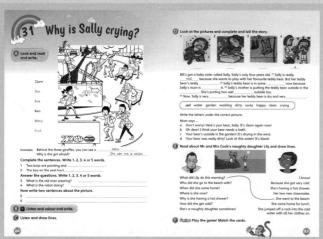

Pronunciation practice 'augh' /ɔ:/ in 'naughty' and 'daughter'. See E.

Flyers word: *look*

Equipment needed

- Movers Audio 31B.
- Colouring pencils or pens. See B.
- Photocopies (one for each group of 3–4 learners, cut up into cards) of the activity on page 124. See F.

Ⓐ Look and read and write.
Reading & Writing Part 6

- Say: *Look at the picture in A and tell me 20 things that you can see.* Ask questions to help: *What animals / clothes / people / parts of the body can you see?*

  Suggestions: *animals:* giraffes, snail, spider, zebra
  clothes: coat, jacket, scarf, shoes, trousers *people:* boys, girls, man *parts of the body:* arms, beard, ear, head, neck.

- Read out the example: *Behind the three giraffes, you can see a zebra.* Ask: *Where can you see a zebra?* (in a cage, behind the giraffes).

  Read out the second example: *Why is the girl afraid? She can see a spider.*

- Learners read 1–4 and write.

  > **Check answers:**
  > (Suggestions) **1** laughing (at something / the girl) **2** his head/foot **3** a coat and a scarf **4** (It's) bouncing a ball

- Write on the board: *This*

  Point to the robot and say: *Complete my sentence! This …?* (robot) *is …?* (bouncing/playing with a ball) Point to the word *This* on the board and say: *'This' can start sentences.* Write the complete sentence on the board: *This robot is bouncing a ball.*

  Write on the board, next to 'This': *Two   There   The* and say: *We can start sentences with 'Two', 'There' and 'The' too.* Choose one of these four words: This, Two, There, The. Write your word on the line in 5. Learners write their word from the board on the line.

  Learners work in groups of 3–4. Learners pass their book to another classmate in their group. (Everyone should have another learner's book.) Say: *Now, look at the picture. Write the second word in a sentence about the picture. This* or *The man / giraffe / spider*, for example. *Two boys / girls / giraffes.* There is or There are. Continue like this, with learners passing on their books until all the sentences in the group are finished. Go round and help learners with vocabulary as necessary. Check that everyone has put a full stop at the end of their sentence.

  Learners in each group look at their sentences and choose the best one.

  Suggestions:

  This girl thinks the spider is scary. **Two** boys have got ice creams.
  There are three giraffes at this zoo. **The** children are at a zoo.

- Say: *Let's see! Who can write the longest sentence about this picture?* Each group writes another sentence starting with one of the words from the board or a different word. The group with the longest (correct) sentence writes it on the board. The other learners clap and say, 'Well done!'

  Suggestion: *The old man is wearing lots of clothes because he's cold and he's sitting on the long seat because he's got a cough and his legs hurt.* (30 words!)

Ⓑ ▶ Listen and colour and write.
Listening Part 5

- Check learners have the necessary colours.
- Learners listen to the conversation twice and colour and write.
- Write on the board: *I coloured …   I wrote … .*

  Check answers by asking different learners to complete the sentences about what they did to the picture.

  1 I coloured the girl's jacket blue.
  2 I coloured the boy's scarf yellow.
  3 I wrote 'Park' above 'Zoo'.
  4 I coloured the spider pink.
  5 I coloured the man's beard brown.

Audioscript

Look at the picture. Listen and look. There is one example.

Girl:	Can I colour one of the giraffes in this picture?
Man:	All right. Which one?
Girl:	I'd like to colour the tallest one.
Man:	OK. Colour that one green, please.

Can you see the tallest giraffe? It's green. This is an example. Now you listen and colour and write.

One

Man:	That girl's having fun! Look!
Girl:	Yes. She likes skipping!
Man:	How about colouring her jacket?
Girl:	OK! I can colour that blue. Is that OK?
Man:	Yes! Good idea!

Two

Man:	Now find the boy in the white trousers.
Girl:	I can see him! He's pointing.
Man:	That's right. Colour his scarf.
Girl:	Can I make it red?
Man:	No. I'd like you to colour it yellow.
Girl:	OK. That's a great colour, too!

Three

Girl:	Can I do some writing here too?
Man:	Yes! Can you see the word 'zoo'?
Girl:	Oh yes, it's by those two boys at the front.
Man:	Yes. Write the word 'Park' above it.
Girl:	You mean like the place you play football in?
Man:	That's right.

Four

Girl:	Oh dear! One of the girls looks really frightened!
Man:	I think she's afraid of that spider. Let's colour that now.
Girl:	OK. I'd like to colour it pink.
Man:	That's fine.
Girl:	Great! There!

Five

Man:	Now, find the person who's sitting on the seat.
Girl:	The boy who's crying?
Man:	No. I mean the old man. He looks cold.
Girl:	Yes, he does! Shall I colour his beard?
Man:	Yes.
Girl:	Can I make it brown?
Man:	Yes. Thank you. This picture looks great now.

C Listen and draw lines.

○ Say: *Listen and draw lines between the names next to the picture in A and the people in the picture.*
Read out these sentences:

1 *Look at Sue! She's really happy today. She loves skipping. Can you see her jumping next to the robot?*
2 *Oh dear! Ben's sitting on a seat. He doesn't look very happy. He hurt his head.*
3 *Can you see my friend Jim? He's bouncing the ball. He isn't a boy! He's a robot!*
4 *Look at those naughty boys! They're pointing at my cousin Clare. She hates spiders. There's a big one in front of her.*
5 *Fred lives in the house next to mine. He doesn't look well today. That's why he's sitting down. He's wearing a scarf too.*

> **Check answers:**
> There should be lines between:
> **1** Sue and girl skipping.　**2** Ben and boy on the seat in front of the girl skipping.　**3** Jim and robot bouncing ball.　**4** Clare and girl looking at spider.　**5** Fred and man with beard sitting down.

D Look at the pictures and complete and tell the story.

> **Movers tip**
> Language like 'there is' / 'there are', the present tense of the verbs 'to be' and 'have got', and the present continuous of action verbs will help candidates to tell the story in Speaking Part 2.

○ Point to the girl in picture 1 and say: *This is Sally. Look at these pictures. They show a story. It's called 'Bear has a wash'. Look at the pictures first.*
Point to the words in the box in **D** and to picture 1 and ask: *Is Sally happy?* (no) *Is Sally sad?* (yes) *Is Sally's bear clean or dirty?* (dirty)
Read out the sentences for picture 1: *Sally is really … ?* (sad) *because she wants to play with her favourite teddy bear. But her teddy bear's really … ?* (dirty).

○ Read out the other sentences. Ask questions. Learners say words from the box to complete the gaps.
Picture 2: *Where's the bear now?* (in the water) *What's Sally's mother doing?* (washing the bear)
Picture 3: *Where's the bear now?* (in the garden) *What's next to the bear?* (two socks)
Picture 4: *Is Sally sad now?* (No, she's very happy.) *Why?* (Because the bear's very clean.)
Learners write the words in the gaps. They tell the story again.

○ Read out **a**: *Don't worry! Here's your bear. It's clean again now!*
Ask: *When does Sally's mum say this, in picture 1, 2, 3 or 4?* (picture 4) Point to the letter 'a' under picture 4.
Learners read sentences b–d and write the correct letters (b, c or d) under the correct picture.

> **Check answers: 1** b　**2** d　**3** c

○ Learners tell the story again, adding the things that Sally's mum says (for example: Oh dear! I think your bear needs a bath, etc), in the appropriate places.

○ Draw two circles on the board. Inside one circle, write: *angry hungry thirsty tired*
Was Sally happy or sad at the start of the story? (sad)
Was Sally happy or sad at the end of the story? (happy)
Why did Sally's mum wash the bear? Was the bear clean or dirty? (dirty)
When the bear was in the garden, was it wet or dry? (wet)
At the end of the story, was the bear clean or dirty? (clean)
Ask learners these questions about Sally and her bear. Add learners' answers (the adjectives) to the circle on the board.
Inside the other circle, write: *drink, eat, wash, dry, sleep, shout, smile, laugh, cry.*

○ Point to the word 'hungry' in the first circle and to the verbs 'shout' and 'eat' in the second circle and ask: *What do you do when you're hungry, do you shout or eat something?* (eat something) Point to these three words again and ask the question again. Learners repeat the question and answer.

○ In pairs, learners choose a different word from the first circle and two different verbs from the second circle (the correct verb and a verb that is a wrong answer to this question) and write another question with: *When you're … do you … or … ?*
Say: *Everyone, stand up. Walk around! Ask everyone in the class your question! Ask me too, please!*
Learners stand up and ask and answer their questions.
Note: with bigger classes, you will probably need to do this in groups.

E Read about Mr and Mrs Cook's naughty daughter Lily and draw lines.

> **Movers tip**
> Practise answering questions that begin with 'What', 'Where', 'Which' 'Who' and 'Why', and recognising answers that match. For example, 'Why … ?', 'Because …' . This will help candidates in Reading and Writing Part 2.

○ Say: *Sally has a cousin called Lily.* Point to the man in **E** and say: *This man is Lily's father, Mr Cook. He's Sally's uncle.* Point to the woman and say: *This is Mrs Cook. She's Lily's* (mum) *and Sally's* (aunt).
Say: *Mr and Mrs Cook are talking about their daughter, Lily.* Point to Mr Cook's first question and Mrs Cook's answer. Ask: *Where did Lily go this morning?* (to the beach)

○ In pairs, learners draw lines between the other questions and answers.

> **Check answers:**
> Who did she go to the beach with?　Her two new classmates.
> When did she come home?　She came home for lunch.
> Where is she now?　She's having a hot shower.
> Why is she having a hot shower?　Because she got very cold.
> How did she get cold?　She jumped off a rock into the cold water with all her clothes on!
> She's a naughty daughter sometimes!　I know!

○ Ask pairs to act out the conversation.

○ Write on the board: *an ugly goat helps Tom*. Underline the first letter in each word. Point to the five letters (a-u-g-h-t) and ask learners to say them. Say: *An ugly goat helps Tom, a-u-g-h-t.*
Learners say the sentence and letters two more times, then write *daughter* on the board, under *a-u-g-h-t:*. Ask: *Did an ugly goat help Tom eat rice?* Say this twice, then point to each letter in 'daughter'. Learners say the question.
Write on the board: *naughty* and say: *Now, an ugly goat helps Tony.* Learners repeat this.
Explain that they can remember the spelling of 'daughter' and 'naughty' by remembering the sentences: *Did an ugly goat help Tom eat rice? Now, an ugly goat helps Tony.*

○ Say to different learners: *Mr Cook, your daughter's naughty*! or *Mrs Cook, you've got a naughty daughter!* Learners answer. *Yes, I know!* Learners say these sentences in pairs. Make sure they pronounce the long /ɔː/ sound in 'naughty' and 'daughter'.

F Play the game! Match the cards.

○ Give a set of 12 cards from page 124 to each group of 3–4 learners. They put the cards face up on a desk so they can all read them.

○ Read out the first half of sentence one: *Sometimes when I'm tired and sick…* . In their groups, learners decide which second card matches this one. (I sleep after lunch.)

○ In their groups, learners match the cards to make four sentences and two pairs of sentences.

○ Check answers by asking one learner to read out the first part/ sentence, and another learner to read out the second part/sentence.

> **Check answers:**
> The best thing to drink when you're thirsty … is a glass of water. / Please go to the bathroom and wash your hands … because they're very dirty. / Would you like another blanket on your bed … because it's very cold today. / Oh dear! The dog's wet again. Can you get me an old towel? / Are you hungry? Shall I make you a chicken sandwich?

77

32 Mary goes shopping

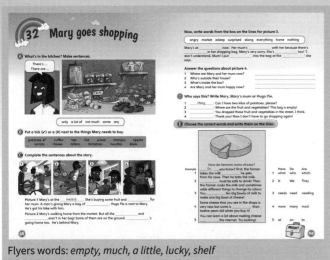

Flyers words: *empty, much, a little, lucky, shelf*

Equipment needed

o Photocopies (one for each pair of learners) of the activity on page 125. See B.

A What's in the kitchen? Make sentences.

o Say: *Look at the picture in A. What food can you see?* Learners put their hands up to answer. (some coffee, pasta, rice, oranges, a carrot, tomatoes, apples, onions)
   Tell learners: *There's no tea – the box is empty!*

o Say: *Listen and point! Point to: the glass bowl on the shelf / the glass bowl on the table / the blue bowl / the plate / the bags on the shelf / the bag on the table / the box on the table.*
   Ask questions about the food items (tell learners to use 'There's' or 'There are' to start their answers).
   Can you see the bowl on the table? What's in that bowl? (There are some/eight oranges.)
   What's on the table? (There are some / four tomatoes / eight onions. There's a bag of rice.)
   Can you see the shelves? (point to the shelves) *How many shelves are there?* (two) *What's on the shelves?* (There's some pasta. There's some coffee. There's a bowl with two apples on the smaller shelf.)

o Point to the carrot and ask: *What's on the plate?* (a carrot) *How many carrots are there?* (one)
   Say: *There's only one carrot.* Point to the word 'only' in the wordbox below the picture in **A**.
   Point to the word 'only' again and ask: *How many apples are there?* (two) Say: *There are …* (only two apples.)

o Learners make sentences with the other words in the box under the picture.
   Suggestions: There are a lot of oranges/onions. There's a lot of coffee.
   There's not much rice. There are some tomatoes. There isn't any tea.

o In pairs, learners ask and answer questions about the food in the picture. For example, one learner asks: *What's in the blue bowl?* The other learner answers *There are a lot of oranges.*
   Suggestions:
   What's next to the rice? (the onions)
   What colour is the box of tea? (pink and yellow)
   How many onions are there? (nine)
   What's on the blue bowl? (white flowers)

B Put a tick or a cross next to the things Mary needs to buy.

o Point to the girl and the kitchen in the picture in **A** and say: *This is Mary and this is her kitchen. Mary goes to the market on Tuesdays. What does she need to buy this week?*
   Point to the word 'potatoes' in the box. Ask: *Why is there a tick after potatoes? Does Mary need to buy potatoes?* (Yes!)
   Learners look at the words in the box and put a tick after the things that are not in the kitchen, or there is not much of, and a cross next to the things she doesn't need to buy because she has them.

> **Check answers:**
> Ask different learners to say sentences about the list with:
> *She needs to buy some …* (tea, potatoes, cheese, carrots, maybe some rice, tomatoes, apples, noodles and kiwis).
> *She doesn't need to buy any …* (coffee, pasta, oranges, onions).

Find the differences.

o Cut up and give out photocopies of the pictures on page 125. Learners work in A and B pairs. They look at their pictures.

o Learner A starts by saying one of the things in their picture, including the number or quantity. For example: Learner A: *In my picture, there are a lot of lemons.*
   Learner B says how their picture is different. For example: *In my picture, there's one lemon.*

Differences:
some / **a lot of** grapes
one / **eight** pineapples
lots of / **two** sandwiches
two / **ten** burgers
not much / **a lot of** milk
lots of lemons / **one** lemon
three / **a lot of** pears
not much / **a lot of** watermelon
a lot of / **not many** chips/fries
20 bottles of water / **one bottle** of water

What's in your kitchen?

o Write on the board in four columns:
   a little   some   a lot of   I need
   Say: *It's great because I live near a really good supermarket. I can buy lots of things there for my picnic this weekend.*

o Say: *I've got a little bread at home.* Write *bread* under 'a little' on the board. Say: *I've got some cheese too.* Write *cheese* under 'some'. Say: *I've got a lot of apples.* Write *apples* under 'a lot of'. Then, say and write four things that you need to buy under 'I need'.
   Learners copy the words from the board into their notebooks and write words for what they have under *a little, some, a lot of.* Then, they write four things that they need to buy under 'I need'.
   Say: *Now you write about the things **you** need for **your** picnic!*

o In pairs, learners ask and answer questions about the things they need. They do not show each other their lists. Each learner has to try and guess four things which their partner needs. For example:
   Learner A: *Do you need any apples?*
   Learner B: *No, I don't.*
   Learner B: *Do you need any bananas?*
   Learner A: *Yes, I do.*
   The winner is the first learner in the pair to guess four of the things on their partner's list.

C Complete the sentences about the story.

o Point to the four pictures. Say: *These pictures show a story. It's called 'A man on a bike helps Mary'. Just look at the pictures first. Now, look at the first picture. Mary's at the market. She's buying some fruit and vegetables for her mum. The man's giving Mary a bag of potatoes.*

o Learners complete the sentences about the first picture by writing one word on each line. Repeat the name of the story and the sentences about picture 1 as necessary.

> **Check answers:**
> vegetables, potatoes

Point to the man with the bike and read the last two sentences about Picture 1: *Hugo Pie is next to Mary. He's got his bike with him.* Ask: *Can you see Hugo? Is Hugo buying fruit or vegetables?* (no)

o Point to picture 2 and ask: *Is Mary at the market now?* (no)
What's on the ground behind Mary? (some fruit and vegetables)
Who's behind Mary? (Hugo Pie)
Learners complete the sentences about picture 2. (All the words they need are in the sentences for picture 1.)

> **Check answers:**
> fruit, vegetables, Hugo Pie

o Point to picture 3. Ask different learners to say sentences. For example: *Mary's at home / in the kitchen. She's with her mum. Her mum is angry. There are no fruit or vegetables in the bag.*

o Learners choose one word from the box to complete the sentences about picture 3.

> **Check answers:**
> home, angry, nothing, surprised, everything, market

o Learners read the questions and write short answers about picture 4.
Suggestions: 1 at the door **2** Hugo Pie
3 Mary's fruit and vegetables **4** yes
In pairs, learners say sentences to tell the story for picture 4.
Suggested story: Mary and her mum are at the door. Hugo Pie is outside. He's holding a box with Mary's fruit and vegetables. Mary and her mum are happy now.

D Who says this? Write *Mary*, *Mary's mum* or *Hugo Pie*.

o Read out 1: *Can I have two kilos of potatoes, please?* Ask: *Who says this? Mary, Mary's mum or Hugo Pie?* (Mary)
Point to 'Mary' on the line.

o Learners read sentences 2–4 and write the person who's speaking on the lines.

> **Check answers:**
> **2** Mary's mum **3** Hugo Pie **4** Mary

o In pairs, learners practise telling the story. They could also act out the story in groups of four (each learner is a different person in the story: the man at the market, Mary, Mary's mum, the man on the bike).

E Choose the correct words and write them on the lines.

> **Movers tip**
> Reading through the whole text in Reading and Writing Part 4 will give candidates an idea of the topic and the structure of the text. Noticing verb forms (singular/plural, affirmative/negative, present/past, etc) will help them complete the gaps which test verbs and pronouns.

o Ask: *Who likes cheese?* Learners say *I do!* or *I don't!* to answer.
Ask: *Who likes pasta? Do you put cheese on your pasta?*
Do you know how to make cheese? What do you need?

o Say: *Read the text. Does the text tell us about eating cheese or making cheese?* (making cheese) *Is a twelve-year-old cheese older or younger than you?*

o Learners read the text about cheese, choose words and write them on the lines.

> **Check answers:**
> **1** which **2** It **3** need **4** more **5** on

o Say: *Read the text in E again and tell me which numbers you find in it.* (ten, one, twelve)
Ask: *How many big bowls of milk are in one big bowl of cheese?* (ten) *How old is some cheese in supermarkets?* (more than twelve years old)

> 📦 **Find out about cheese**
> o Learners choose different cheeses and find out about them.
> o They find out what kind of milk is used (cow, sheep, goat), how old the cheese is when we find it in shops, etc.
> o They work in small groups and present their findings to each other.
> o Learners can also find a recipe that has their cheese in it. They tell other learners how to make it.

33 Last weekend, last week

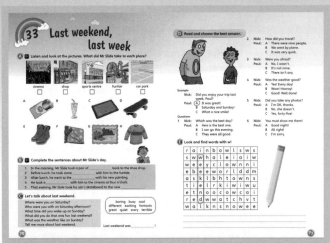

Equipment needed

o   Movers Audio 33A.

A ▶ Listen and look at the pictures. What did Mr Slide take to each place?

o   (Books closed.) Say: *Can you tell me seven places that you can find in a town?* Learners put their hands up and tell you different places.
    Say: *Open your books. Look at page 70. Did you say any of the places you can see in A?*

o   Point to the pictures of the places in **A** and say: *Listen to Mr Slide and Alice. Which place did Mr Slide go to this morning? Why did he go there?* Play the first part of the audio. Learners answer the questions. (He went to the shoe shop. He needed to take some boots back.)

o   Learners listen to the rest of the audio and write letters in the boxes under the pictures.

> **Check answers:**
> shop E   funfair A   sports centre G   cinema B   car park D

o   Say: *Look at the pictures in A. Put a star * next to your favourite place.*
    Draw a circle round the last place you were in.
    Put a tick (✓) next to the nearest place to your house.
    Point to your favourite place in **A** and say for example: *My favourite place is (the funfair). I love (going on the rides) there.*
    Point to a place you went to yesterday and say for example: *I was (at the shops) yesterday.*
    Point to a place near your home and say: *There's (a cinema) near my house.*
    In small groups, learners show their star, circle and ticks and say sentences about these places.

o   Read out these sentences. Learners listen and say which place you are talking about.
    You go to these places to buy things like food or clothes. (shops)
    This is a place where people can play tennis, badminton or basketball. (a sports centre)
    Some people put their cars in this place when they go shopping. (a car park)

o   Say: *Listen. These places are not in the pictures in A, but you find them in towns and cities too. What are they?*
    You can shop for food, clothes and sometimes books in this big store. (a supermarket)
    There are lots of different shops inside this big place. (a shopping centre)
    This place is often outside and people go there to buy things like fruit and vegetables. (a market)

o   Write on the board: *a library   a bookshop   You go here to …*
    This is a place where … .   People who want to … .
    Say: *Work in pairs. Write a sentence about a library and another sentence about a bookshop. You can make sentences that start with the words on the board.*

o   Pairs of learners write their sentences on a piece of paper. Stick the pieces of paper on the classroom walls. Learners move around and read the sentences. They look to see if they all wrote the same sentences. You could also give a prize for the best pair of sentences.

Audioscript

Mr Slide is talking to Alice. What did Mr Slide take to each place?

Girl:	Hello, Mr Slide. Did you have a busy day?
Man:	Yes, I did, Alice! My Saturdays are always busy! I took lots of things to different places.
Girl:	Where did you go this morning?
Man:	I went to the shoe shop.
Girl:	Why?
Man:	I needed to take some boots back. I bought them last week but they're too small!
Girl:	Oh dear!
Man:	And then I went to the funfair.
Girl:	Did you take your tablet with you?
Man:	No, only some crayons. I wanted to draw and colour a picture.
Girl:	Exciting!
Girl:	What did you do after lunch?
Man:	Let me think…. Oh yes! I went to the sports centre. The man who works behind the desk wants to buy one of my new paintings!
Girl:	Wow! That's good!
Man:	Yes, I'm very happy about that.
Man:	And I went to the cinema this afternoon.
Girl:	To see the film that starts at four o'clock?
Man:	Yes, that's right. I took a milkshake with me because I get thirsty sometimes.
Girl:	So do I!
Girl:	What about this evening?
Man:	I went to the new car park. It was really cold and I didn't take a sweater with me…
Girl:	Oh! But why did you go there?
Man:	I wanted to try my son's new skateboard!
Girl:	Brilliant!

B Complete the sentences about Mr Slide's day.

o Learners close their books. Say: *Mr Slide went to lots of different places that day. Which five places did he go to?* (shoe shop, funfair, sports centre, cinema, car park) Learners open their books and in pairs, complete the sentences about Mr Slide's day.

> **Check answers:**
> 1 boots 2 crayons 3 sports centre 4 milkshake 5 car park

o Ask: *Where did you go last weekend?* Learners answer. *Did you go in the morning? The afternoon? The evening? What did you do there? Who did you go with? Did you have fun?*

o Learners work in groups. Ask: *What is the most fun thing to do in a city?* Groups choose one activity. Ask one learner from each group to write their activity on the board. The class then votes for the activity that is most fun.

C Let's talk about last weekend.

o Tell two stronger learners to ask and answer the questions in **C**. For the last two questions, they choose words from the box to talk about the weather and their weekend.

o In pairs or groups of three, learners ask and answer the questions.

o Each learner chooses one word from the box to describe last weekend and writes it on the line.

D Read and choose the best answer. Reading & Writing Part 2

o Point to the boy in the picture. Say: *This is Paul. Paul was on holiday with his school last week. His uncle is asking him questions about his trip.*

o Read out the example and the three possible answers. Ask: *Why is A the right answer?* (It's the only one that answers the question.) *Saturday and Sunday could answer a question like When did you go on holiday? What a nice smile!* doesn't really answer a question.)

o Learners read the rest of the conversation and choose the best answer.

> **Check answers:**
> 1 C 2 B 3 A 4 A 5 C 6 B

E Look and find words with *w*.

o Point to the box in **E** and say: *In this box, there are 21 words with the letter 'w' in them.*
Point to the word 'weekend' and the circle round it and ask: *Which days are weekend days?* (Saturday and Sunday) *Do you like weekends?* (yes!) *Which two words make the word 'weekend'?* (week and end) Say: *The weekend is the end of the week! Hooray!*
Say: *Find 20 more words with the letter w! Look across and down* (move your hand to help them understand the direction of the words.)

> **Check answers:**
> Across (top to bottom): rainbow, bowl, whale, clown, world, town, kiwi, cow, watch, walk, snow.
> Down (left to right): sweater, website, yellow, brown, sandwich, wind, wave, swim, swimsuit.
> **Note:** The word 'low' is also in the box, in the eighth column. This word is a Flyers word.

o Say: *In pairs, look in your Fun for Movers book and find pictures for six of the words you found. Write the word and the page number in your notebooks.*
The first pair to find six pictures says *Stop!* To check answers, the two learners say the page number, everyone finds that page and then the two learners point to the picture and say a sentence. For example: *There are three bowls in this picture.* (Unit 32 A, page 68)

Suggested pictures:
bowl 28, 33, 68, 102
brown 8, 10, 11, 21, 22, 23, 27, 29, 41, 51, 61, 63, 67, 75, 77, 79, 82, 84, 86, 94, 96
clown 49, 73, 88, 89
cow 9, 10, 58, 79, 82
rainbow At the top of all the first pages of the unit! 19
sandwich 27, 45, 47, 62
snow 20, 21, 44, 54, 59
sweater 14, 29, 31, 42, 89, 99, 102
swim 38, 47, 50, 61, 92, 93
swimsuit 14, 47, 61, 92, 93
town 46, 48
walk 6, 13, 45, 47, 59, 63, 68, 74
watch noun - 81, 86
wave (sea) 23, 38, 44, 61, 88, 92, 95
website 35, 53
whale 9, 93, 104
wind 18, 20, 87
world 35, 102
yellow 29, 31, 35, 38, 43

o Say: *Now, I want you to write the words in alphabetical order on the lines in E. Write the word 'bowl' on the line under the box in E. Now, write the other 20 words after 'bowl'. Let's see who's the quickest!* Learners write the words.

> **Check answers:**
> brown, clown, cow, kiwi, rainbow, sandwich, snow, sweater, swim, swimsuit, town, walk, watch, wave, website, weekend, whale, wind, world, yellow

Play *Where were you? Bingo!*

o (Books closed). Ask: *Can you remember the five places you saw in A?* Learners tell you the five places. Write all the words on the board.
Say: *I need fifteen places. Can you tell me ten more words for places in a town?* Write their words on the board.

Movers places: bus station/stop, beach, café, car park, cinema, hospital, library, market, park, playground, school, shopping centre, shop, sports centre, square, station, store, supermarket, (swimming) pool, zoo

o Learners write the seven days of the week in their notebooks. They choose seven places from the list on the board and write a different one next to each day of the week.

o Say different sentences about the places on the board. For example: *I was at the supermarket on Friday last week. I was at the sports centre yesterday.*
Note: Write down the places you mention.
If learners have written places next to the days you say, they cross them out.

o The winner is the first person to cross out all the days and places. Check answers by telling the learner to say the seven places they have crossed out and the day you went to that place. For example: *On Tuesday, you went to the park.*

34   What did you do then?

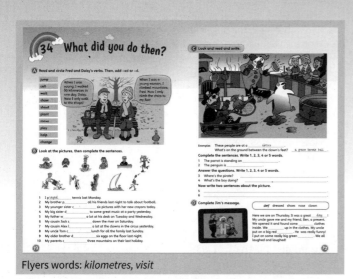

A Read and circle Fred and Daisy's verbs. Then, add -ed or -d.

○ Point to the people in the picture in **A** and ask: *Where are these people?* (in a park) *What are they doing?* (sitting, talking) *What's the weather like?* (cold, windy) *Read their sentences. What are their names?* (Daisy and Fred) *What are they talking about?* (when they were young and now)

○ Ask: *What do you do when I talk to you?* Mime somebody listening. *(We listen.) What did you do when I talked to you yesterday?* Mime somebody listening. *(We listened.)*

Write on the board: We listen / We listen*ed.*

○ Learners look at the picture of the two old people and circle the past and present verb forms in their speech bubbles. (was, walked/walk, climbed/climb)

Ask two learners to pretend to be sitting on a bench and role play the conversation. Make it fun by telling them to use 'old' voices.

○ Write on the board: *called   waited   changed*

Say: *Find these verbs next to the picture!* Point to the words on the board and ask: *How do we make the past simple form of these verbs?* (We add '-ed' to the end of 'call' and 'wait'. Because 'change' ends in 'e', we only need to add 'd' to the end of the verb to make the past tense form.)

Note: If possible, refer to regular past simple endings in the learners' first language to compare.

Learners add '-ed' or '-d' to the end of the words in the purple boxes so that all the verbs are regular past simple.

○ Point to the verb 'jump'/'jumped' and ask: *Do you think the man jumped a lot when he was young?* (yes) *Do you think he jumps a lot now?* (no) *You're the old man! Tell me about jumping!* (**Suggestion:** When I was young, I jumped a lot. Now, I never jump!)

○ Point to the verb 'play'/'played' and say: *In pairs, write two sentences for the woman. Write what she played when she was young and what she plays now.*

Suggestions: When I was young, I played baseball / basketball / tennis / the guitar / the piano. Now I only play board games / card games.

B Look at the pictures, then complete the sentences.

Movers tip

In Reading and Writing Parts 4 and 5, the verbs that candidates have to write in the gaps will be in both present and past forms. Answers will always appear in the vocabulary box (Part 4) or in the story text (Part 5) in the form that is needed. Recognising past tense forms will help them choose the correct verbs.

○ Ask: *How many pictures are there in B?* (11) *How many people are laughing?* (one) *Which person doesn't look happy?* (The boy with the eggs.)

○ Ask different learners: *Which picture do you like best? Why?* (For example: *The boy in the boat, because I like sailing.*)

○ Point to the sentences in **B** and ask: *How many sentences are there?* (10) Read out the example: *I played tennis last Monday.* Say: *Find a picture for this sentence!* (the girl who's playing tennis). Write *play* on the board. Ask: *When did the girl play tennis?* (last Monday)

Add -*ed* to the end of 'play' on the board: *played*

○ Teach/revise spelling rules with past simple. In pairs, learners complete the verbs in sentences 2–10.

Note: The first letter of each word and the pictures are there to help them.

Note: The name 'Alex' is a name for both boys and girls. Other names like this on the Movers wordlist are: 'Kim' and 'Sam'.

Check answers:
2 phoned   **3** coloured   **4** danced   **5** worked   **6** sailed
7 laughed   **8** cooked   **9** dropped   **10** climbed

○ Ask: *Which picture have you not used?* (the boy who's playing basketball)

Say: *Let's write a sentence for this picture!* Write on the board: *My friend …*

Ask different learners to come to the board and write. Each learner adds one word to the sentence. (For example, My friend Peter played really well in his basketball game yesterday.)

○ Ask: *Which is the longest sentence in B?* (sentence 7 = 13 words)

Say: *Read this sentence! Now, close your books! Who can tell me the sentence?*

Write on the board: *My cousin Alex laughed a lot at the clowns in the circus yesterday.* (leave gaps between 'Alex' and 'laughed', 'lot' and 'at', 'clowns' and 'in', and 'circus' and 'yesterday'.)

Say the sentence, pausing where the gaps are. Explain that in English, we say words in groups like this.

Say: *Say the sentence, please!* Learners read it, pausing between the word groups.

○ Erase 'yesterday'. Learners read the sentence and add yesterday. Erase 'My cousin Alex'. Learners say the whole sentence. Erase 'laughed a lot', then 'at the clowns in the circus'. Each time, learners say the whole sentence.

At the end, say: *Well done!*

Flyers words: *kilometres, visit*

C Look and read and write.

Reading & Writing Part **6**

o Point to the picture in **C** and say: *Jim had a fun day last week. Who is Jim in this picture?* Learners guess it's the boy. Ask: *Who is Jim with? His mother? His aunt? His grandmother? And his sister? His best friend?* Learners decide and choose names for the older woman and the girl.

o Ask: *How many people can you see in the picture?* (five) *Where are they?* (at a circus) Point to and read the first example: *These people are at a circus.* Say: *That's right! Everyone is at the circus!*

Point to the ball between the clown's feet and ask: *What's this?* (a green tennis ball) *Where's the ball?* (between the clown's feet). Point to the second example and its answer.

o Say: *Read 1 and 2 and write 1–5 words to complete the sentences. Then, write 1–5 word answers to 3 and 4.*

> **Check answers:**
> (Suggestions)
> **1** a tennis racket
> **2** jumping (into some water)
> **3** in the (red) ship
> **4** (He's) laughing and clapping

o Say: *Now, write two sentences about the picture. Write them on the lines in 5 and 6.*

Check answers by asking different learners to say their sentences. Accept any answers. Encourage learners to extend their sentences if they can. Make this a fun activity. Remind learners that lots of different answers will be correct for this part of the test.

Suggestions:

The ship is red.

The pirate likes playing tennis.

These children like coming to the circus.

I can see a funny pirate on the ship.

The penguin is standing by the pool.

The girl is laughing because she loves penguins.

I like the clown but I like the pirate and penguin more.

D Complete Jim's message.

o Say: *Jim went to the circus one day last week. He had lots of fun there. What did he enjoy most at the circus? What do you think?* Learners answer.

o Point to the picture in **D** and say: *Jim wasn't with his grandmother and sister at the circus on Thursday, he was with his uncle and his friend Ben on Thursday. What did Jim dress up as?* (a clown) *Did he enjoy being a clown?* (yes)

Read out the first two sentences of the message: *Here we are on Thursday. It was a great day!* Point to the word 'day' on the line in the second sentence and to this word in the box next to the screen. Say: *Read and choose and write words on the lines to complete the message.*

> **Check answers:**
> clown   dressed   nose   shoes

Ask: *Do you like dressing up in funny clothes? Would you like to be a clown one day and work in a circus? Why? Why not?*

Find five differences between the pictures.

Speaking Part **1**

o Ask: *Who were the two old people in the park in A? What were their names?* (Fred and Daisy). Learners look at the two pictures on page 115. Ask: *Which person in A climbed mountains when she was young?* (the old woman, Daisy) Say: *The woman in the pictures is Daisy when she was younger.*

o In pairs, learners find five differences between the two pictures and think of the words they need to say what the differences are.

o Check answers by saying: *In picture 1 Daisy's wearing a blue jacket, but in picture 2 she's ….* .

Ask each pair to complete a sentence, repeating differences if necessary so that all pairs have the opportunity to speak.

> **Check answers:**
> Daisy's wearing a blue / **red** jacket.
> The weather's cloudy / **sunny**.
> There are three / **four** mountains.
> There's a bear / There **isn't a** bear.
> The man's taking a photo / **reading**.

Play the game! Who did this?

o Say: *Write the names of four people you know. But not the names of people in this class!*

o Say: *Next to each name, write one thing that you know or think that each of the four people did last week. You can use the verbs from A to help you.* (Tell learners to use their imagination if necessary!)

For example: *Mario played tennis on Tuesday. Ana played computer games. Pablo called lots of friends. Susie planted some flowers.*

o Form pairs of learners who do not know each other very well, if possible.

Learners swap lists. Their partner reads the sentence and tries to guess who the person in each sentence is and asks a question about what that person did. For example:

Learner A: *Is Mario your brother?*

Learner B: *Yes.*

Learner A: *Is Mario good at tennis? / Does Mario play tennis every week? Did you play tennis with Mario?*

Learner B: *Yes./No.*

Optional extension: Listen and write words

o Say: *Listen and write the words you hear.*

fifty / questions / yesterday / answered / Alex

Say: *Now, write the words in alphabetical order!* (Alex answered fifty questions yesterday.)

Do the same with these:

the / Fred / town / near / lived / zoo (Fred lived near the town zoo.)

changed / jeans / Wednesday / on / his /Ben (Ben changed his jeans on Wednesday.)

Learners could draw a picture for one of the sentences and write it at the bottom.

83

35   What a morning!

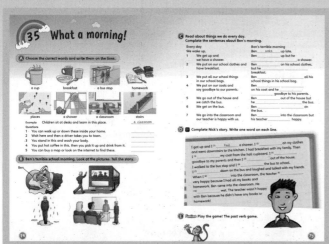

Pronunciation practice Linking: *woke up, got up, put on, got on, went into.* See D.

Flyers words: *diary, late*

Equipment needed

- Movers Audio 35D.
- Photocopies of page 126 (one for each group of 3–4 learners) cut up into cards. See B.

A   Choose the correct words and write them on the lines.

Reading & Writing Part 1

- Say: *Look at the pictures. How many pictures are there?* (eight)
  Say: *How many sentences can you see?* (6: 1 example + 5 sentences)
  Say: *You don't need to use one of the words under two of the pictures.*

- Say: *Look at the words under the eight pictures.*
  How many words have got 'a' in front of them? (four)
  What does this tell us about these words? (They're singular.)
  Are any of the words plural? Do they end with the letter 's'?
  (yes, stairs and places)

- Read out the example: *Children sit at desks and learn in this place.*
  (a classroom)
  Ask: *Is a classroom a place?* (yes) *Do you learn things in a classroom?* (yes)

- Learners read the sentences and write the words on the lines.
  Before you check answers, tell learners to make sure they have copied the words correctly (including the 'a' in front of 'cup', etc). In pairs, they check they have the same answers and that their partner's answers are spelt correctly. If not, they look at the sentences where they have different answers and check them again and check the spelling of the words under the pictures.

- Ask : *Which words helped you choose your answers?*

> **Check answers:**
> 1   stairs (*walk, up or down, inside your home*)
> 2   a bus stop (*wait here, driver takes you, to town*)
> 3   a shower (*stand, wash your body*)
> 4   a cup (*hot coffee, in, pick up, drink*)
> 5   places (*map, look, on the internet, find*)

- Ask: *Which words and pictures have we not used?* (homework, breakfast) Write on the board: *Homework: You … this in the … after you … home from school.*
  Breakfast: People … this in the … . It isn't lunch!
  Say : *Tell me words to complete the sentence about homework.* (do, evening, come)
  Which words complete the sentence about breakfast? (eat, morning)
  Ask: *What do people eat in the evening?* (dinner)

B   Ben's terrible school morning. Look at the pictures. Tell the story.

Speaking Part 2

- Teach/revise the word 'late'.
  Say: *This class starts at (10 o'clock). You have to be here at (10 o'clock). I have to be here at (10 o'clock). If I come here after (10 o'clock), I'm late. If you come here after (10 o'clock), you're late!*

- Say: *Look at these pictures. They show a story. It's called 'Ben's terrible school morning'. Look at the pictures first.*

- Point to the first picture. Say: *Ben's in bed. He's waking up. He looks at the clock and thinks, 'Oh no! I must get up and go to school!' Now you tell the story.*
  1   To make this Speaking Part 2 as authentic as possible, tell learners in pairs, to tell the rest of the story, saying two or three sentences about what they can see happening in each picture.
  2   To give learners more support, continue as follows.

- Point to the second picture. Different learners suggest sentences about this picture. Ask these questions to help them if necessary:
  Is Ben at home now? (no)
  Is he on the bus? (no)
  Are his friends on the bus? (yes)
  Has he got his school bag with him? (no)
  Has he got a coat on? (no)

- Point to the third picture. **Suggested questions:** *What's Ben doing?* (walking)
  What's the weather like? (It's raining.)
  Is Ben happy? (no) *Why not?* (Because he's wet.)

- Point to the fourth picture. **Suggested questions:** *Where is Ben now?* (in the classroom / at school) *Is his teacher happy?* (no) *Why not?* (He's late.)

- Give out the photocopies of page 126 (made into sets of cards) to groups of 3–4 learners.)
  Say: *Read the sentences that Ben wrote in his diary about his terrible morning.*
  Say: *Three cards go with the first picture and two cards go with each of the other pictures. Groups match the cards to the pictures.*

- Point to the small pictures on each of the cards. Learners tell you the order they put the cards in by saying the names of the things on each card.

> **Check answers:**
> **(Picture 1)** star, flower, moon; **(Picture 2)** sun, square ;
> **(Picture 3)** eye, phone; **(Picture 4)** toothbrush, radio

- Read out the sentences from Ben's diary (in the correct order).
- Learners work in groups of six. One learner in each group reads out the sentences from Ben's diary. The other learners listen and mime the story. One learner in each group could be Ben, one learner the teacher and the others the people on the bus and in the classroom. They change roles each time.

C   Read about things we do every day. Complete the sentences about Ben's morning.

- Ask learners to tell you different things they do in the morning. (I get up. I have breakfast etc.)

- Point to the example: 'We wake up. Ben woke up late.'
  Underline the words 'wake' and 'woke' in these sentences. Explain that 'wake' is an irregular verb and 'woke' is the past form.
  Note: If appropriate, it would be helpful to point out to learners that there are both regular and irregular past verb forms in their own language.
  Make sure that learners understand that the first sentence is in the present tense, because it is about something that we do every day. The second sentence is in the past because it is about Ben's terrible morning (yesterday).

- Learners read the sentences about things we do every day and then complete the sentences about Ben's terrible morning with the correct past form of the verbs.

  Point out that in some sentences they need to write the negative form ('didn't') because **his** morning was terrible. When they have to write the negative, there are two lines for them to write on.

  Note: Learners can use the sentences on the cards about Ben's morning to help them.

  > **Check answers:**
  >
  > **1** got, didn't have   **2** put, didn't have   **3** didn't put   **4** didn't put, didn't say   **5** went, didn't catch   **6** didn't get   **7** went, was not

- Ask learners to tell you the other verbs and their past forms in the sentences. Write them on the board: get / got, do / did, put / put, go / went, is / was

D ▶ Complete Nick's story. Write one word on each line.

> **Movers tip**
>
> Candidates should be familiar with the past simple forms of the verbs on the Movers wordlist. Many of these verbs are in this unit. See page 124–125 of the Student's Book for the full list of irregular verbs on the Movers wordlist.

- Point to the picture of the boy. Say:

  This is Nick. He's in Ben's class. Can you see him in the pictures in B? (Learners point to this boy in picture 4.)

- Ask: *Did Nick catch the bus yesterday?* (yes)

  Was Nick late for school? (no) Say:

  Nick's morning was <u>very different</u> to Ben's terrible morning.

- Read out the first example sentence about Nick: *I got up and I had a shower.* Point to the word 'had' on the line in this sentence.

- Learners read and complete the text. Tell them that the sentences in the second part of C can help them and that they can look at the list of verbs on pages 124–125.

  > **Check answers:**
  >
  > **2** put   **3** took   **4** said   **5** went   **6** caught/took   **7** sat   **8** went/came   **9** was   **10** was

- Say then write these sentences on the board. Different learners come up and write *Ben* or *Nick* in each gap.

  1   *… had a shower.*
  2   *… had breakfast.*
  3   *… didn't take his coat.*
  4   *… took his school bag with him.*
  5   *… walked to school.*
  6   *… was wet.*
  7   *The teacher smiled at … .*
  8   *The teacher wasn't happy with … .*

  > **Check answers:**
  >
  > Nick: 1, 2, 4, 7 Ben: 3, 5, 6, 8

- Say: *Listen to Nick.* Play sentence 1 on the audio. Say: *woke up, got up.* Explain: *because up starts with a vowel sound /ʌ/, the /k/ and /t/ from 'woke' and 'got' carry on:* /wəʊkʌp/, /ɡɒtʌp/. *Because 'on' and 'in' also start with the vowels /ɒ/ and /ɪ/, we say got on* /ɡɒtɒn/ *and went into* /wentɪntuː/. Learners listen to 1 again and repeat Nick's sentence.

  Play sentences 2–4. Learners listen and repeat Nick's sentences.

Audioscript

One
Boy: I woke up, then I got up.

Two
Boy: I put on my clothes.

Three
Boy: I got on the bus.

Four
Boy: I went into the classroom.

- Say: *Talk about this morning in pairs. Talk about the things you did at home, how you came to school, your first lesson.* Learners tell each other about their morning. Remind them to pronounce 'woke up, got up, put on, got on, went into' like Nick!

- Read out the start of the text in **D**: *I got up … .* Ask: *Where was Nick when he got up?* (in his bedroom) Write *bedroom* on the board.

  Continue asking learners to read out the sentences in the text and asking where Nick did each thing. Write each place on the board: *bathroom, bedroom, kitchen, hall, street, bus stop, bus, school, classroom*)

- Say: *Now, let's tell the last part of each story about Ben's and Nick's school days.* Point to the word *classroom* on the board and say: *It was the end of the school day. Nick and Ben were in the classroom.*

- Divide the class into two groups – A and B. Group A write what Ben did that evening. Group B write what Nick did. They try and use all the words from the board.

  Suggestions: Ben went out of the school and got on the bus. He sat at the back of the bus. He got off the bus at the bus stop outside his home. He went inside. Ben said hello to his parents but he didn't put his coat in the cupboard. He did his homework. He had dinner with his family in the kitchen. He went upstairs to his bedroom and took off his clothes. He went into the bathroom. He had a shower then cleaned his teeth and went to bed.

  Nick went out of the school and got on the bus. He sat at the back of the bus. He got off the bus at the bus stop outside his home. He went inside. Nick said hello to his parents and put his coat in the cupboard. He did his homework. He had dinner with his family in the kitchen. He went upstairs to his bedroom and took off his clothes. He went to the bathroom but he didn't have a shower. He washed his face and hands, then cleaned his teeth, went to bed and went to sleep.

- Form pairs of learners – one learner from group A and one learner from B. They read out their sentences and compare Ben and Nick's evenings.

E Play the game! The past verb game.

- Write a past simple verb on the board. For example: *went*.

- In pairs or small groups, learners take it in turns to think of another past simple verb (regular or irregular) either starting with 'w' or with 't'. A learner from the team then writes this on the board, below the relevant letter:

  ```
  w  e  n  t
  o
  r
  k
  e
  d
  ```

- The next team then thinks of a verb and writes it either under 't' or next to 'd' (depending on the verb) and so on.

  ```
  w  e  n  t
  o        o
  r        o
  k        k
  e
  d  a  n  c  e  d
  ```

- Give a point to any team that spells a verb correctly. If the team whose turn it is can't think of a verb that fits, they don't get a point. They cannot use the same verb more than once.

36 Could you do it?

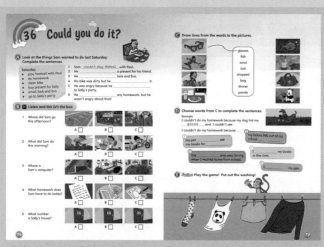

Equipment needed
- Movers Audio 36B.
- A4 paper, cut up into four squares, string and one clothes peg for each learner. See E.

A Look at the things Sam wanted to do last Saturday. Complete the sentences.

- Point to the boy in the picture and say: *This is Sam. Sam was in bed last Saturday.*
  Ask: *Was Sam OK?* (no) *Why was his nose red? What was the matter with him?* (He had a bad cold and a temperature.)
- Learners look at Sam's diary. Say: *Sam wanted to do lots of things on Saturday. What was the first thing Sam wanted to do?* (play football with Paul)
  Ask: *Could Sam do that?* (no)
  Ask: *Why not?* (Because he had a cold / was in bed.)
- Look at the example with learners: *Sam couldn't play football with Paul.* Ask: *Did Sam play football with Paul?* (no) *Why could Sam not play football?* (because he was in bed / he had a bad cold and a temperature)
- In pairs, learners complete 2–6 using 'couldn't' and other words in Sam's diary.

> **Check answers:**
> 2 couldn't buy   3 couldn't email   4 couldn't clean
> 5 couldn't go   6 couldn't do

- Ask: *When did you last have a cold? Did you have a cough? Did you come to school?*

B ▶ Listen and tick the box. Listening Part 4

> **Movers tip**
> For Listening Part 4, candidates should practise reading each question carefully (especially the question word). Then they should look at each set of three pictures and think about how each picture might answer that question.

Note: There is no example in this Listening Part 4. In *Cambridge English: Movers*, candidates would listen to an example question.

- Say: *Sam was better on Sunday. Look at the pictures in 1. Which places can you see?* (football field / shops / zoo)
  Say: *Listen to Sam talking to his uncle on Sunday evening.*
  Play question 1. Learners listen. Point to the answer (B – he went to the shops). Ask: *What did his mum buy for him?* (new sports shoes)
- Tell each learner to look at questions 2–5 and to read each

question and look at the three pictures. They write a word that they think they will hear on the audio in big letters on a piece of paper. (for example, for question 1, they could write *football, shop,* or *zoo* because they can see these things in the pictures.).

Suggestions: 2 garden / cook / bike   **3** stairs / living room / bedroom   **4** writing / reading / drawing   **5** number / 16, 18, 21 / door

- Play the audio for questions 2–5. When learners hear their words, they stand up and hold up their piece of paper. After each question, see if all the learners are standing up. If not, ask the learners who are sitting: *Which word did you write?* (They may have missed the word or maybe it wasn't said).
- Play the audio for questions 2–5 again. Say: *Listen and tick the box.*

> **Check answers:**
> 2 B   3 A   4 C   5 B

- Ask different learners: *What was the last thing that you bought? How do you help at home? What do you like cooking? How often do you clean your bike? Where's the computer in your house? How often do you email your friends? What homework do you have to do today? What number of the street is your house/flat?*
- Ask: *Which questions did I ask?* Learners put up their hands to say the questions that they remember. Say: *Well done! That's your question!* Continue until all the learners have a question. (More than one person can have the same question.) (With big groups, pairs of learners get a question.)
  Learners ask and answer their questions in groups of 5–6.

Audioscript

Look at the pictures. Listen and look.

One
Where did Sam go this afternoon?
Uncle:	Did you go to the zoo this afternoon, Sam?
Sam:	No, Uncle Jim. We went shopping. Mum bought me some new sports shoes.
Uncle:	That's good!
Sam:	I know, but I wanted to play football!
Uncle:	Why didn't you?
Sam:	I couldn't. I've got a cold.

Two
What did Sam do this morning?
Sam:	I was busy this morning, Grandpa!
Grandpa:	Oh! What did you do? Did you work in the garden?
Sam:	No, but I cooked our lunch!
Grandpa:	Wow! That's clever!
Sam:	Yes! I wanted to clean my bike too, but I didn't.

Three
Where is Sam's computer?
Sam:	I moved my computer yesterday. It's not in my bedroom now.
Woman:	Oh! Why?
Sam:	My sister wants to do her homework on it and I don't want her in my bedroom!
Woman:	So is it in the living room now?
Sam:	No, in the hall by the stairs.

Four
What homework does Sam have to do today?
Sam:	I've got to do my homework today, Mum.
Mum:	Have you got to do some writing or read your book?
Sam:	No, I've got to draw a map of an island. That's all.
Mum:	That's good.

Five

What number is Sally's house?

Sam: I couldn't go to Sally's party yesterday.

Girl: Oh. I like Sally. Where does she live?

Sam: She lives at number 18, Farm Street.

Girl: That's funny. My cousins live at number 16 in that street, and my grandma lives at number 21!

C Draw lines from the words to the pictures.

○ Say: *Look at the pictures. Point to the glasses. Now, point to the <u>word</u> 'glasses'. Can you see the line between the <u>picture</u> of the glasses and the <u>word</u> glasses?*
   Draw lines between the other pictures and words. Learners draw lines.

> **Check answers (by asking questions):**
> *What are these?*
> *You pick these up and put them on when you want to see better.* **(glasses)**
> *This is a kind of weather. It can be difficult to walk quickly in it.* **(wind)**
> *This animal lives in water.* **(a fish)**
> *This is an animal too. In most countries, you can only find it in a zoo.* **(a panda)**
> *This is when you can't find something. You … it.* **(lost)**
> *People carry things in this when they go on trips.* **(a bag)**
> *You eat this is the evening.* **(dinner)**
> *When you had something in your hand and it fell and now it's on the ground, you … it.* **(dropped)**

Now ask more questions about the pictures:
What colour are these glasses? **(pink)**
Oh dear, what is the boy running after in the wind? **(his hat/cap)**
What colour is the fish's tail? **(dark) orange)**
What's the panda eating? **(leaves)**
The man lost his train … . **(ticket)**
Whose face is on his bag? **(a clown's)**
What's on this dinner plate? **(beans)**
How many apples did the woman NOT drop? **(one)**

D Choose words from C to complete the sentences.

○ Ask: *I know that <u>you</u> always do all your homework. But some teachers say that some children <u>don't</u> always do their homework! Here are some funny stories from teachers. Children say why they couldn't do their homework!*

○ Read out the example: *I couldn't do my homework because my dog hid my ……glasses…… and I couldn't see.* Point to the dog in the picture and ask: *What's the dog got in its mouth?* (some glasses) *What's it doing?* (hiding the glasses)

○ Learners complete sentences 1–5 with words from **C**.

> **Check answers:**
> **1** fish/panda, dinner **2** bag **3** wind **4** dropped
> **5** lost/dropped

○ Ask: *Which sentence do you think is the best?* Learners vote for the best one.

Optional extension:

Learners work in pairs to think up funny reasons of their own. Ask different pairs to come to the front of the class and write their reasons on the board. For example:

> because I had to go to the moon last night.
> because Mum cooked it by mistake.
> because I gave it to an alien.
> because my baby brother put it in the bath.
> because my sister dropped paint on it.

The class votes for the funniest reason.

E Play the game! Put out the washing!

○ Give each learner a square of paper.
   Say: *Everyone! Choose one of the words from C. Write it in big letters on your piece of paper!*

○ Say: *Now, listen to this story. Hold up your word when you hear it!*

○ Read out the story, pausing slightly between each sentence. (You could also mime the story to help learners understand it.) Learners hold up their word when they hear it, then put their hands down when they hear the next word from C.

   There was a very strong wind yesterday. Great! I could fly my new kite! My mum and I went to the park to fly it. The kite's orange and has a green fish on it. The kite was inside a big purple bag. It was very difficult to walk in that wind. I had to hold on to my glasses because the wind was really strong. I had to hold on to the bag too! In the wind, the kite flew really well. But then, my glasses fell off in the wind and I dropped the kite. Mum ran after it, but she couldn't catch it. We lost the kite! I picked up my glasses and we went home.
   Now, my uncle works at the zoo. He phoned me and said: 'Sam, did you lose your kite?' 'Yes' I said, sadly. 'Well, I think I found it!' he answered. 'Come to the zoo!'
   My kite was in the panda's cage! It was in a tree there. My uncle climbed the tree and moved the kite. It dropped to the ground. To say thank you to my uncle, we invited him for dinner!

○ Two learners come to the front of the classroom. Give them the string. They each hold one end of the string. Take a peg and put it on the string.
   Say: *This is a washing line. But today, we're not putting clothes on the line. We're putting words.* Put the pegs in a small box near the clothes line.

○ Read out the story again, very slowly. When learners hear their word, they come and peg their word on the washing line. Some words are in the story twice. This word is taken off the line and pegged again!

○ With stronger classes, learners could tell the story after they have heard it a few times.

Optional extension:
Other washing line games

○ Learners say sentences about the story using the words on the line. For example, a learner says: *Sam's kite had a green fish on it* and takes the word 'fish'.

○ Learners say sentences to define one of the words on the washing line. For example, a learner says: *This is a kind of weather. It's difficult to walk in it.* and takes the word 'wind'.

○ Learners make their own story using some of the words on the washing line and then tell it to the rest of the class.
   Note: If you don't have a washing line and pegs, learners could stick their pictures on the wall or put them on the classroom floor or learners could stand in order holding their words in front of them.

37 Mr Must changes his job

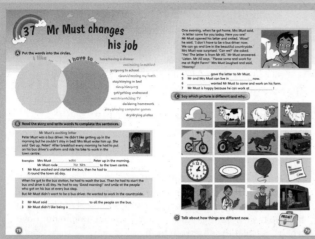

Flyers words: *diary, letter* (as in *mail*), *uniform, stay, job*

Equipment needed

o   A letter sealed in an envelope, 'Mr Must' should be written on the front of the envelope. The letter inside should read: 'Dear Mr Must, please come and work for me at Right Farm. Mr All.' See B.

A Put the words into the circles.

o   Ask: *What do you like doing every day?* Write some of your learners' answers on the board. For example: *I like eating, drawing, playing on the computer, watching TV, sleeping.* Ask: *Which is the most exciting – eating, drawing, playing on the computer, watching TV or sleeping?*

o   Ask: *What do you have to do every day?* (I have to clean my teeth, get dressed, go to school, do my homework.) Write some of these answers on the board too and ask: *Which is the most boring?*

o   Point to *stay/staying in bed* in **A** and say: *On a school day, can you stay in bed or do you have to get up?* (We have to get up) *In the holidays, can you stay in bed?* (yes)

Say: *Look at the activities in A. In pairs, choose the things you **like doing** and the things you **have to do**.* Then, write the things you **like doing** in the yellow circle using the *-ing* form (having a shower, eating breakfast) of the verb and the things you **have to do** in the orange circle using the infinitive form (have a shower, eat breakfast) of the verb.

o   Walk around and help if necessary. Accept any reasonable answers.
Note: Some learners might put the verbs in both circles: For example, they might **like eating** eat breakfast and **have to** eat breakfast.
Note: 'Like' can be followed by either '-ing' or the infinitive, but don't practise that now.

o   Ask different learners these questions. Stress the bold words and make sure learners stress the word that is different in their answers.
*Where do you like watching TV? In the **bathroom**?* (No – in my **bedroom**!)
*When do you have to clean your teeth? After a **game of hockey**?* (No – after **breakfast/dinner**!)
*When do you get dressed? When you go to **bed**?* (No – when I **get up**!)
*When do you sleep? When you're **hungry**?* (No – when I'm **tired**!)
*Where do you have a shower? In the **hall**?* (No – in the **bathroom**!)
*When do you have to dry your hair? When it's **wet**?* (Yes!)

B Read the story and write words to complete the sentences.

Reading & Writing Part 5

o   Show learners your letter (the letter to Mr Must). Explain that 'letter' is the same word for a letter like a, b, c or for something you write and send someone.

o   Say: *This story is called Mr Must's exciting letter.* Read out the first four sentences of the story in **B** slowly and use a different voice for Mrs Must.

o   Learners read the first and second parts of the story. Ask: *What does Mr Must do?* (He's a bus driver.)
Does Mr Must like being a bus driver? (no)
Where would Mr and Mrs Must like to live? (in the countryside)

o   Look at the example sentences with learners. For the first example, learners must find the words in the text that give this answer. (in the morning … Mrs Must woke him up) For the second example, he rode his bike to work and he worked in the town centre.
Learners read sentences 1–3. Tell them they only need 1, 2 or 3 words to complete each sentence.
In pairs, they find the words in the text that they need. Learners underline the words they need in the text and write them in the gaps.

Check answers:
1 drive   **2** Good morning!   **3** bus driver

o   Learners read the third part of the story. Ask: *Are Mr and Mrs Must happy at the end of the story?* (yes) *Why?* (because they can live in the countryside / on the farm)
Ask: *What did Mrs Must say at the end of the story?* (Hooray!) Tell learners that this is another way of saying 'That's great!'

o   Learners read the third part again and complete 4–7.

Check answers:
4 Mrs Must   **5** the (beautiful) countryside   **6** Mr All
7 Right Farm

o   Ask two volunteers to role play the last part of the story when Mr Must comes home and opens the exciting letter. Give them the letter to open and read out. Encourage them to say *Wow!* and *Hooray!*

Read and complete the sentences.

o   Say: *Take a pencil. Write numbers at the start of each line of the first two texts in B.* Learners write 1–9. Say: *Find the word 'like' in the story in B.* (line 1) *Put your hand up when you find it.* When all the learners have their hands up, ask one learner to read out the sentence and another learner to write it on the board. (Lines 1–2: *He didn't like getting up in the morning.*)

o   Say: *Now I want you to find the things Mr Must had to do. Draw a line under them all.* Give learners time to draw lines.
Ask: *In which line is the first thing that Mr Must had to do?* (Lines 3–4: he had to put on his bus driver's uniform and ride his bike.)
Say: *Mr Must didn't like getting up in the morning or* (putting on his bus driver's uniform.) *Mr Must didn't like getting up in the morning, putting on his bus driver's uniform or … ?* (riding his bike to work)
Continue like this, asking different learners to repeat the sentence with the things Mr Must didn't like doing until they have the sentence with all of them.
Mr Must didn't like getting up in the morning, or putting on his bus driver's uniform, or riding his bike to work, or washing the bus, or starting the bus, or driving it, or saying 'Good morning' or smiling,
In pairs, learners say the sentences to each other. Their partner points at any action in the text that their partner forgets to say!

Compare before and now.

o Divide the class into two groups (A and B). Learners in group A look at the sentences on page 112. Learners in group B look at the sentences on page 114 of their book. Each group of learners completes their sentences with appropriate verbs.

> **Check answers:**
> **Learner A:** wear / put on, had, wash/clean, stay, lived
> **Learner B:** love/like, wash/clean, have, wear / put on, say

o Form pairs of learners – one learner from each group. Learner A reads out a sentence (sadly), each time starting with: *When I was a bus driver … .*
Learner B listens, then reads out their matching sentence (happily), starting with *Now, because I work on a farm … !*
Example: Learner A: *When I was a bus driver I had to wear a uniform.*
Learner B: *Now, because I work on a farm, I can wear the clothes that I like!*

C Say which picture is different and why. Speaking **3** Part

o Ask: *How many pictures are there?* (16)
Say: *Look at all the pictures. What am I talking about?* Read out these sentences. Learners say things/people they can see in the 16 pictures.
People ride these. (horse, bike, motorbike)
You find these animals on some farms. (cow, sheep, goat, horse)
These animals give us milk. (cow, sheep, goat)
These can move. (cow, sheep, goat, horse, bike, motorbike, truck, a bus driver, doctor, farmer, teacher)
You can pick these up and carry them. (balloon, clock, plate, letter)
These things start with the letter 'c'. (clock, cloud, cow)
Say: *Say/write all the things in the pictures in C in alphabetical order!*
(balloon, bike, bus driver, clock, cloud, cow, doctor, farmer, goat, horse, letter, motorbike, plate, sheep, teacher, truck)

o Ask: *What can you see in the first four pictures?* (a cloud, a cow, a sheep, a goat) Write on the board: *Which one is different? Why?*
Suggestion: A cow, a sheep and a goat are animals. The cloud is different because it's not an animal.

o In pairs, learners ask and answer the questions on the board. Ask different pairs to tell the class about the differences.
Suggestions:
2 The truck is different because you drive it. You ride a horse, a bike and a motorbike. / The horse is different because it's got legs.
3 The letter is different because it's square. The clock, plate and balloon are round.
4 The doctor is different because she's a woman. The teacher, bus driver and farmer are men. / The farmer is different because he is outside.

D Talk about how things are different now.

o Ask learners to imagine life 100 years ago. What was different? Ask: *Did people wear T-shirts?* (no) *Did people have computers?* (no)

o Write on the board: *People couldn't write on their computers. They had to write on paper.*

o Write on the board:
TV emails cars phones supermarkets toys tablets games books

o In pairs or groups of three, learners think of as many differences as they can and write sentences using 'couldn't' and 'had to'.

o Ask each pair or group to read their sentences to the class.
Suggestions:
TV/books (People couldn't watch TV, they had to read books.)
Emails/letters (People couldn't write emails, they had to write letters.)
Cars (People couldn't drive cars, they had to walk or ride horses.)
Phones (People couldn't talk by phone, they had to speak to people who lived near them or write letters.)
Supermarkets (People couldn't buy everything in one big shop. They had to buy things in different shops.)
Toys (Children couldn't play computer games. They had to make their toys.)
Tablets/computers (People couldn't work on computers. They had to do their work on pieces of paper.)
Games (Children couldn't play on a tablet. They had to play board games.)
Books (People couldn't read e-books. They had to read paper books.)

---

 100 years

Pre-teach 'invented' and 'inventor'.
Learners look on the internet or in encyclopedias and other books for information about when different things that we have in our homes and cities were invented. They draw a timeline and put the inventions in the different years. Learners can add their timelines to their project files.
Suggestions: bike (1818 or 1884) lift/elevator (1852) phone (1876) camera (1888) movies (1893) helicopter (1936) (home) video camera (1963) the internet (1969) CD (1972) DVD (1995)

38 Playing and working

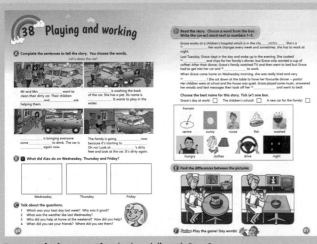

Pronunciation practice /w/ and /haʊ/. See C.

Flyers words: *same*

Equipment needed

O   Movers Audio 38B.

A Complete sentences to tell the story.

> **Movers tip**
>
> Some candidates find it difficult to tell the story in Speaking Part 2. Train learners to just look at one picture at a time and to think of just two things to say about what's happening there. That way, it won't look so difficult.

O   Learners look at the story. Point to the first picture and ask: *Is this car clean or dirty?* (dirty). Point to the last picture and say: *Oh dear! Silly dog! Is the car clean or dirty again now?* (dirty!)

O   Learners work in groups. Say: *Look at the sentences that tell the story. Choose one or two words to complete each sentence.* Learners choose answers and write them on the lines.

O   When everyone has finished, ask the groups to add two more sentences somewhere to their story and to choose a title for their story. They can write their extra sentences in their notebooks. Walk around and help with ideas and vocabulary if necessary.

O   Ask different groups to read out their titles and completed story.

Suggested story:

Mr and Mrs Chips want to clean their dirty car.

Their children Peter and Daisy are helping them.

Daisy is washing the back of the car.

She has a pet. Its name is Sausage.

It wants to play in the water.

Peter is bringing everyone some pink lemonade to drink.

The car is very clean again now.

The family is going inside now because it's starting to rain.

Oh no! Look at Sausage's dirty feet and look at the car! It's dirty again.

B ▶ What did Alex do on Wednesday, Thursday and Friday?

O   Say: *Alex lives in the house next to the family in the story in A. She was busy on Wednesday, Thursday and Friday last week. Listen and draw the things she saw, did or ate.* Learners listen and draw three pictures in their notebooks. Stop the audio to give them time to draw. Prompt them if necessary to ask: *What did she see? What did she do? What did she eat?*

Suggested answers:

Wednesday: monkeys on a screen

Thursday: two girls fishing by the river

Friday: a plate with fish and potatoes

Audioscript

Man:	Hi Alex!
Girl:	Hello! I had a great day on Wednesday!
Man:	What did you do?
Girl:	My dad took me to the cinema to see a film about monkeys!
Man:	Oh yes. I saw that film yesterday! It was fantastic.
Girl:	My cousin Sally came to see me on Thursday.
Man:	What did you do with her?
Girl:	We went fishing by the river on Thursday.
Man:	Did you catch any fish?
Girl:	Yes. Two.
Girl:	Sally slept at my house that night. The next day, Friday, Mum made us a great lunch.
Man:	What was that?
Girl:	Fish and and chips with tomato sauce!
Man:	Is that your favourite meal?
Girl:	Yes! I love it!

O   Learners write the seven days of the week in their notebooks. They write two things they did on each of those days last week. Ask them questions to help them with this.

Suggested questions:

What did you do on Monday after you got up?

What did you eat and drink for breakfast on Tuesday?

Which two things did you do on Wednesday?

Where did you go last Thursday? Why?

Did you play on a computer on Friday?

Who were you with on Saturday? Did you have fun?

Did you send any texts on Sunday? Who to?

O   In groups of 3–4, learners talk about and compare their days. They decide if their weeks were different or the same. They could also draw a picture of their best day or a poster with words or a word cloud to show the things they did.

C Talk about the questions.

O   Say: *Find the question words in 1–4. How many 'w's are there?* (seven) *How many 'h's?* (seven) *How many 'h's come after a 'w' which is at the beginning of a word?* (six – Which, Why, What, Who, When, Where) *How many 'w's' come after a 'h', at the end of the word?* (one – How)

O   Show learners how your mouth changes position. For 'Wh', you put your lips forward and push the air out. For 'How', your mouth is open for the /ha/ then it pushes forward for the /aʊ/.

O   In pairs, learners practise saying the questions in **C**. Their partner listens and looks at their mouth to check they are pronouncing /w/ and /haʊ/ correctly.

O   Learners answer the questions in groups of four.

D Read the story. Choose a word from the box. Write the correct word next to numbers 1–5.

Reading & Writing Part 3

O   Point to the picture of the nurse. Say: *This is Grace. What's her job?* (She's a nurse.) *Where do nurses work?* (in hospitals)

O   Say: *Read the first two sentences of the story. What kind of hospital does Grace work at?* (a children's hospital)

O   Point to the word 'nurse' on the first line in the story and to the picture and word 'nurse' in the box. Learners read the story, choose other words from the box, and write them next to numbers 1–5.

○ Learners choose the best name for the story. (Grace's day at work!) Ask: *Why is 'The children's school!' not the right name for the story?* (There isn't a children's school in the story.) *Why is 'A new car for the family!' not the best name?* (The car in the story isn't new and the story is not about the car.)

○ Read out these sentences about Grace and her family. Learners correct them.

   1 *Grace had breakfast in the morning last Tuesday because she had to work in the afternoon.* (No! Grace had breakfast in the evening because she had to work at night/that night.)

   2 *Grace had breakfast in the morning.* (Grace had dinner in the morning.)

   3 *After work, Grace read a book and phoned her friend.* (After work, Grace played some music and answered her emails and text messages.)

○ Say: *I'm Grace and you are my children. Here's what I did last Tuesday and Wednesday. Tell me what you did!*

   For example: *I got up in the evening.* (Learners: We got up in the morning.)

   Suggested sentences:

   I had hot chocolate in the evening. (We had fish and chips.)

   I went to the hospital. (We went to bed.)

   I worked all night. (We slept all night.)

   I had dinner in the morning. (We had breakfast)

   Note: You could say or write the key words learners need to help them on the board. (fish and chips, to bed, slept, breakfast)

Let's talk! Ben and Anna's week.

○ Say: *Let's read about Anna and Ben's weeks. Last week, they were on holiday like Alex!*

   Learners work in A and B pairs. Learner A looks at the information about Ben's week on page 113 of their book and Learner B looks at the information about Anna's week on page 114 of their book.

   Say: *Anna and Ben did the same five things last week.*

   Ask: *What did they do?*

   Answers:

They watched TV.	They went shopping.
They listened to the radio.	They read a story.
They played hockey.	

○ Say: *Anna and Ben both did these five things but they did them on different days.* Learner A asks questions to find out when Anna did each of the five things.

   Learner B asks about Ben. For example:

   Learner A: *Did Anna play hockey on Monday morning?*

   Learner B: *No, she didn't.*

   Learner B: *Did Ben watch TV on Monday morning?*

   Learner A: *Yes, he did.*

○ Learner B writes *watched TV* in the box for Monday morning. Learners continue like this in their pairs until they have both written the five activities in the correct boxes.

○ Check answers by asking different learners to say sentences to compare the things Ben and Anna did. For example: *Ben played hockey on Wednesday morning, but Anna played hockey on Monday afternoon.*

○ Ask: *Which morning were Anna and Ben NOT busy?* (Friday) *Which two evenings did they not do anything?* (Monday and Wednesday)

E Find the differences between the pictures.

> **Movers tip**
>
> For Speaking Part 1, practise identifying and describing typical differences that candidates might find in the two pictures. These often relate to colour, number, size, shape, position, activity and weather.

○ Point to the two pictures. Say: *Look at these pictures. They look the same, but some things are different.*

○ Choose a learner to say a sentence about one of the differences in the pictures. (See below for answers.)

○ In pairs, learners say sentences about the other four differences. (They could write them if you prefer.)

   Suggestions:

   1 The nurse is wearing a hat in the first picture, but she **isn't wearing** a hat in the second picture.

   2 The table is round / **square**.

   3 She's eating an apple / some **soup**.

   4 There's a radio / **TV** on top of the cupboard.

   5 There's a picture of a kangaroo / a **panda** on the wall.

F Play the game! Day words.

○ Write on the board: *Saturday*. Learners work in pairs or groups of three. They write down words beginning with each letter of 'Saturday'. The words can be nouns, verbs or adjectives.

○ Give points for every correctly spelt word. Give learners four minutes to do this. Pairs or groups give their list of words to another pair, who checks the words. Teams get an extra point if they have words for all the letters in 'Saturday'.

   Suggested words:

   S – nouns: *sandwich, shoe, shop, shower, snow, seat, shopping* verbs: *sail, shop, shout, show, skate, start, say, see, sing, sit, swim* adjectives: *short, small, slow, sad, safe, sweet*

   A – nouns: *alien, apple, armchair, animal, apartment* verbs: *ask, answer* adjective: *afraid*

   T – nouns: *tomato, tennis, T-shirt, table, trip* verbs: *take, talk, try, throw, travel* adjectives: *tall, thin*

   U – noun: *uncle* verb: *understand* adjective: *ugly*

   R – nouns: *rabbit, radio, rain, rainbow, river, roof* verbs: *run, read, rain* adjectives: *right, round*

   D – nouns: *door, desk, dog, doll, dolphin, duck, DVD* verbs: *drink, draw, do, don't, dry, dress up* adjectives: *different, dirty, difficult*

   A – (see above)

   Y – noun: *yesterday* adjectives: *yellow, young*

○ If you have time, write the word for another day on the board. This time, groups write one word for each letter as quickly as possible The first pair or group to write words for all the letters shouts *Stop!* Everyone stops writing.

   The winners are the group or pair with the most points.

39   We've got lots of things to do

Pronunciation practice strong and weak 'the' (*the morning,*
the afternoon and *the evening*). See 'In, at or every?'

Flyers words: *hard* (adv), *noisy, tidy* (v)

Equipment needed

- Movers Audio 39D.

In the morning

- Ask: *What do you do in the morning before you come to school?* Write learners' suggestions on the board. For example: *clean my teeth, get dressed, have breakfast, have a shower, wash my hair, find my school books, put my things in my school bag.*
- Say: *I do some of those things too.* Mime putting some toothpaste on your toothbrush then cleaning your teeth. Ask: *What am I doing?* (putting toothpaste on your toothbrush, cleaning your teeth)
- Ask learners to listen and mime the actions you say.
  Suggestions: get out of bed, put on your shoes, wash your face, open the door and go downstairs, put on your coat, wave goodbye to your parents.

In, at or every?

- Teach/revise: 'o'clock'. (Learners will not have to use other clock times in this unit. Those are taught at Flyers level.)
- Write on the board: ... *the morning*   ... *the afternoon* ... *the evening*.
- Read out each part of the day using weak pronunciation of 'the' /ðə/before morning and strong pronunciation of *the* /ði:/ before afternoon and evening as these both start with vowels. Check pronunciation of these weak and strong forms of 'the' before 'morning', 'afternoon' and 'evening' throughout the lesson.
- Talk to learners about when these different parts of the day start and end. In Britain, we think morning starts at about six o'clock and ends at twelve o'clock. We think the afternoon ends at about six o'clock and the evening ends at about eleven o'clock.
- Ask: *Do we say **in** or **at** for these parts of the day?* (in) Write 'in' in front of 'the morning', 'the afternoon' and 'the evening' on the board.
- Ask: *What's the word for the part of the day when we are sleeping?* (night)
- Draw a moon on the board and write *night* next to it. Say: *We usually say **at** night.* Write *at night* on the board, too.
- Ask: *What can we see outside at night? Is it noisy or quiet at night?* Write some of the answers on the board.
  Suggestions: We can see the moon and stars outside at night. We can see bats and birds which don't fly in the day. It is quiet at night because most people are sleeping.

- To revise 'every', ask different learners: *Do you dream every night? Do you do your homework every day? Do you wash your bike every weekend?* etc.

A   When do you do these things?

- Say: *We sleep at night but in the day we're .. .?* (awake). *When we're awake, we do lots of different things.*
  Learners look at the pictures. Ask: *Which picture is different?* (the last one) *Why?* (This person isn't awake / is asleep / is sleeping.)
- Point to the first three pictures. Ask: *What are these people doing?* (washing their face, cleaning their bike, doing their homework) Ask: *When are these people doing these things?* (**1** in the morning, **2** in the evening, **3** in the afternoon) Point to the last picture. Ask: *And when is this person sleeping? In the afternoon?* (No, at night.)
  (The times in the pictures will also help learners choose the right answers.) Learners complete the answers on the dotted lines under each picture.
- Teach/revise: on Monday (morning / afternoon / evening) and at the weekend.
  Learners look at the questions 'Do you ...?' 'When do you ...?' Ask a learner: *Do you write text messages?* If the learner answers *Yes, I do,* ask: *When do you write text messages*? *In the afternoon? Every evening? At the weekend?* If the learner answers *No, I don't,* ask another *Do you…?* question or: *Who writes text messages in your family?* Ask another learner: *Do you give food to your pet?* and then continue as before.
- Learners work in A and B pairs. Learner A asks Learner B the three questions in the blue box. Learner B asks Learner A the three questions in the orange box.

B   Choose the correct words and write them on the lines.   Reading & Writing   Part 4

- Learners look at the picture. Ask: *What can you see?* (a man/farmer, a cow, sheep and chickens) *Where do you see these animals?* (on a farm) *Who wants to be a farmer one day? Why?*
- One learner reads out the question in the yellow circle. *Is it easy, difficult, boring or exciting to be a farmer?* Other learners answer with their choice of adjective.
- Learners quickly read the story without adding the missing words. Ask: *Which animals did Farmer Jack go and see first in the morning?* (cows) *How many breakfasts did he have?* (two) *Did he sometimes have to work at night?* (yes) *Do you think he liked being a farmer?* (yes/no)
- Learners look at the text again. Look at the example together. Ask: *Do we say 'He likes telling his grandchildren about when he **is**, **was** or **were** young?'* ('was', because he's not young now and we can't say 'were young' because Jack is only one person!)
- Learners choose the other missing words.

> **Check answers:**
> **1** came   **2** in   **3** there   **4** at   **5** every

- Ask: *What do you think Farmer Jack did on Sunday evenings when he didn't work?* (watch TV, have a long bath, read his favourite story, listen to music, etc.)
- Divide learners into groups of four and give each group a large sheet of paper. Tell them to draw lines on their piece of paper like this. One learner writes *on the farm* in the middle box.

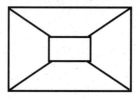

- Say: *You work on a farm!* In their groups, learners talk about the jobs they have to do and then each learner writes two jobs on one side of the paper. If they don't know how to say something, they could draw a quick picture of the job but you might like to teach 'a **barn**' and 'to **water** flowers / plants / vegetables'. When groups have thought of eight different jobs, they call out *We're tired!* When all the groups are 'tired', or have no further ideas, ask groups about the jobs they do.

  Suggestions: wash the truck / the cows, plant / clean / water vegetables, feed / give food/water to chickens / sheep / cows / horses / goats, put the chickens' eggs / fruit / vegetables into boxes, tidy the chickens' house/barn, paint the farmhouse windows, milk the cows, cut the grass, clean floors, put vegetables into the truck, drive to the market, etc.

C Draw lines between the question and the answer.

- Ask: *Did Farmer Jack always work on Sunday evenings?* (no) Write on the board: *always, often, sometimes, never.*

  Revise these words if necessary. Ask: *How often do you do homework?* (every day = always, four days a week = often, two days a week = sometimes, no days = never)

- Learners look at the four pictures, the four questions and the four possible answers. In pairs, they draw lines to a suitable answer for each of the questions.

- Ask four different pairs to come to the front of the class and role play their conversations. Learner A is an interviewer and mimes holding a microphone, Learner B mimes doing each of the four tasks and answers the interviewer's questions.

- Point to the four questions under the pictures and say: *These questions are about more things some children do to help their parents. How can we end each question? You choose!*

  In pairs, learners decide how to end each question.

  Suggestions:

  Do you carry the shopping?   Do you work in the garden?
  Do you tidy your bedroom?   Do you paint the walls?

- Learners choose four of the eight 'Do you … ?' questions in **C** and copy them into their notebooks adding the answer to each one. They could illustrate their four conversations with a drawing.

D Listen and write.   Listening Part 2

> **Movers tip**
> For Listening Part 2, make sure candidates are aware of the types of answers they have to write on the form. These often include numbers and names of people or places that will be spelt for them.

- Learners work on their own, looking at the example and then listening and completing the form for a test practice. Alternatively, you could offer more support and general practice as follows.

- Learners look at the picture of Charlie. Ask: *How old is he? Guess!* Learners answer. Learners then look at the form. Point at questions 1–5. Ask different learners: *How can we ask these questions?* Write appropriate questions on the board.

  Suggestions:

  What's Charlie's family name?

  How old is Charlie?

  Which day does he give lessons?

  When are Charlie's lessons?

  How many children are in the class?

  What does Charlie want to teach?

- Learners choose possible answers and write them in their notebooks.

- Play the whole audio. Learners listen and complete the form.

> **Check answers:**
> **1** 28 **2** Saturday(s) **3** afternoon **4** 12 **5** hockey

- Ask: *Do you have sports lessons? When is the lesson? How many children are in the class? Do you enjoy your sports lessons? Which sports do you do?*

What's your sports teacher's name? What's your sports teacher like? Is it difficult/easy to be a sports teacher?

Audioscript

Listen and look. There is one example.

Girl: Excuse me. I'm doing some homework about being a sports teacher. Can I ask you some questions about your job?

Man: OK …

Girl: First, what's your name?

Man: Charlie Smith.

Girl: Do you spell your family name S-M-I-T-H?

Man: Yes. Well done …

Can you see the answer? Now you listen and write.

One

Girl: Can I ask another question – how old are you?

Man: I'm twenty-eight.

Girl: Pardon? Did you say twenty-eight?

Man: Yes, that's right.

Two

Girl: And when do you give tennis lessons at this sports centre?

Man: I give children tennis lessons here every Saturday.

Girl: Oh!

Man: Saturday is my favourite day of the week!

Girl: It's mine too!

Three

Girl: When is your tennis class? Is it in the morning?

Man: No, I only teach tennis in the afternoon.

Girl: In the afternoon?

Man: Yes.

Four

Girl: And how many children are there in your tennis class?

Man: There are twelve children in my class.

Girl: That's a lot!

Man: I know, but I like having twelve children in my class and everyone enjoys it.

Girl: OK!

Five

Girl: And my last question. Would you like to teach another sport, too?

Man: Yes!

Girl: Football?

Man: Not really but I'd like to teach hockey.

Girl: Hockey! Wow! That's my favourite sport!

Man: Well, it's a great game …

E What about you? Complete the sentences.

- In pairs, learners complete the sentences with ideas of their own. Ask each pair to come and write one of their ideas on the board.

  Suggestions: 1 put my homework in my school bag **2** listen to a story **3** play computer games with my brother **4** go to the cinema

- Ask volunteers to come to the front of the class, read the beginning of one sentence then mime their answer. Others guess what they are doing.

Play the game! The long sentence.

- Ask learners to repeat this sentence: *Every day I get up.*

- Ask one learner to say the sentence again and to add another action to it. For example: *Every day I get up and have breakfast.*

  The next learner repeats this and adds another action. For example: *Every day I get up and have breakfast and get dressed.*

- The game continues. A learner is eliminated if they forget one of the actions or if they repeat an action that another learner has said.

40 People who help us

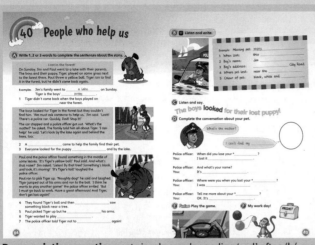

Pronunciation practice past simple regular ending '-ed' after /k/, /p/, and /s/ sounded as /t/. See C.

Flyers words: *missing, police officer, job*

Equipment needed
- Movers Audio 40B.
- Colouring pencils or pens. See D.

A Write 1, 2 or 3 words to complete the sentences about the story.

Reading & Writing Part 5

Movers tip

In Reading and Writing Part 5, the questions always follow the order of the story. But words in the story might be in a different order from the words in the questions. For example: 'On Sunday' might be at the beginning of the sentence in the story but at the end of the question.

- Point to the name of the story and to the first and second pictures. Ask: *Who do you think is lost in this forest?* Learners suggest answers.
- Point to the second picture and say: *This is Jim and this is Paul. Where are they?* (in the countryside / in a forest)
  Ask: *What are they doing?* (shouting) *Why are they shouting?* Learners suggest answers. Say: *Well, let's read the story to see!*
- Read the first sentence of the story and show learners that the first example gives the same information, but in two different ways. ('Jim, Paul and their parents' becomes 'Jim's family.' 'On Sunday' is at the beginning of the sentence in the story but at the end of the example sentence.)
- Read out the second example: *Tiger is the boys' puppy.* Ask learners to find this information in the story. (The boys and their puppy, Tiger …) Say: *So what kind of animal is this story about? A tiger or a puppy?* (a puppy) Teach/revise 'pet'. *So do you think the boys' pet, their puppy, is lost in this forest?* (Yes!)
- Learners read the story and write the missing words in questions 1–7. Tell them to underline the parts of the story where they found their answers.
- Check answers by asking different learners to each read out a completed sentence. They should also say where they found their answers.

Check answers:

1 some/the grass **2** police officer **3** behind the/some trees
4 Jim **5** jumped out of **6** another game **7** get lost

B ▶ Listen and write.

Listening Part 2

- Teach/revise Flyers words 'police officer' (seen in **A**) and 'job'. Ask: *What do police officers do?* (drive cars, find people/things, help people) *What colour clothes do police officers in our country wear?* (accept correct answers) *What's my job?* (You're a teacher!)
- Point to the picture and ask: *What's this man's job?* (He's a police officer.)
- Say: *In the story about Tiger, who came and helped the family?* (a police officer) Point to the police officer's note book. Say: *This is the police officer's notebook. He wants to ask Jim some questions. Listen to Jim and the police officer and write Jim's answers.*
  Play the audio. Learners listen to the example then complete the answers. Let them listen twice.

Check answers:
1 afternoon **2** Wild **3** 87 **4** lake **5** brown

Audioscript

Listen and look. There is one example.

Police officer:	Hello. I'm a police officer and my name's Ben. What's the matter?
Jim:	We can't find our puppy.
Police officer:	Your puppy? Oh dear! Well, I can help you.
Jim:	Thanks, Ben.

Can you see the answer? Now you listen and write.

One

Police officer:	When did you lose your puppy?
Jim:	We lost him this afternoon.
Police officer:	You lost him this afternoon?
Jim:	Yes, and his name is Tiger.
Police officer:	Tiger. OK!

Two

Police officer:	And what's your name?
Jim:	I'm Jim Wild.
Police officer:	Jim Wild? Do you spell that W-I-L-D?
Jim:	Yes, that's right.

Three

Police officer:	Where do you live, Jim?
Jim:	My address is 87 City Road.
Police officer:	Did you say number 85?
Jim:	No, I said number 87.
Police officer:	OK. Sorry.

Four

Police officer:	Where were you when you lost Tiger?
Jim:	We were by the lake.
Police officer:	Was your puppy in the water?
Jim:	No.

Five

Police officer:	And what colour is Tiger?
Jim:	He's brown, black and white.
Police officer:	Pardon?
Jim:	Tiger's body is brown and black but his feet are white.
Police officer:	OK. Thank you. Now let's go and try to find him!

C Listen and say.

o Say: *Find the word 'looked' in the lost puppy story.* Learners circle 'looked' in line 1 of paragraph 2. Ask: *Did the boys look for a lost kitten?* (no) *What did they look for?* (their puppy/Tiger)

o Write on the board: *The boys looked for their lost puppy.* Point to the '-ed' ending on 'looked' and ask: *How do we say this? Listen carefully because these two letters sound like one different letter.* Repeat the sentence making sure you pronounce '-ed' as /t/. Learners practise the pronunciation. You could forward chain this sentence chorally:
The boys looked > The boys looked for > The boys looked for their lost puppy!

o Write on the board:
Lily looked when Jim jumped and Daisy danced on her desk! Circle the three '-ed' endings. Ask three different learners to come to the board, rub the three '-ed' endings out and write big red 't' letters instead. Make sure learners understand that the words we read and write must end in '-ed' but when we hear or say them, they end in a /t/ sound. The class chants the sentence.

o Write on the board:
............*cooked when* ....*hopped and* ....*skipped and* ....*bounced on his* ....
In pairs, learners choose how to complete the sentence.
Suggestion:
Kim cooked when Hugo hopped and Sam skipped and Ben bounced on his bed.
Different pairs say their sentence. Check the pronunciation of all the /t/ endings!

D Complete the conversation about your pet.

o Check that learners have their colouring pencils or pens.
Point to the police officer's face and say: *Now you are talking to a police officer because **your** pet is lost. The police officer is asking you lots of questions.* Point to the police officer and ask: *What's the police officer's first question?* (What's the matter?)

o Point to the empty circle and speech bubble. Say: *This is you! Draw your face now.* Learners draw their own face.

o In pairs, learners choose a pet animal (real or imaginary). Then, on their own, they write the animal (cat, dog, horse, goat, etc) in their own speech bubble and next to all the stars* in the conversation.

o Learners then choose and write their own answers to the police officer's questions. Encourage learners to help each other in pairs if necessary.

o Pairs then role play their conversations, taking turns to be a police officer or themselves. Choose one or two pairs to role play their conversations to the rest of the class.

E Play the game.

o Teach/revise: 'o'clock'. Learners will only have to use 'o'clock' in this task. They won't have to use other time expressions.
Learners look at the picture on page 115 at the back of their books.
Say: *You can only see these two drivers' hands.* Point to the first picture. Ask: *Is this driver a man or a woman?* (a man) *What's his name? You choose!* Write the chosen name on the board (for example: *Jim*).

o Point to the second picture and ask: *Is this driver a man, too?* (no, a woman) *What's her name? You choose!* Write the chosen name on the board (for example: *Anna*).

o Divide learners into groups A and B. Groups then work in pairs. Group A pairs should complete all 14 sentences to talk about the woman's day and Group B pairs, all 14 sentences about the man's day. Walk round and help if necessary.

o A and B group pairs now take turns to give information about each driver's work day. If answers aren't different, learners in group B should quickly change their answers!
Learner from group A: *Anna lives in Green Street.*
Learner from group B: *Jim lives in a house.*
Learner from group A: *Anna gets up at six o'clock.*
Learner from group B: *Jim gets up at seven o'clock.*
Change the A and B order half way through, for example:
Learner from group B: *Jim has a burger for lunch.*
Learner from group A: *Anna has pasta for lunch.*
Note: You may prefer to ask learners to write words to complete these sentences about a driver (real or imagined) for homework.

F My work day!

o Learners ask a family member or friend about their job.
Note: Learners may find it more fun to write about an imagined person's job.

o Using the following questions, learners complete an interview text.
Good morning! Can I ask you about your job?
Do you work inside or outside?
Is your job exciting or boring?
Do you have to work on a computer?
Why do you like your job?

o Learners draw or find a picture of a person doing this job to illustrate their interview script.

o Learners choose a partner to play the role of the adult and then, using their script, they role play the interview in class.

o Learners add their interview script and illustrations to their project file. Alternatively, display learners' interview scripts and illustrations on a classroom wall if possible.

41 I had a great birthday

A Complete sentences about the picture.

> **Movers tip**
>
> In Reading and Writing Part 6, learners can write sentences about the people in the picture (what they are wearing and doing, where they are, etc) and about any other different things they can see. Encourage learners to use their imaginations to add more details. See example sentences below.

○ Draw a big circle on the board. At the top of the circle, write *birthdays*. Ask different learners to say and write words in the circle connected to birthdays.

Suggestions: party, friends play, games, dance, sing, listen to music, invite, presents, cake, enjoy

○ Point to the picture. Ask: *Where are these people?* (at a birthday party) *How many people can you see?* (eight)

○ Read out the first sentence: *Two people have got numbers on their clothes.* Ask: *Is this sentence correct about the picture?* (yes)

○ Say: *Look at the picture and read sentences 2 – 6. Write 1–5 words on each line to complete the sentences.*

> **Check answers:**
>
> (Suggestions) **2** any shoes   **3** filming the birthday party
> **4** some balloons   **5** playing guitars   **6** sandwiches and glasses

○ Say: *Let's write more sentences about this picture! Look at sentence 1. This sentence is about what two people are wearing. Now you write a sentence about two different people in this picture. You can write about their clothes, their hair or what they are doing!* Learners work in pairs. Give them a minute to write a sentence then ask different pairs to read out their sentence.

Suggestions

Two people are playing guitars / wearing pink dresses / have got very long blond hair.

○ Read out sentence 2: *The young girl who is dancing isn't wearing any shoes.* Ask: *Why isn't this girl wearing any shoes?* (because she doesn't like wearing shoes / they hurt her feet, etc) Write one of your learners' suggestions on the board: *The young girl who is dancing isn't wearing any shoes because they hurt her feet.*

Write on the board: *The person who's got a beard …* Ask: *Who can tell me more about this person? What's this person doing? What's this person holding? Why are they doing that?*

Point to the first half of the sentence on the board again and say: *Make a longer sentence, please!* Learners work in pairs. They copy the words from the board and finish the sentence with their own choice of words.

Suggestion

The person who's got a beard is holding a camera because he's making a video / videoing/filming the party.

Optional extension:

Learners could make another sentence about the woman with the cake.

Suggestion

The woman who is coming into the room / wearing a pink dress is carrying a cake because it's her daughter's birthday.

Write names and draw lines.

○ Point to the name 'Lucy' next to the picture and also the line which goes from this name to the girl in the picture who is singing.
Say: *This is Lucy. We can see her birthday party in the picture.*

○ Point to the four dotted lines below 'Lucy'. In pairs, each learner chooses four people in the picture and thinks of names for them. They write each name on a different line on the left and draw a line in pencil from the name to the person in the picture.

○ Draw four lines on the board. Ask one learner: *What are your four names? Can you spell them for me?* Write a name on each line on the board.

○ In pairs, learners ask each other to say and spell their four names. Learner A asks Learner B to say and spell the four names that they chose. Learner A then writes these names on the four lines to the right of the picture. Learner B then asks Learner A to say and spell their four names and then writes these on the lines to the right of their picture.

○ Ask the same learner who told you the four names you wrote on the board: *Who's (one of the names they chose, for example: Paul)?* The learner describes Paul to you. They shouldn't point to the boy. They should describe him or talk about what he's doing / holding / where he is. For example: *Paul has got curly black hair. Paul is the boy who's playing the guitar. Paul is in the band.*

○ In pairs, learners take it in turns to ask about the names and describe the people they drew lines to. The listening learner draws a line between the four names on the right and four people in the picture. When they have both done this, they check that they have drawn lines between the same names and people in the picture.

B Read and choose the best answer.

○ Point to the girl in the picture in **B**. Ask: *Who's this?* (Lucy, the girl who is singing in the picture in **A**.)
Remind learners that it is Lucy's birthday party we can see in the picture in **A**.
Say: *Lucy is talking to her friend Alex.*
Tell learners to read out what Alex says in 1 and 2.
Ask: *Was Alex at the birthday party?* (no)

○ Ask a learner to read what Alex says in 1.
Read Lucy's answer: (C) Thanks!
Ask: *Why does Lucy say 'thanks?'* (Because Alex says 'Happy birthday!')
Learners think of things that Alex could say/ask for the wrong answers *Don't worry!* and *Me too!* to be right.
Suggestions: *I didn't bring you a present! I love parties!*

○ Learners read the rest of the conversation and choose the best answers for 2–5.

> **Check answers:**
>
> **2** A   **3** C   **4** A   **5** B

C Read the story. Choose a word from the box. Write the correct word next to numbers 1–5.

> **Movers tip**
>
> In Reading and Writing Part 3, each word and its picture can only be used once. Remind candidates to cross out answers as they use them. You could suggest they choose the missing words they find easier first, then read the text again to choose the missing words that they find more difficult. Remind candidates that three of the options in the box should not be used.

○ Learners work on their own for a test practice. Check that they understand the instructions. They read the story, look at the example and then find and write the missing words. If you would like to give learners more support, begin by writing these questions on the board:

Who is the story about?

Where did they go?

Why did they go there?

○ Learners look at the text. Read the text aloud as far as *different animals.*

○ Check the answers to the questions on the board. Ask: *Who is the story about?* (Jack and his sister and parents)

Where did they go? (to Forest Farm)

Why did they go there? (It was Jack's birthday.)

○ Learners look at the example in the story: *It was my **birthday** last weekend.* Ask: *Where can you see the word 'birthday'?* (under the picture of the birthday cake)

○ Learners read the story and write the missing words on the lines.

> **Check answers:**
>
> **1** zoo **2** sheep **3** bought **4** close **5** surprised
>
> (*windy, lunch* and *hid* were not used)

○ Say: *Now look at the three names for the story. Which is the best?* Learners talk together in pairs and choose a name for the story. Ask: *Is the story about one of Dad's pets?* (no) *Does Jack's mother make a cake in the story?* (no) *Did Jack have a great day at the farm?* (yes) Say: *Yes, that's the correct answer! Tick that box!*

Let's talk about you and your birthdays.

○ Ask the following questions round the class. Write each one on the board after it has been answered. Learners copy the questions into their notebooks.

1 How old are you? Do you like birthdays?

2 What presents did you get for your last birthday?

3 What food is good to eat at parties?

4 Who do you invite to your parties?

○ Learners interview another person in the class about their birthday and write their answers (1–4 words for each question) in their notebooks.

D Find the presents and draw lines.

○ In pairs, learners read the definitions and find the answers in the word wheel. They can circle each answer and draw a line to its definition.

> **Check answers:**
>
> **1** scarf **2** towel **3** sausages **4** bike **5** chocolate

○ Ask: *Which three letters don't make answers?* (a b t) *What word can these letters make?* (bat). *Is this the thing you hold in your hand and hit balls with or the animal that only flies at night?* (learners decide, but 'bat' is the missing present!) Ask: *Which is a more exciting present? A bat?* (mime hitting a ball) *Or a bat?* (mime flapping your wings) *Show me!* Learners mime hitting a ball or flapping their wings. *Which is a better present to take with you to the sports centre? Show me!* Learners mime hitting a ball!

○ Divide learners into groups of 3–4. Give each group a sheet of paper. Say: *Write the six presents – a scarf, a towel, sausages, a bike, some chocolate and a bat – on your piece of paper.* One learner in each group writes the six presents. Say: *Now listen and write.* (Pause between words.)

Write *a grandma, a best friend, a pet dog, a sister, a father, a new baby.*

○ Write on the board: .... *is/are for* ....

Ask: *Which present is best for which person or animal?* Each group talks and matches presents saying, for example: *The towel is for the baby! The sausages are for the dog!* Groups then take turns to tell the other groups. Did everyone match the presents in the same way?

E Play the game! Birthday presents.

○ In pairs or small groups of 3–4, learners write a list of presents they would like for their next birthday. They should write as many presents as possible in 2–3 minutes.

○ Learners pass their list on to another pair/group.

○ Tell learners that you have a shop and you like giving people presents. Anyone whose list includes something you are giving away can have that present. Say: *Today, we have lots of things to give you. First, some kites. Would you like a kite?*

○ Any pair/group which has written 'kite' can put a tick next to that word and win a point.

○ Continue until you have given away all the presents. The winning team is the one with the most points/presents.

Suggestions for presents:

doll	guitar	app	board game
robot	plant	phone	hat
toy car	model boat	comic book	poster
laptop	teddy bear	roller skates	skateboard
balloons	camera	DVD	flowers
sweets	shorts	pen	watch
cinema ticket	flowers	tennis racket	ball
jeans	painting	puppy	e-book

F 🧰 **Plan your party!**

○ Learners work in groups of 3–4. Say: *You want to have an exciting birthday party. Think about your party.*

Where is your party? What games can you play? Can you have music there? What food can you have?

○ Each group makes a poster about their party. Groups draw pictures on their poster or find pictures in magazines to cut out and glue on the poster. They add the information about their party.

○ Display the posters on the classroom walls. Learners walk round and decide which party they would like to go to.

Note: If learners have each made a party poster, they could add it to their project file at the end of this activity.

42 An exciting week for Alex

Equipment needed

- ○ Movers audio 42B and 42D.
- ○ (Optional) A photocopy of the objects on page 127, cut up. See E.

○ Say: *I like cleaning things!* Write *cleaning things* on the board. Ask six different learners: *What things do you like doing?* Learners suggest different activities. Write their chosen activities under yours. For example:

cleaning things

sleeping

eating chips

playing computer games

watching TV

listening to music

going for a walk

○ Point to 'cleaning things' and say: *I think cleaning things is great. Cleaning things is better than playing computer games! Do you think cleaning things is better than playing computer games?* (no!)

○ Point to the seven activities and ask: *Which do you think are good things to do? Which are bad things to do?* Learners suggest answers.

○ Teach/revise: 'better' and 'best', 'worse' and 'worst'.

Write on the board ....*is better than*............

............*is the best.*

............*is worse than*............

............*is the worst.*

○ In pairs or small groups, learners talk about which activities are good, bad, better or worse than others and which are the best or the worst. They then use the structures on the board to write four sentences. For example: *Sleeping is better than watching TV. Eating chips is the best. Going for a walk is worse than listening to music. Cleaning things is the worst.*

Ask groups to read out their sentences.

Ⓐ Which was Alex's best school day?

○ Point to Alex. Say: *This is Alex. She's talking about her school week.* In pairs, learners read Alex's speech bubbles and, as quickly as possible, find the answer to 'Which was Alex's best school day last week?' Pairs work quickly and quietly to solve the puzzle and put up their hands when they have the answer (Wednesday).

○ Write on the board:

My best day last week was............because..............

My worst day last week was............because..............

Learners complete the sentences with their own ideas for their weeks. They write a day and then a reason. Walk around, help with ideas and check their answers.

○ 'Wednesday' is often spelt and pronounced incorrectly by learners in this age group. Ask learners to call out the spelling of 'Wednesday' and write it on the board. You might like to draw a pencil next to the word to show this is how we write the word. Practise the pronunciation of Wednesday chorally. Say:

Wednesday is an exciting day!

On Wednesday we play and play.

So tell me what's your favourite day?

Is it Wednesday? Say Wednesday!

○ In a tired voice, say: *It's Wednesday today!* Ask: *Am I happy, sad or tired?* (tired)

Write on the board: *happy, tired, sad, angry, busy, afraid, surprised.* In groups of 3–4, each learner secretly chooses one of the adjectives and says *It's Wednesday today!* in that way. Others in the group guess how the learner is feeling. For example: *You're afraid!*

Ⓑ ▶ Listen to Alex telling her grandfather about her week. Where did Alex go with each of these people? Listen and write a letter in each box.

Listening Part 3

○ Ask 3–4 different learners: *What do you do at weekends? Do you sometimes go into the town/city? What do you like doing there? Which places do you like to go to in the town/city?*

Write learners' favourite things to do and places to visit on the board.

○ Say: *Look at the pictures in B. Which places can you see?* (a river, a concert, a circus, a city, a cinema, a shopping centre, a funfair, a (swimming) pool)

○ Say: *Alex likes going to different places, too.* Point to the first sentence in B and ask: *Who's Alex talking to?* (her grandfather) *What's she talking about?* (her week)

Play the audio. Learners listen to the example and then write letters in the boxes below the pictures of the people. Play the audio twice.

○ Check answers by asking learners where Alex went with these people. For example,

Where did Alex go with her aunt? (She went shopping / to a shopping centre / to the shops.)

Where did Alex go with her mum? (She went to a concert / see her favourite band.)

Audioscript

Listen and look. There is one example.

Alex is telling her grandpa about her exciting week. Where did Alex go with each of these people?

Man:	Hi Alex! Did you have a good school holiday?
Girl:	Yes, Grandpa! I was so busy! I went to lots of different places. On Monday, I went to the shops with my aunt.
Man:	Did you buy anything?
Girl:	A new video game and some roller skates!

Can you see the letter F? Now you listen and write a letter in each box.

Man:	What did you do on Wednesday?
Girl:	Erm… Let me think. Uncle Jack and I caught a bus. It had no roof!
Man:	Wow!
Girl:	We could see all the city buildings. We sat in the front seat.
Girl:	And Friday was good.
Man:	What did you do that day, then?
Girl:	Mum got us tickets to go and see my favourite band.

Man:	Brilliant! Was that in the afternoon?
Girl:	No, the evening. It's more exciting then.
Man:	And where did you go on Tuesday?
Girl:	Dad took me swimming. I enjoyed that a lot.
Man:	Did you go to the circus too? I love watching the clowns.
Girl:	Me too! But no, we didn't go to see that.
Man:	Well, what about Saturday? Where did you go that day?
Girl:	To the funfair with some of my classmates! I went on lots of rides. It was great.
Man:	Weren't some of the rides scary?
Girl:	Grandpa!!?? No! I'm very brave!
Girl:	And on Thursday one of my cousins invited me to the cinema.
Man	What was the film about?
Girl:	A boy and a boat. He went to an island in it.
Man	How big was the boat? Was it huge?
Girl:	No, it was a little one, Grandpa.

C 🧳 **A day in the city.**

o   In small groups, learners collect ideas for things they would like to do on an imagined city trip, for example: go for a ride on a river boat, go to the circus, have a picnic in the park, walk round the city centre, take photos of animals at the zoo. They each draw a picture of part of the day, then write a collective diary entry and glue their pictures around it to make a collage. Display these on the classroom wall if possible.

D ▶ **Charlie's going to the zoo. Listen and draw circles around his correct answers.**

o   Learners look at the picture. Ask: *Who are these people?* (a boy and a man / a father and his son)

o   Point to the conversation and ask: *What's the boy's name?* (Charlie) *What are Charlie and his dad talking about?* (Charlie's lunch/food)

o   In pairs, learners read the conversation and circle Charlie's correct answer.

o   Play the audio. Learners listen and check their answers.

> **Check answers:**
> Yes, please, Dad!   Cool!   Good idea!   All right!   No, thanks!
> Yes. Don't worry!

o   Ask one pair to role play the conversation.

o   Working in pairs or small groups, learners write a different version of the conversation in their notebooks. They copy Dad's first question and all Charlie's correct answers but change Dad's other lines. Encourage learners to be creative when they choose new lines for Dad to say/ask. For example:
Well, here are some cheese and mango sandwiches.
How about taking some lemonade, too?
What about some of Grandpa's chocolate?
Would you like to buy a lion at the zoo?
And have you got your phone and map?

Audioscript

Man:	Charlie, it's your school trip to the zoo today! Would you like to take something to eat?
Boy:	Yes, please, Dad.
Man:	Well, here's a milkshake and some chicken and salad sandwiches.
Boy:	Cool!
Man:	How about taking some orange juice, too?
Boy:	Good idea!
Man:	What about some of Grandma's coffee cake? It's really nice.
Boy:	All right!
Man:	And would you like to buy an ice cream at the zoo?
Boy:	No, thanks!
Man:	And have you got your ticket, Charlie?
Boy:	Yes. Don't worry!

E **Find the differences between the pictures.**

o   Say: *Look at these pictures. They look the same, but some things are different.* (Point to picture 1.) *In this picture, the man is sitting down, but here* (point to picture 2) *he's standing. What other different things can you see?*

o   In pairs, learners find the differences and express them in sentences. Check answers by asking different pairs to say one of their differences.
Suggestions: In this picture:
the clown's nose is red, but here it's **blue**.
a puppy is singing but here a **parrot** is singing.
a man is with the boy but here a **woman** is with the boy.
the hat is on the ground but here it's **on the man's head**.
the man with the guitar has got a beard but here he **hasn't got** a beard.
you can see the sun but here there is a **cloud**.
the boy's sweater is green but here it's **yellow**.
the clown's scarf is short but here it's **long**.
the clown has got three balls but here he's got **two** balls.

o   Ask different learners questions about the people and things that are in the picture.
Do you think the people know the man's song?
Do you like the clown's scarf?
Can you throw three balls like this clown? Is it difficult?
Do you like clowns? Do you laugh at them?
Do you know any English songs? Can you sing one?

F **Play the game! Say thanks.**

o   Write the following expressions on the board:
Brilliant! Cool! Hooray! Fine! Good! Yes, please. Thank you. OK. All right. No, thanks. Oh dear. Oh no! Don't worry.
Explain that you are going to offer learners different things and they have to answer, using these expressions. Use the pictures that you have photocopied from page 127. Alternatively you could use pictures from magazines.

o   Choose a learner and show them the picture of the motorbike. Say: *(Julia), here's a motorbike for you.* (Julia): *Great!*

o   Julia then turns to another learner and offers them the motorbike.
(Julia): *Pablo, here's a motorbike for you.*
(Pablo): *Thanks!*
Repeat this a few times then change the offer/request.
Suggestions:
Would you like a new computer?
I bought this camera for you.
Do you want me to buy you a new toothbrush?
Let's buy that app on the internet.
You must do your homework now.
Can you help me wash the bathroom floor?
Shall I buy you a ticket for the film?
Would you like some chips?
Do you want me to show you that new music website now?
How about buying that model truck?
I need to water the plants. Can you do that for me?
We need to fix the basketball net.
It's not raining now! We can go outside and skateboard!

43 My holidays

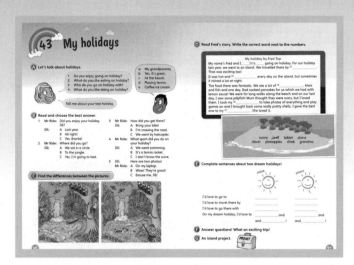

A Let's talk about holidays.

○ Say: *Let's read and talk about holidays.*

○ Read out question 1: *Do you enjoy going on holiday?* Ask: *Who's asking this question, the girl or the boy?* (the girl) *What's the boy's right answer? Is it 'Coffee ice cream'?* (no) *Is it 'Yes, it's great!'?* (yes) Learners draw a line between 1 and b. Ask two learners to ask and answer the question in open class.

○ Make sure learners see that one of the answers is wrong for all the questions. Learners draw lines between questions 2–4 and their matching answers. Check answers by reading out the questions in turn. Different learners answer them.

> **Check answers:**
> 2 e   3 a   4 d

○ Point to the options in the boy's speech bubble and ask: *Which was the wrong answer?* (At the beach.) In pairs, learners think of another question for this answer. Ask 3–4 pairs to ask their question and give the answer.
Suggestions:
Where are you now?
Where do you go swimming?
Where's your holiday home/boat?

○ Say: *Tell me about your last holiday.* Ask different learners for one short sentence each. For example: *It was funny/terrible! / It was sunny/cloudy. / I went swimming.* Write around ten of their suggestions on the board.

○ Learners choose three short sentences that relate to their own holiday and write them in their notebooks.

○ If learners know these countries, ask: *Would you like to go to America? To Australia? Why? / Why not?*

B Read and choose the best answer.

> **Movers tip**
> In Reading and Writing Part 2, the first person in each conversation question/answer turn isn't always the same. Point out that sometimes names are reversed. You could role play the conversation to make this clear. When they finish choosing their answers, candidates should always quietly read the conversation again to check it makes sense.

○ Learners look at the first sentence:
Say: *Mr Ride is Jill's teacher. He's asking Jill about her holiday.*

○ Ask: *How many questions does Mr Ride ask Jill?* (five) Ask learners about his questions. If learners think the answer is *yes*, they sit down. If they think the answer is *no*, they stand up.
Does Mr Ride ask about the weather? (no, stand up)
Does Mr Ride ask about the place? (yes, sit down)
Does Mr Ride ask about the food? (no, stand up)
Does Mr Ride ask about sport? (yes, sit down)

○ Make sure learners see why A and B are not correct answers for 1.
Say: ***Last year.*** is wrong because that answers a 'When..?' question. Ask: *What's a good 'When …?' question for this answer?*
Suggestions:
When did you go to the mountains?
When did you take these photos of the jungle?
Say: *'All right' is wrong because that can answer a 'How about …?' or 'Let's …' suggestion. It means 'OK!'* Ask: *What's a good 'How about …?' question or 'Let's …' sentence for this answer?*
Suggestions:
How about going to New York?
Let's swim in the lake!

○ Learners look at questions 2–5. Tell them to cross out <u>one</u> wrong answer to each question. Ask the class to vote for one option to cross out in each case.

○ In pairs, learners choose the correct answer from the remaining two options. Again, have a class vote and end with the class voting for one correct answer for each question.

> **Check answers:**
> 2 B   3 C   4 A   5 B

C Find the differences between the pictures.

Speaking Part 1

○ Learners look at Jill's two holiday photos. Ask: *Where did Jill go on holiday?* (to the jungle) *Can you see Jill? What's she doing in the second picture?* (swimming) *Which animals did she see in the jungle?* (a monkey, a snake, bats, parrots)

○ Say: *Can you see a boy in these pictures too?* (yes) *He's Jill's brother.* Ask the class to choose a name for Jill's brother and write it on the board.

○ Say: *These pictures look the same, but some things are different.* Hold up your book and point to the boat in the first picture. Say: *In this picture the boat is brown, but here* (point to the second picture) *it's yellow.*

○ Tell learners you are going to say that again and this time you want them all to say 'yellow' together. Repeat the prompt. Learners all say: *But here it's yellow!*

○ Ask: *What other differences can you see?* Point to the first picture and say: *Jill's brother is climbing the tree, but here he's …* (fishing)

○ Point to the first picture each time you prompt the following differences:
There are four parrots, but here there are … (**three** parrots)
The monkey is holding a flower, but here the monkey is holding a … (**banana**)
The snake has a short body, but here it has a … (**long** body)
Jill is taking a photo, but here she's … (**swimming**)
There is one bat, but here there are … (**two** bats)
Note: In the Movers Speaking Test, the examiner will say something about the first picture each time, but will only use prompts to help learners talk about differences if they need more support. After talking about the example difference, learners will only need to talk about four more differences.

D Read Fred's story. Write the correct word next to the numbers.

o Learners look at the first line of the story. Ask: *Who wrote this story?* (Fred Top) *What's the story about?* (Fred's holiday)

o Read out the first sentence. Point to the word 'love' in the example sentence and where it is crossed out in the island picture.

o Learners read the story. In pairs, they complete the text with words they can see in the island picture. Say: *Be careful! Two of these words are wrong answers!*

> **Check answers:**
> **1** plane **2** sunny **3** pineapples **4** tablet **5** grandma

o Ask: *Would you like to go on holiday to an island? What can you do on an island holiday?*

Write on the board: *on the island in or on the sea*

Say: *Think of five fun things you can do on an island and five fun things you can do in or on the sea.*

Learners work in pairs and write suggestions in their notebooks. Walk around and help with vocabulary if necessary. You might like to teach/revise: camping, sandcastles, surfboard, waves, windsurfing, water skiing, underwater.

o Ask pairs for their suggestions and write them on the board under the appropriate heading. Alternatively pairs come to the board and write suggestions on the board themselves.

Suggestions:

on the island – run on the sand, play games on the beach, climb coconut trees / rocks, look for animals, take photos, swim in a waterfall, go for walks in the jungle, draw pictures / write messages on the sand, find different fruit to eat, sleep in the sun, pick flowers, go fishing, have a picnic, look for shells on the sand, look at rock pools, camp, make sandcastles, read a book, listen to music.

in or on the sea – go for a swim, play ball games in the sea, catch fish, go sailing, go on a boat trip, play on surfboards, go water skiing, go windsurfing, swim underwater to look for shells/fish, jump up and down in the waves.

o Ask the class to vote for their three favourite on the island activities and their three favourite in/on the sea activities.

o Divide learners into two teams and tell the class to stand up. Say you are going to ask questions about the story. The learner who puts up their hand first and then correctly answers the question can sit down again. Accept one-word answers.

o Ask some or all of the following questions:

Did a boy or a girl write this story?	(a boy)
Where did he go?	(to an island)
How did he go there?	(by plane)
Was the weather good?	(yes)
Did it rain in the day?	(no)
What fruit did Fred eat?	(kiwis / (and) pineapples)
What did his father cook?	(pancakes)
What did Fred do in the morning?	(swam / went swimming)
What did Fred take with him on holiday?	(a tablet)
What did Fred bring home?	(shells)
Did he give one shell to his grandfather?	(no)

E Complete sentences about two dream holidays!

o Say: *Fred had a great holiday! I'd love to go to Australia! I'd love to travel there by balloon! I'd love to go there with (the name of a famous person). When I'm there, I'd love to go swimming and sailing. For me, that's a dream holiday! Now you choose dream holidays.*

Learners work in pairs. Both learners read the sentence starters and write their own sentence completions in the 'mine' column. Then they look at their partner's answers and copy them in the 'yours' column.

o Say to 2–3 pairs: *Tell me about your dream holiday.* Learners read out their 'own' answers. Say: *And tell me about your partner's dream holiday.* Learners read out the 'yours' answers changing 'I'd love to ...' to 'He'd love to ...' or 'She'd love to ...'

Ask the class: *Whose dream holiday is the most exciting?*

F Answer questions! What an exciting trip!

o Make sure learners understand the difference between a 'trip' and a 'holiday'. A trip is usually a journey to a place you want to visit but you might come home again on the same day.

o Learners work in small groups of 4–5. They think of an exciting trip (real or imagined) and write answers to the questions on page 113 at the back of their books. Make sure everyone understands the questions before they start their group work. Encourage learners to be creative with their answers. Learners then draw a picture in the box to illustrate their holiday answers.

G An island project

o Learners use the internet to find out about an island which they would like to visit.

They print out (or cut out from magazines) images of their island, for example: pictures of the shore, the island landscape, the people and animals that live there, the food that grows there, etc.

o Learners could draw a map of the island and show or write where it is. They could find out about the weather there and draw charts.

They could find out about what kind of jobs the people do there. (fishing, working in hotels, growing bananas, making sugar, etc.)

o When they have collected all their information, learners make a poster or a booklet about their island. Display these on the classroom walls if possible. Learners could later add their island information to their project file.

44 Along the beach

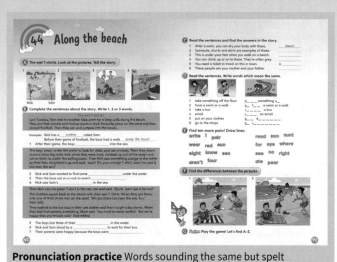

Pronunciation practice Words sounding the same but spelt differently. See E.

Ⓐ Look at the pictures. Tell the story. Speaking Part 2

○ **Note:** In the Movers Speaking Test, learners only need to say two or three sentences about each picture in order to tell the story. In this activity, learners are more supported, but if you want to give your class a more authentic test practice, make sure they answer your questions about the pictures in complete sentences.

○ Say: *Look at these pictures. They show a story. It's called 'The wet T-shirts'. Look at the first picture. Sam and his brother Nick are at the beach. Their clothes are on the sand by the sea. Sam and Nick are playing football. Now you tell the story.*

○ Different learners suggest sentences to tell the story. Ask learners questions to help them if they find this difficult.
Picture 2: *What are the boys doing now?* (swimming under the water) *What are they looking for?* (shells)
Picture 3: *What are Sam and Nick doing now?* (sitting on some rocks) *What's Nick taking from the water?* (an orange T-shirt)
Picture 4: *What are Sam and Nick doing now?* (standing next to a bus stop / waiting for a bus) *Where are they going? Guess!* (home) *Are their T-shirts wet?* (yes)

Ⓑ Complete the sentences about the story. Write 1, 2 or 3 words.

> **Movers tip**
> In Reading and Writing Part 5, the sentences that candidates have to complete always appear in the same order as in the story, but some key words in the sentence completions may be different from the key words in the story. For example: *the water / the sea, brothers / boys* and *tried to find / looked for.*

○ Say: *This is Sam and Nick's story.* Learners read the first sentence.
Ask: *When did the boys go to the beach?* (last Tuesday)

○ Learners read the first part of the story. They should not read the questions.

○ Write the first example sentence on the board:
Nick has a <u>brother</u> called Sam.
Ask: *How do we know that Sam is the name of Nick's brother? Find the information in the story and draw a line under your answer.*
Write the sentence on the board: *Sam and his <u>brother, Nick</u>.*
Write the second example sentence on the board:
Before their game of football, the boys had a walk <u>along the beach</u>.
Ask: *Can you find this information in the text? Draw a line under the words!*

Write the important parts of the sentences on the board:
Sam and his brother Nick went for a long walk along the beach. They … then played football.

○ Learners read the rest of the story and complete sentences 1–7.

> **Check answers:**
> **1** ran and jumped   **2** shells / sea animals   **3** the (sailing) boats
> **4** (orange) T-shirt   **5** shoes   **6** bus stop   **7** (both) safe

Ⓒ Read the sentences and find the answers in the story.

○ Read out sentence 1: *After a swim, you can dry your body with these.*
Ask: *What can people dry their hands or face or bodies with?* (towels) *Where is this word in the story?* Learners find the word 'towels' on line 2.
Read out sentence 2: *Swimsuits, shorts and skirts are examples of these.* Say: *Listen! When you hear me read the answer for this sentence, say 'Stop!'*
Read out the first two sentences of the story in **B**. Learners say *Stop!* when they hear you say 'clothes'.
Last Tuesday, Sam and his brother Nick went for a long walk along the beach. They put their towels and clothes [down …]
They write the word *clothes* on the dotted line after sentence 2.

○ Make sure that learners understand that all the answers are in the story and that the words they need are in the order they read them in the story. In pairs, learners read sentences 3–6, find the words in the story and write them on the lines.

○ Ask different learners to take turns to read out one sentence of the story. Other learners listen and mime what is happening.

> **Check answers:**
> **3** sand   **4** rocks   **5** bus   **6** parents

Let's talk about you and the beach.

○ Ask different learners these questions about the sea and the beach.
Do you live near a beach?
Are you good at swimming?
When do you/people go to the beach?
What things do you/people like doing on the beach?
What's better: swimming in the sea or in a swimming pool? Why?
Do you like jumping in the waves? Or are you afraid of them?
What's your favourite sea animal? Fish, sharks, whales, penguins or dolphins?
Are you frightened of any sea animals? Which ones? Why?
Note: If you have lots of students in your class, write these questions on the board. Learners ask and answer them in small groups.

Ⓓ Read the sentences. Write words which mean the same.

○ Check that learners understand 'pick up' in 1 by picking up your bag from the floor.
Say: *I'm taking my bag off the floor. I'm picking my bag up.* Point to the first letters of 'pick' and 'up' and to the lines to show how many letters are missing. Learners complete the words 'pick' and 'up' on the first line.

o   Learners read the other clues and write the missing letters on the lines.

o   Say: *We put on our clothes in the morning. We get dressed. What do we do before we have a shower or a bath? We don't put on our clothes, we …* (take them off) *We don't get dressed, we …* (get undressed)

o   Ask the following questions. Learners stand up if their answer is *yes* and sit down if it is *no*:
   1   Did you go for a swim in the sea last week?
   2   Did you catch a bus to school this morning?
   3   Did you have a walk in a jungle last weekend?
   4   Did you get dressed in your favourite clothes this morning?
   5   Do you often go shopping?
   6   Did you send any emails this week?

o   Ask learners how many of the questions they can remember. Volunteers come to the board and write one of the questions you asked. Challenge them to write all six questions.

o   In pairs, learners ask and answer these questions.

E Find ten word pairs! Draw lines.

o   Write on the board: *sea*. Ask: *Can you think of another word that sounds like 'sea' but means something different?* (see) Learners look at the words and draw a line between 'sea' and 'see'.

o   In pairs, learners look at the two blocks of words. Say: *There are ten more word pairs here that sound the same but look different. Can you find them? Draw lines.*

Check answers:

write/right, I/eye, pair/pear, wear/where, red/read (past simple)
sun/son, eight/ate, know/no, aren't/aunt, four/for

o   Write on the board: *sun/son*. Say: *Can we make a sentence or a question that has both these words in it?* Learners make suggestions, for example: *My son likes sitting in the sun.*

o   In their pairs, learners then choose two other pairs and try to write their own sentences. Ask 3–4 pairs to read out one of their sentences or questions.

Suggestions:

I write with my right hand.
I've got a fly in my eye!
Look at that pair of pears.
Where's the hat that I wear to school?
I read 'The Red Balloon' yesterday.
My friend ate eight burgers.
I know there are no cakes in the kitchen.
My aunt and uncle aren't here.
I had four computer games for my birthday.

F Find the differences between the pictures.

Speaking **1** Part

o   Ask learners to cover picture **2** and to tell you what they can see in picture **1**.
   Suggestions:
   Two children are swimming in the sea.
   A man and a boy are looking at a shell.
   There's a towel on the sand.
   There's one cloud.
   It's sunny.
   A bird is flying.
   A dolphin is jumping out of the water.

o   Say: *Now look at both pictures. They look the same but some things are different.*
   Point to picture **1** then **2** and say:
   Here, there are two children swimming in the sea, but here there are three children.
   What other different things can you see?

o   In pairs, learners find the differences and make sentences about them.

o   Ask different learners to say their sentences about the differences.

Check answers:

The man and boy are looking at a shell. / They're **playing with a beach ball**.
The towel is purple and yellow / **blue and pink**.
The hat is on the boy's head / on the **sand**.
There's a dolphin / a **whale** in the sea.

G Play the game! Let's find A–Z.

o   Ask learners to call out the alphabet in English. Go round the class with the next learner saying the next letter. Write the letters on the board.

o   Learners look again at all the words in the story in **B** and find words that begin with as many different letters of the alphabet as possible. Learners write their words in alphabetical order in their notebooks.

Note: There are no words beginning with K, V, X or Z.

Words in the text:

A   a, added, along, and, animals, around, at
B   back, be, beach, big, boats, both, boys, brother, bus, but, by
C   careful, caught, climbed, clothes
D   Dad, down
E   everything
F   favourite, feet, football, for
G   get, got, green
H   happy, he, his, home
I   in, into, it
J   jumped
L   last, long, look
M   me, more, Mum, must
N   near, Nick
O   of, on, one, only, orange, out
P   parents, picked, place, played, put
Q   quick
R   ran, rocks
S   safe, said, sailing, Sam, sand, sat, saw, sea, shells, shoes, some, something, stop, swam
T   that, the, their, them, then, there, they, those, tired, to, too, told, towels, T-shirt, Tuesday
U   under, up
W   walk, walked, was, watch, water, waves, we, went, were, wet, when, with
Y   you, your

Optional extension:

o   Ask learners to make sentences using the words they found in the text.

45 Treasure!

Equipment needed

○ Colouring pencils or pens. See B.

A Look and read. Choose the correct words and write them on the lines.

Reading & Writing Part 1

○ Write on the board: *a pirate*. Ask: *What kinds of things do we read about pirates in stories?* Write learners' ideas on the board. Ask questions to prompt answers if necessary. For example:
What do pirates wear? (scarves, trousers, shirts, hats)
What do pirates look like? (Ugly! They sometimes have beards and moustaches!)
How do pirates travel round the world? (They sail in boats/ships.)
What are pirates good at finding? (treasure)

○ Read out the example: *This person is in stories and sometimes he has a parrot!*
Ask: *Do most children like reading stories about pirates?* (Yes!)
Point to the picture of the pirate in **A**. Ask: *Has this pirate got a parrot?* (no) *What's this pirate wearing?* (blue and white trousers, a green and white shirt, a red scarf and a black and white hat) Point to the answer on the line in the example: a pirate.

○ Learners read the other sentences and write their answers on the lines.

> **Check answers:**
> **1** a ticket **2** the sky **3** maps **4** islands **5** treasure **6** a ship

○ Tell one learner to choose a picture. The other learners have to guess which picture has been chosen. They ask questions about it, for example:
Is it a person? No, it isn't.
Is it green? No, it isn't.
Is it the boat? No, it isn't.
Is it the treasure? Yes, it is.

○ Learners do the same in pairs for a minute or two.

B Colour the words you can make from the name of the film!

○ Write on the board: *Pirates and Parrots.* Point to the words and say: *'Pirates and Parrots' is the name of a film. Look at the letters in these three words. Can we make the word 'tests' from these letters?* (yes)

○ Ask a volunteer to come up to the board and circle the letters they need to write 'tests' (the last three letters of pirates and the last two letters of parrots).

○ Learners look at **B**. Point to 'tests' in the first box. Ask: *What colour is this box?* (yellow) *It's yellow because we can make this word.*

○ Say: *Look at the other eight words in their boxes. Colour the words that you can make. Be careful! There are some that you can't make! Don't colour those! You can colour the boxes yellow or another colour. You choose!* Learners work in pairs and colour boxes.
Check answers by reading out the words and asking: *Did you colour this box?* Learners call out *yes* if they did or *no* if they didn't.
Coloured boxes: parents, apps, seats, parties, pandas

○ Ask: *Why can't you colour 'trousers'? Which letter is missing?* ('u') *And which letter do you need to write 'sisters'?* (We need three 's's and there are only two!) *What about 'dinner'?* (We need another 'n'). Write the three missing letters *u, s* and *n* on the board. Ask: *What word can we make from these three letters?* (sun)

○ Write on the board: *Treasure Island.* Pairs write similar puzzles, writing six or seven words in boxes, some of which can be made from the name of this famous book and some which can't. Say: *Make your words four letters or more long! And only have one wrong letter in words that you can't make, please!*
Walk round and help if necessary.
Pairs swap puzzles to check the words and colour the correct boxes.
Suggestions for correct words:
trees, aunt, nurse, stars, reads, eats, learns, needs, sails, tries.
Suggestions for incorrect words:
grass, lakes, plant, skates, uncle, bear, dances.

C Write 1, 2 or 3 words to complete the sentences about the story.

Reading & Writing Part 5

> **Movers tip**
> In Reading and Writing Part 5, the answer will never be longer than three words. Candidates should only use words they can see in the story.

○ Say: *This story is about going to see the film that's called Pirates and Parrots!*
Learners read the first part of the story. Point to the pirate in the first picture in **C** and ask: *Who's this?* (Dan) *Did the child who's telling this story see this film in a cinema or at home?* (in a cinema)

○ Say *Tell me about Dan.* (He's a famous pirate and he's very strong. He has a black beard and moustache.)
Point to the parrot and ask: *What's the parrot's name?* (Clever) *Whose parrot is this?* (Dan's)

○ Read the first example sentence, pausing at the gap. *The boy and his … ?* (parents) *read about the film on the internet.* Explain that although the answer might also be 'mum and dad' these are NOT the words we read in the story so 'mum and dad' is the wrong answer here.
Read the second example. Ask: *Where did the family see the film?* Point to the answer in the story (the Star Cinema). Ask: *How many words are in this answer?* (three). Remind learners they should not write more than three words in the gap.

○ Learners complete sentences 1–2.

> **Check answers:**
> **1** a (famous) pirate **2** parrot

○ Point to the second picture in the story.
Ask: *Where are Dan and Clever now?* (on an island / on the beach) *Who are they with?* (more pirates) *What are the pirates doing?* (eating, climbing trees)

○ Learners read the next part of the text and complete sentences 3–5.

> **Check answers:**
> **3** small island **4** find **5** went to sleep

○ Point to the third picture. Point to the box of treasure. Ask: *What's this?* (treasure)

○ Learners read the last part of the story and find out where the pirates found the treasure (under the sand). They then complete sentences 6 and 7.

> **Check answers:**
> **6** treasure   **7** sang / danced / sang and danced

D   Talk about differences between pictures 2 and 3.

○ Point to the second and third pictures again.
Say: *Some things are different in these pictures. For example, in this picture there are some coconuts on the tree, but in this picture there are no coconuts in the tree. What other different things can you see?*

○ Learners suggest sentences to describe the differences. To help them, you could write these words on the board:
day/night, the bowl, eating/singing, climbing / playing the guitar, treasure, hat, dancing

> **Check answers:**
> In this picture (2) it's day, but in that picture (3) it's **night**.
> There's a pineapple and some coconuts in the bowl / only a **pineapple**.
> Dan and the parrot are eating/**singing**.
> A pirate is climbing the tree / **playing the guitar**.
> There is no treasure / **a box of** treasure.
> Dan's hat is on the sand / on **his head**.
> No pirates are dancing. / **Two** pirates are dancing.
> You can see the sun / the **moon**.
> The sea is blue/**purple**.

Look at the last picture. Listen! Is this right or wrong?

○ Learners look at the last picture again while you say seven different things about the picture. Say: *When I say something that is <u>right</u> about the picture, nod your head.* (Demonstrate this.) *When I say something that is <u>not right</u> about the picture, shake your head.* (Demonstrate this.).

○ Make sure learners have understood what you want them to do then read out the following sentences:

All the pirates in the picture are dancing.	(Learners shake heads)
You can see the moon above the sea.	(Learners nod heads)
The treasure box is open.	(Learners nod heads)
The parrot is on Dan's head.	(Learners shake heads)
Someone is cooking the pirates' dinner.	(Learners shake heads)
There's a coconut on the sand by Dan.	(Learners nod heads)
There are fourteen pirates in the picture.	(Learners shake heads)

○ Say: *Now listen to some questions and write about the last film you saw.* Tell learners if they can't remember the last film they saw, they can invent information.
Learners write the numbers 1–5 in their notebooks. They listen to the five questions and write their answers next to each number.
Say: *You don't have to write long answers. Write short answers to my questions. You can write one, two, three or four words.*

   1   *What was the name of the last film you saw?*
   2   *Which day did you go?*
   3   *Who did you watch it with?*
   4   *Did you enjoy the film?*
   5   *What was the film about?*

○ Ask five different learners these questions again. Learners read out their answers then talk about their films in pairs or small groups.

E   Let's write five-line poems!

○ Write the following words on the board: *pirates, islands, maps, trees, parrots, pineapples, coconuts, treasure, sand, noises, ships, waves.*

○ Write on the board: *clever.*
Say: *'Clever' is a good name for a clever parrot. What can we say about Dan the pirate. Is he clever?* (yes/no) *Is he strong?*
Say: *Now tell me more about Dan the pirate. He's …?* Write learners' suggestions on the board.
Ask for words to describe 'islands' and 'noises' in the same way.

Suggestions from Movers wordlist
boring, brave, cool, dangerous, different, exciting, famous, fantastic, huge, loud, scary, silly, strong

○ Say: *Work in pairs now.* Point to the words on the board and say: *Choose one of the words on the board and write it in your notebooks.*
Pairs choose and write their word, for example: 'pirates' or 'maps'.

○ Say: *Under your word, write two more words that you think of about your first word.*
Examples:

pirates	***maps***
sail sea	*rivers roads*

○ Say: *On the next line, write a question about your first word.*
Examples:

pirates	***maps***
sail sea	*rivers, roads*
Where do they go?	*Can you read them?*

○ Say: *Under that, write an answer to that question.*
Examples:

pirates	***maps***
sail sea	*rivers, roads*
Where do they go?	*Can you read them?*
To islands	*Yes, I can.*

○ For the last line in the poem, tell learners to write an adjective to describe the first word and then write the first word again.
Examples:

pirates	***maps***
sail sea	*rivers, roads*
Where do they go?	*Can you read them?*
To islands	*Yes, I can.*
scary pirates	*silly maps*

○ Learners could illustrate their poems with a drawing. Display the poems around the classroom.

46   A day on the island

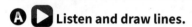

Pronunciation practice Sentence stress (*The **pirate** in the **big boat** has a **black hat** on his **head***). See C.

Equipment needed

O   Movers Audio 46A.

Ⓐ ▶ Listen and draw lines.   Listening Part 1

> **Movers tip**
>
> In Listening Part 1, candidates have to name the people so, before they listen, they should look at the people in the picture and think about what they are doing and wearing, where they are, etc. If two people are doing the same or wearing the same clothes, they should look for other differences because this might be tested.

O   Learners look at the picture. Ask: *Would you like to go to this beach? What can you do at this beach?* Learners answer. For example: go sailing / fishing / play games / read comics / find shells / sleep.

O   Say: *Find five things that start with the letter 's'.*
     (**Suggestions:** sand, sea, shell, sun, shoes, shark, shorts).
     Say: *There's a line from the name Jack to one of the boys on the beach. What colour is that boy's T-shirt?* (red and white)
     Ask: *What's he doing?* (looking for something)
     Where is he looking? (on the sand near/under the plant)

O   Play the audio stopping after the example. Ask: *What's Jack looking for?* (his glasses)

O   Learners listen to the rest of the conversation and draw lines from the names to the people in the picture. Play the audio twice.

> **Check answers:**
> Lines should be drawn between:
> **1** Sally and girl hiding behind rock.
> **2** Peter and boy lying on ground with his eyes closed.
> **3** Sam and boy calling the parrot.
> **4** Vicky and girl holding her foot.
> **5** Alex and boy pirate on boat.

O   Say: *You didn't need one of the names. Which one?* (Grace)

Audioscript

> *Look at the picture. Listen and look. There is one example.*
> Boy: The children are enjoying the island.
> Woman: Yes, they are, but what's the matter with that boy?
> Boy: Oh! You mean Jack. He's looking for his glasses. He dropped them near that plant.
> Woman: Oh yes! I can see them now.
> *Can you see the line? This is an example. Now you listen and draw lines.*

> *One*
> Boy: Look at Sally!
> Woman: Where?
> Boy: There. She's the girl who's hiding behind that big rock.
> Woman: Oh yes! I can see her. She's playing with her friend.
> *Two*
> Boy: There's Peter.
> Woman: Which one's he?
> Boy: There. I think he's sleeping in the sun.
> Woman: I think he's awake, but his eyes are closed because it's sunny.
> *Three*
> Woman: Who's that boy? The boy who's calling the parrot?
> Boy: Oh, that's Sam.
> Woman: Why's he doing that?
> Boy: Because the parrot's not in its cage. Look! The door's open.
> Woman: Oh dear!
> *Four*
> Boy: Vicky doesn't look very happy.
> Woman: Which one's she?
> Boy: She's the girl who's holding her foot.
> Woman: Did she hurt her foot on that shell?
> Boy: Yes, I think she did.
> *Five*
> Boy: And there's Alex. He's very funny.
> Woman: The boy on the boat?
> Boy: Yes!
> Woman: I like his pirate hat!
> Boy: Me too!

Ⓑ Look and read and write.   Reading & Writing Part 6

O   Learners look at the picture in **A** again. Read out the first example: *The pirate on the ship is wearing a black hat.*
     Read out the second example: *What is the person in the small boat doing? fishing* Ask: *Where's the small boat?* Learners point to the boat. Ask: *Is there a man in this boat? Is he fishing?* (yes)

O   Say: *Read 1–4 and write 1–5 words. Then, write two sentences on the lines in 5 and 6 about people or things in the picture in A!* Learners write words and sentences.

> **Check answers:**
> (Suggestions) **1** some glasses / a headache   **2** the coconut tree
> **3** a (bird) cage   **4** behind the rock

Ask: *What colour are the glasses?* (blue and black). Explain that they can write words like blue, big, etc to complete the sentences.
Ask: *Is the cage big or little?* (little) *Is the rock little or big?* (big)
Explain that they can add adjectives to their answers to the questions.

O   Ask different learners to read out one of the sentences they wrote in 5 or 6. Encourage learners by saying: *Well done! Brilliant!*

Suggestions

Simple sentences: One person is looking for his glasses. There are no big waves in the sea. You can see the sun in the sky.

Compound sentences: The boy is sad because he hurt his foot on the shell. One person is asleep because he's tired. The ship has only got one sail and there's only one person on the ship.

Ⓒ Listen and say.

O   Say: *Look at the sentence in C. Some words in this sentence are more important than the other words.* Read out the sentence making sure that you stress the bold words: *The **pirate** in the **big boat** has a **black hat** on his **head!***

O   Ask one learner to only read out the bold words: *pirate, big boat,* black hat, head.

- Ask: *When (Maria) says 'pirate, big boat, black hat, head' what do you know about this pirate?* Learners suggest answers: *He's got a big boat. He's got a black hat. He's got a head!*
- Ask another learner to only read out the smaller words: *The, in the, has a, on his.* Ask: *When (Tony) says 'the, in the, has a, on his' what do you know about this pirate? Can you tell me about him?* (no)
- Learners work in pairs. Repeat the sentence to the class then say: *Now tell your friend about this pirate. When you read out the sentence, make the big words more important than the small ones. Say the big words more slowly and more loudly because those words tell you a lot about this pirate.* Learners repeat the sentence to each other.

  Optional extension:
- Write on the board: *red   parrot   flying   moon*
- In pairs, learners copy the words into their notebooks leaving spaces between the words. They decide how to make a sentence and fill the gaps with function words, writing them in small letters. Pairs then practise saying their sentence. For example, *The **red parrot** is **flying** to the **moon**.* Check learners begin their sentences with a capital letter and add a full stop at the end.
- Pairs then choose their own four words and write sentences using large letters for the 'important' words.
- Ask different pairs to read out their sentence. Check that the sentence stress is correct!

D Say which picture is different and why.   Speaking **Part 3**

- Point to the first set of four pictures.
  Say: *Look at these four pictures. One is different.*
  Ask: *Which one is different?* (the last one – the rock on the sand)
  Why is it different? (You can swim in the sea, a river and a lake but you can't swim in a rock / on the sand! The sea, a river and a lake have water in them but the rock picture doesn't have any water in it.)
- In pairs, learners look at the other three sets of pictures and talk about which picture is different and why.
- Check answers by asking one pair of learners to say which picture is different and why. If the other learners in the class agree, they say: *Yes, you're right!* If they don't agree, they say: *Try again!*

  Suggested answers:
  Set 2: The seat is different. You can travel on a bike, a boat and a helicopter but you **sit** on a seat.
  Set 3: The plate is different because it's **yellow**. The towel, the bag and the boat are red.
  Set 4: The girl who isn't awake / who is asleep is different because she is **sleeping** / **lying down**. The other three girls are all awake / standing up.
- Say: *Look at the first four pictures again. You can't swim on a rock but what can you do?* If necessary, prompt learners to suggest you can climb a rock. Learners suggest two other things you can climb, for example: a tree, a mountain.
- Now quietly, in pairs, learners do the same with the three other sets focusing on the picture that is different.
  They think of two other things you can sit on, for example: an armchair, a mat.
  They think of two other things that can be yellow, for example: the sun, a lemon.
  They think of two other people (or animals) you could show in pictures that are sleeping, for example: an old man, a cat.

  Optional extension:
- Pairs could then draw their own new sets of four pictures. Three should be the same in some way and one picture should be different. If learners have internet access or magazines they could cut up, they could find pictures to make sets. Pairs could then swap sets with other pairs and talk about the differences.

E Listen, write the words, questions and answers.

- Learners listen and write words in each of the coloured boxes.
- Say: *Write these words in the blue box: Sam, pair, has, of, yellow, a, glasses, got*
  Now write these words in the red box: like, sharks, does, about, Alex, reading, on, internet, the
  And put these words in the green box:, was, his, beach, the, Peter, with, at, today, friends
  And these words in the yellow box: Grace, did, dressing, enjoy, like, pirate, a, up
- In pairs, learners check they have the same words in the blue box as their partner. They then make a question by unjumbling the words and writing it in the blue question box. Remind them to use a capital letter for their first word. Check this first sentence. Continuing in pairs, learners then unjumble and write the other three sentences.

  Check answers:
  blue question box: Has Sam got a pair of yellow glasses?
  red question box: Does Alex like reading about sharks on the internet?
  green question box: Was Peter at the beach with his friends today?
  yellow question box: Did Grace enjoy dressing up like a pirate?

- Ask four volunteers to come to the front of the class and divide the rest of the class into two groups A and B. Tell group A that they always answer *yes!* and group B *no!*
  Volunteers read out one question from their question boxes.
  Group A answers the question with the *yes* short form answer.
  Group B answers the question with the *no* short form answer:
  Yes, he has! / No, he hasn't!
  Continue in the same way for the three other answers:
  Yes, she does! / No, she doesn't!
  Yes, he was! / No he wasn't!
  Yes, she did! / No, she didn't!

F Write your question and yes or no answer.

- Asking learners for help, write on the board:
  Has…?   Yes, she has. No, she hasn't.
  Does…?   Yes, he does. No, he doesn't.
  Was…?   Yes, she was. No, she wasn't.
  Did…?   Yes, he did. No, he didn't.
  Learners then think of their own question and answer and write them on the lines. Encourage them to be creative. For example:
  Did the monster live on the moon? No, he didn't.

G Play the game! Guess my question.

- Choose a picture from the Student's book (for example, the picture on page 56). Say: *I wrote a question about this picture. Can you guess it?*
- Draw five lines on the board. Add a question mark at the end:
  ....?
- Learners suggest words for the question. For example:
  Learner A: *is*
  You write *is* where it appears in the sentence.
  Is ....
  Learner B: *a* Teacher: *No, that's not in this sentence.*
  Continue until the sentence is complete.
  Suggested answer: *Is the purple bat sleeping?*
- Learners answer the question using 'yes' or 'no' or a short form answer.
  Each pair of learners chooses another picture. They write a question about it and draw lines on a piece of paper. Another pair of learners guesses their question and answers it.

47   The different things we do

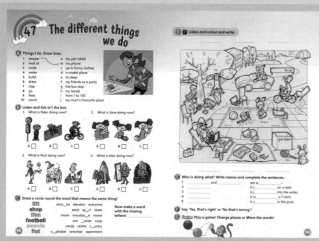

Flyers word: *over*

Equipment needed

○   Movers Audio 47D.

○   Colouring pens or pencils. See D.

A   Things I do. Draw lines.

○   Ask: *What can you do with a ball? You can … (kick / catch / throw / play with a ball). What can you open?* (a door, a window, a box)
What can you cook? You can cook … (eggs, burgers, pasta)
What can you ride? (a bike, a motorbike, a horse)
What can you drive? (a bus, a car, a lorry)

○   Learners look at the two columns of words and the picture of the girl answering her phone. Look at the first verb: 'answer'.
Ask: *What can you answer? Can you answer a train?* (no) *Can you answer your best coat?* (no) Point to the line from 1 to b. Learners say in chorus: *You can answer a phone!*
Ask: *Who answers the phone at home? Is it OK to answer a phone when you're eating with your family / working in class / driving a car?*

○   Learners draw lines between 2–10 and the letters to show the match. Each of the endings should be used only once.

○   Check answers by asking different learners to read out each verb phrase using *I can …* at the beginning.

> **Check answers:**
> **2**g   **3**f   **4**j   **5**d   **6**c   **7**h   **8**e   **9**a   **10**i

○   Ask: *Do you like building models of planes, buildings or trains? Is it fun to build cities in computer games?* Learners answer.
Ask different learners: *Where do you catch a train / clap your hands / water plants? And where do you answer my questions?*
Suggested answers:
I clap my hands at a concert / sports game.
I water plants on the balcony / in the garden.
I answer your questions in this classroom / in our playground.

○   Learners work in pairs to write three 'Where do you … ?' questions. Pairs then ask and answer each other's questions. If possible, ask 2–3 pairs to come to the front of the class and mime one of their questions. The class guesses the question and answers it.

B   Listen and tick the box.

> **Movers tip**
> When learning new vocabulary, learners should learn words that go together, for example: *colour a picture, take a photo, make a mistake, have a shower, wait for a bus, dress up in funny clothes, hurt a foot.* Learners should also understand the difference between what someone did (past simple) and what they are doing now (present continuous). Collocations and tense distinctions are tested in all parts of Cambridge English: Movers, especially in Listening Part 4.

○   Say: *Look at the pictures and read the four questions. Is the answer A, B or C? Listen and tick the right box.*

○   Read out the script below twice if necessary.

One	*What's Peter doing now?*
Boy:	*Peter's the boy who's in the road, waiting for the bus. He couldn't ride his bike to school today because he jumped off the wall in his garden yesterday and he hurt his foot badly.*
Two	*What's Jane doing now?*
Woman:	*Before lunch, Jane phoned her best friend and now she's writing texts to invite everyone in her class to a party. She wants to read her favourite comic today, too. She can do that this evening.*
Three	*What's Paul doing now?*
Man:	*Paul's doing his homework downstairs because his mum can help him there. He doesn't like making mistakes! And he needs a shower! He played football at school this afternoon.*
Four	*What's Alex doing now?*
Girl:	*Alex saw a really funny film at the cinema yesterday. It was about a girl who travelled to the moon. Now she's dressing up in some clothes that look like the ones that the people wore in the film.*

> **Check answers:**
> **1**A   **2**B   **3**C   **4**B

C   Draw a circle round the word that means the same thing!

○   In pairs, learners look at the word groups on the right, find the missing letters and complete the words. Ask different pairs to spell one word: earache, sport, moustache, soccer, country, alphabet.
Ask: *What were the missing letters?* (c o h s o l) *Which word can we make from these?* (school) Learners write it on the line.

○   Ask: *Do you know another word which means the same as truck?* (lorry). *What about another word that means the same as eraser?* (rubber). Explain that we sometimes have two different words to talk about the same thing because American English is sometimes different from British English.

○   Learners read the six words in the first column and each set of three words and circle the word that means the same as the first word.

> **Check answers:**
> elevator, store, movie, soccer, candy, apartment

○   Ask: *Do you think the coloured words or the words with the circle round them are the American English words?* (The circled words are more likely to be used in American English.)

○   In pairs, learners think of six sentences. Each sentence should include one of the six correctly paired words, for example: *I love eating sweets.* Pairs take turns to read out one of their sentences. It might be fun for learners to try to read their sentences out in exaggerated British or American accents!

D   ▶ Listen and colour and write.   Listening Part 5

○   Learners look at the picture. Ask: *Where's this swimming pool?* (in a garden) *Is the swimming pool big?* (No, it's small.) *How many grown-ups can you see?* (two) *How many children are there in the picture?* (five)

○   Play the example. Say: *There are two laptops in this picture. Which laptop must we colour – the one on the ground or the one that the mother's holding?* (the mother's laptop) *What colour must it be?* (green) *What's the mother doing? Is she looking at a website?* (No, she's writing an email.)

○   Check that learners have colouring pencils or pens. Play the rest of the audio twice. Learners listen and colour and write.

Check answers:
1 Colour father's car – yellow.
2 Colour boy's sweater (boy on bike) – red.
3 Colour biggest book – blue.
4 Write 'games' under 'garden'.
5 Colour girl's hair (girl in tree) – brown.

○ Say: *The girl and the man didn't talk about two people in this picture. Which ones?* (the boy and girl in the pool)

Audioscript

Look at the picture. Listen and look. There is one example.

Man: Do you like this picture?
Girl: Yes. It's a great swimming pool!
Man: The mother's writing emails on her laptop.
Girl: Oh yes! Can I colour that?
Man: Yes, please. Make it green.

Can you see the green laptop? This is an example. Now you listen and colour and write.

One
Man: The father's driving his sports car. He's coming home.
Girl: I'd like to colour his sports car! It's so cool!
Man: Good idea! Make it yellow.
Girl: All right. Wow! It looks fantastic now.

Two
Girl: That boy's naughty!
Man: The boy who's riding the bike?
Girl: Yes! Can I colour his sweater?
Man: Yes, colour it orange.
Girl: Can I colour it red? I like that colour more.
Man: OK!

Three
Girl: Why are all those things on the rug?
Man: The children did their homework there, I think.
Girl: Oh! Can I colour the biggest book?
Man: Yes. Colour it blue, please.
Girl: All right. I'm doing that now.

Four
Man: There's a box next to the pool. Can you see it?
Girl: Yes, I can.
Man: Good. Write 'games' under the word 'garden' on that box.
Girl: Does this family have lots of fun in this garden, then?
Man: Yes, they do.

Five
Man: Look! The woman's daughter is in the tree.
Girl: She's good at climbing! Can I colour her hair?
Man: Yes. You choose the colour for her hair.
Girl: How about brown?
Man: OK! Thanks. This picture looks a lot better now!

Ⓔ Who is doing what? Write names and complete the sentences.

○ Say: *Look at the picture again. Let's choose names for everyone in this family.* Learners offer suggestions, for example: Mr and Mrs Nice, Eva, Anna, Tom and Hugo. Agree on one set of names and write those on the board. Say: *Now you write these names on the lines above and below the picture.* Learners then draw a line from each name to the appropriate person in the picture.

○ Point to the father and the boy on the bike. Ask: *What are their names?* (*Mr Nice* and *Tom*) Write on the board: *Mr Nice* and *Tom* are ....! Ask: *What are they both doing?* *The word you need begins with w.* (waving) Write *waving* on the line on the board. Learners complete sentence 1 with the names and 'waving'.

○ Learners complete sentences 2–5.

Check answers:
2 (name of mother) sitting,   3 (name of girl in pool) jumping,
4 (name of girl in tree) wearing,   5 (name of boy in pool) swimming

Ⓕ Say 'Yes, that's right' or 'No, that's wrong'!

○ Give each learner a sheet of paper and tell them to write *Yes, that's right!* on one side and *No, that's wrong!* on the other side.

○ Learners close their books and try to remember the picture. Say: *When I say something about the picture, think, 'Is that right or wrong?' and hold up your answer.* Say: *A woman is writing a message.* Learners hold up their answer ('Yes, that's right!' or 'No, that's wrong!').

○ Ask one learner to count the 'Yes, that's right!' answers and another learner to count the 'No, that's wrong!' answers. They report back saying: *(12) people think that's right! (three) people think that's wrong.* Do the same with these five sentences choosing different people to count the answers.
   A rabbit is jumping into a box. A cat is wearing a pair of glasses. Everyone in the picture is smiling. There's a tennis racket on the grass. Some leaves are falling from the tree.

○ Learners then open their books again and check the picture to see how many of their answers were correct.

Check answers:
A rabbit is jumping into a box. (no)
A cat is wearing a pair of glasses. (no)
Everyone in the picture is smiling. (yes)
There's a tennis racket on the grass. (yes)
Some leaves are falling from the tree. (no)

Optional extension:

○ Learners work in small groups. Each group chooses another picture from the book and writes five sentences about it (at least one of them should be wrong).

○ Two groups then work together. Group A shows Group B the picture giving them 30 seconds to remember it before reading out their sentences. Group B hold up their 'Yes, that's right!' or 'No, that's wrong cards'. Group B then shows their picture and Group A answers with yes or no cards.

Ⓖ Play a game! Change places or Mime the words.

○ Choose a game that suits your class size and space.
   Change places. (In a big classroom or outside in the playground.)

○ Teach the instruction 'Change places!' Learners all stand (or all sit) in a large circle. Ask them a question from the list below. All the learners who answer 'yes' to this question change places with another person whose answer is also 'yes' (for example A and B swap places, or A swaps places with B, B with C, C with A, etc). If only one person answers 'yes' they stay where they are. Those whose answer is 'no' also stay where they are.

Suggested questions:
Did anyone phone you this morning?
Are you good at swimming?
Did you catch a bus to school today?
Do you often text your friends?
Did you ride a bike last weekend?
Can you drive a car?
Did you listen to any good music yesterday?
Do you live in the town centre?

Mime the words.

○ Learners play in teams of 4–5. Each learner in the team chooses a word combination (for example: clap your hands) from this unit and writes it on a small piece of paper.
   Collect the pieces of paper and put them in a hat.

○ Taking turns, one learner from each team comes to the front of the class and picks a word combination from the hat. The learner then draws a picture of it on the board or mimes it to the other people in their team. The team has one minute to guess. Teams win a point for every correctly-guessed word combination.

48 We want to do this one day

Equipment needed

o Photocopies (one for each pair of learners) of the questionnaire on page 128. See E.

o Story prompts. See D.

A What are your answers? One day, would you like to … ?

> **Movers tip**
>
> In Speaking Part 4, candidates often need to answer Who/What/Where questions, and Yes/No questions. Although Yes/No answers are fine, encourage learners to also give short form answers like: Yes, I would. No, I don't. Make sure they listen carefully to the modal or auxiliary verb and its tense in the question so they do this correctly.

Note: At Movers, 'Would you like?' is most often used plus a noun for offers, for example: 'Would you like some milk?' Appropriate answers are 'Yes/No.' or 'Yes, please.' / 'No, thank you.' but we can also answer with 'Yes, I would.' / 'No, I wouldn't.'

In this activity, the questions are not offers but asking about things people want to do. Appropriate answers are more likely to be: 'Yes.'/'No.' or 'Yes, I'd like to do that.' / 'No, I don't want to do that.' or 'Yes, I would.' / 'No, I wouldn't.'

'One day' + 'I'd like to…' or 'I'd like to …' + 'one day' is often used to mean 'I'd like to do this sometime in the future'. Learners will not have to produce this in the test, but should recognise the meaning of this structure.

Make sure learners understand the meaning of this before you start this activity and teach appropriate answers: 'Yes.'/'No.' or 'Yes, I'd like to do that.' / 'No, I don't want to do that.' or 'Yes, I would.' / 'No, I wouldn't.'

o Write the question on the board: One day, would you like to … ?

Look at the first picture together. Ask: What is this child doing? (sailing round an island). Complete the question on the board: … sail round an island? and then ask 3–4 learners the same question: One day, would you like to sail round an island? Learners answer for example: Yes, I'd love to do that. No, I don't want to do that!

o In groups of 3–4, learners write questions for the other seven pictures. The structure is on the board, but walk around and help with vocabulary if necessary.

Suggestions:

One day, would you like to climb a mountain / travel to the moon / sleep under the stars / fly above the clouds / make friends with an alien / ride on an elephant / walk under a waterfall?

o Groups work with other groups asking or answering (or ask questions in open class).

Note: If you think it would be helpful, explain we can put 'one day' at the beginning or end of a question or answer.

Optional extension:

Learners work in groups. Each group chooses an adventure they think is really exciting. Groups then tell the rest of the class. For example: We would like to make friends with an alien one day!

Learners could choose their own adventure, write their sentence: I'd (really) like to ……………………… one day! and illustrate their sentence with a picture.

B Read and choose the best answer.

Reading & Writing Part 2

> **Movers tip**
>
> Reading and Writing Part 2 tests functional responses. Candidates need to choose an answer that makes sense, for example, if a person suggests doing something, the reply might be an agreement (Yes, let's do that! OK! Good idea! etc). or a refusal (Not today. Sorry, I can't do that. No, I don't want to do that etc).

o Ask different learners questions about books and reading:
Do you like reading?
Do you often go to the library?
Do you have to read a lot of books for school?
Do you like reading stories on the internet?
Do you or your parents read e-books?
Do you like reading funny, sad or exciting stories?
Would you like to read a story about a famous or important person?

Learners answer the questions using short answers and saying why they do or don't do these different things. For example (answers to the second question):
Yes, I do. I like going to the library. We always go on Saturdays. Our library has lots of good books.
No, I don't. I don't like going to the library. / There isn't a library near my home. We never go there.

o Learners look at the picture. Ask:
How many people can you see? (two – a boy and a girl)
What are they doing? (talking)
What has the girl got in her hand? (a book)

o Learners look at the example.
Ask: What are these children called? (Tom and Zoe)
Who's asking the question? (Tom)
Who's answering the question? (Zoe)
Say: Read Tom's question. (What are you reading about?)
Ask: Which is the best answer for Zoe to say?
Is it 'Along the beach'? (no)
Is it 'I can't practise today'? (no) Tom didn't ask Zoe to practise or do any sport.
Is it 'A really cool woman'? (yes!) Zoe's reading about a really cool woman.
Point to the circle round the letter B.

o Point to answer A. (Along the beach.) Ask: What's this answer telling us about? (a place) Is Tom's question asking about a place? (no) What's a good question for this answer? (Where did you go?)

o Point to answer C.
Ask: What's a good question for this answer? (Can you practise today?)

○ Learners read the text and circle the best answers.

Check answers:
1 A   2 C   3 C   4 C   5 A   6 B

○ In pairs, learners role play the conversation between Tom and Zoe.

C Read the story. Choose a word from the box. Write the correct word next to numbers 1–5.

Reading & Writing Part 3

○ For an authentic test practice, tell learners to read the story, choose the five missing words from the box and write them in the gaps. Then they choose the best name for the story and tick that box.

If you would prefer to give learners more support, you could complete the activity in the following way.

○ Point to the story. Say: *This is a story about Zoe and the book she is reading.* (Point to the girl in the picture in **B**.)

○ Write on the board:
What was the woman's name?
How old was she?
Learners read the first part of the story to find the answers to these questions. (Mary Banks, 22)

○ Ask learners: *Where could people learn more about Mary?*
Learners read the second part of the story and answer this question. (on a website, in a comic)

○ Say: *Now read the last part of the story.* Give learners plenty of time to read through to the end in silence then ask: *What does Zoe want to do now?* (sail around the world)

○ Learners read the story again and, in pairs or on their own, choose one of the words under the pictures for each gap and write them on the lines.

Check answers:
1 whales   2 tired   3 page   4 buy   5 swim

○ Learners look at the three possible names for this story.
Ask: *Which is the best name for the story?* (Learning about Mary)
Did Zoe's father have a boat? (No – so the first name for the story is not right.)
Did Zoe have a sailing lesson? (No – so the third name for the story is not right.)

D Write a story about a story! Choose words.

○ Ask questions about reading and writing stories. You could ask these in open class with learners putting their hands up to answer, or write them on the board for learners to answer in small groups.
Do you like reading stories? What kinds of stories are best?
What was your favourite story when you were young?
Where do you like reading most? Have you got a favourite place?
Do you or does anyone in your family like writing stories?
What kinds of stories do you/they write?
Do you/they like writing on a computer or with a pencil or pen?
Which is best?

○ Say: *Let's write some really short stories now.*
Write on the board the following prompts:
Day?   It's .... and
Boy's name?   ....
Where?   is going to the ....
Boy's name?   .... has got a new e-book.
Where?   It's on his ....
What?   His e-book is about ....
Boy's name?   .... likes reading about
What?   .... because one day,
Would like?   he would like to .... !

○ Say: *You can write this short story now. Choose the missing words.*
Learners work in pairs. They talk together and write their four sentence 'story about a story' in their notebooks. Point out that the boy's name should always be the same and the two 'What?' gaps should be the same word too.
Walk round and help with ideas if necessary while learners copy the story on the board, adding their own choice of words in the gaps. For example:
It's **Saturday** and **Jack** is going to the **park**. **Jack** has got a new e-book. It's on his **tablet**. His e-book is about **the moon**. **Jack** likes reading about **the moon** because one day, he would like to **live there**!

○ Pairs take turns to read out their four sentence story to the rest of the class. Learners vote for the funniest/best story.

○ Ask more questions:
Is it better to write a story or read a story?
Is it better to read a story or watch a film?
Is it better to watch a film or play a computer game?
Is it better to play a computer game or play a game outside?
What do you like doing best? Writing stories, reading stories, watching films, playing computer games or playing games outside?
Pairs talk together and decide. Ask the questions again. Pairs put up their hands to show their answers.
Ask: *So what do most of you like doing best?* Learners answer.

E Let's see! How well do you know your friend?

○ Copy and cut up one questionnaire on page 128 for each pair of learners (Learner A and Learner B).

○ In pairs, learners read their questions and write what they think their partner would answer, using short answers. (Yes, I am. / No, I'm not.) They write their partner's name in the space at the top.

○ Learners ask each other the questions and tick the answers they guessed correctly.

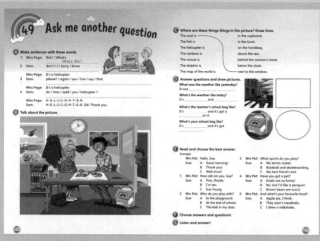

Equipment needed

o   Colouring pens or pencils. See D.

Ⓐ Make sentences with these words.

> **Movers tip**
>
> Practise using greetings (*Hi! Hello! Good morning! Good afternoon!*) naturally and teach candidates how to ask someone to repeat a question and to clarify meaning if necessary. This will help them to become more communicative and fluent and to feel more confident in the Speaking.

o   Point to the small picture and say:

This is Sam and this is Miss Page, his English teacher. What are they looking at? (a helicopter on a computer) *Sam doesn't know this word in English.*

Point to Miss Page's purple jumbled words and her question ('What's this?') in 1. Make sure learners see that the jumbled word that begins with a capital letter must be the first word in a question or answer.

o   Learners put the words in the right order in 2,3 and 4.

> **Check answers:**
>
> **2**   Sorry, I don't know.
>
> **3**   Can you say that again, please?
>
> **4**   How do you spell helicopter?

o   In pairs, learners choose a picture of something in their book, for example the giraffe on page 51 or the castle on page 63 and role play (like Sam and Miss Page) asking and answering about meanings and spellings.

Note: Remind learners that it's fine to say 'Pardon?' or 'Sorry?' or 'I don't understand.' if they would like to hear something again because they haven't fully understood something.

Ⓑ Talk about the picture.

o   Learners work in pairs to list as many things as they can see in the picture. Give learners a time limit to do this (two minutes). Say: *Count your words! How many words have you got?* Pairs count the number of things they have listed then pairs work together to compare answers. Ask: *Did anyone find 20 things?*

Suggestions: bags, boat, book, bottle, boy, clock, coat, cupboard, dolphin, door, dress, drink, fan, fish, floor, girl, glasses, helicopter, map, mouse, numbers, pen, pencil, pictures, rainbow, shoes, socks, sweater, table, wall, water, woman

o   Learners look at the picture. Ask: *How many people can you see?* (three)

How many are standing? (one) *How many are sitting down?* (two)

Who are these people? Guess! (a mother and her son and daughter / a teacher and two students)

Where are they? (at school / in a classroom)

What's the girl doing? (looking/pointing at a picture) *And the boy?* (smiling/hiding behind the door)

o   Say: *Let's talk about how the woman and the girl in this picture are different.* For example: *The girl's hair is blonde, but the woman's hair is … ?* (black)

The girl's hair is long, but the woman's hair is … ? (short)

The girl's hair is straight, but the woman's hair is … ? (curly)

o   Ask: *What about their clothes? How are those different?* Learners talk about the differences in pairs. Ask 3–4 pairs to talk about one difference.

Suggestions:

The woman's wearing glasses, but the girl **isn't wearing** glasses.

The girl's wearing a green sweater, but the woman's wearing a **pink dress**.

The girl's sweater has words on it, but the woman's dress has **flowers** on it.

The girl's wearing socks, but the woman **isn't wearing** any socks.

o   Choose two things in your classroom that learners could talk about, for example, two different walls (or what they can see from two different windows). In groups of 3–4, learners say how they are different. Ask 3–4 pairs to talk about one difference.

For example:

This wall has a window, but that wall hasn't got a window.

This wall is white, but that wall is grey.

There's a clock on this wall, but there's a map on that wall.

There are pictures on this wall, but there are no pictures on that wall.

o   Say: *Now listen carefully to some questions about this picture.* **You choose** the answers.

Learners work in pairs or small groups. Read the sentences below, pausing after each question to give learners time to use their imaginations and to suggest answers. They choose and write their answers on a piece of paper or in their notebooks. Ask:

What day is it? And is it the morning or afternoon?

How old are the children?

Why is the girl pointing at the book?

What's in the picture on that page?

What's the girl saying?

What's the woman saying?

What's the boy thinking?

What are the books in the cupboard about?

What's the name of the pet fish?

What's in the girl's school bag?

What's in the woman's handbag?

What's this classroom like? Is it big? Small? New? Old? Hot? Cold?

What's outside the classroom?

○ Give learners some extra time (two or three minutes) to look at the classroom picture again and to complete their answers or to think of other information they would like to add about the picture. Walk round and help with ideas if necessary.

When learners have finished, ask different groups for their ideas about this picture. Make sure learners understand that there are no wrong answers!

○ Write learners' suggestions for names on the board. The class chooses a set of three names. They can use the boy's name again in **D**.

C Where are these things in the picture? Draw lines.

○ Point to the coat in the picture in **B**.

Ask: *What's this?* (a coat)

Where is it? (next to the window) Point to the line between 'The coat is' and 'next to the window.'

○ Learners draw lines to make sentences about where each thing is.

> **Check answers:**
> The fish is in the bowl. The helicopter is above the sea.
> The rainbow is on the handbag. The mouse is in the cupboard.
> The dolphin is below the clock. The map of the world is behind the woman's head.

○ Ask: *Where's the star?* (on the girl's hair) *Where's the bottle?* (on the table / next to the glass)

Say *yes* or *no*.

○ Read out these sentences about the picture in **B**.

Learners nod their heads if they think the sentence about the picture is right so their answer is 'yes'. Learners shake their heads if they think the sentence is wrong so their answer is 'no'.

1   All the people in the picture are wearing socks. (no)
2   We can see a classroom door and it's closed. (no)
3   The woman is pointing at a map. (no)
4   There are two words on the girl's sweater. (yes)
5   The clock on the wall is square. (no)
6   A fish is swimming in a glass bowl. (yes)

D Answer questions and draw pictures.

○ Teach/revise 'What's it like?' by asking learners: *What name did you choose for the boy in B?* Learners answer (for example: Ben). Write two questions on the board and ask learners to answer them:

What does Ben like doing?   *He likes … ?* (playing football)
What is Ben like?   *He is … ?* (thin and he's funny)

Explain that when we answer 'What's someone like?' we say what we know about someone (He's nice.) or what we see when we look at someone (He's thin and he's got brown hair.)

○ Ask learners to describe different objects in the picture in **B**, for example: *What's the coat like?* (It's long. It's purple) You might like to teach 'pockets' (Flyers) and 'buttons' (non YLE vocabulary) so learners could add: *It's got big pockets. It's got round, black buttons.*

Ask: *What's our classroom like? / What's the classroom like in picture B?* (It's got green walls and a green door. There's a window in the door. The floor is brown. There's a table and a cupboard in it. etc)

○ Read the first question in **D**: *What was the weather like yesterday?* Point to the weather picture and ask: *It was … ?* (cold, windy and cloudy) Learners write *cold, windy and cloudy* on the line.

Read the third question in **D**: *What's the teacher's school bag like?* Point to the picture of the teacher's school bag and ask: *It's … ?* (grey) *and it's got a … on it?* (rainbow) Learners write *grey* and *rainbow* on the lines.

○ Learners look outside at the weather today, draw a picture of the sky in the empty square and complete the weather answer. Learners draw their own school bag in the empty circle and complete the school bag answer.

○ Ask one learner: *What's the weather like?* Ask learners: *What's your school bag like?*

E Read and choose the best answer.

○ Point to the girl in the picture in **B**.

Say: *I think this girl's name is Sue. She's taking her Movers Speaking Test today.*

Point to the woman. Say: *And I think this woman's name is Mrs Pat. She's talking to Sue and asking her some questions.*

○ Look at the example. Ask: one learner to read Mrs Pat's greeting (Hello, Sue.)

Say: *Look at the three answers. When Mrs Pat says 'Hello, Sue.' Can Sue say 'Thank you!'?* (no) *Can she say 'Well done!'?* (no) *What does she say?* (Good morning!) *That's right! Good morning is a nice way to say 'Hello!' to Mrs Pat. Draw a circle round the letter A.*

○ Learners read the rest of the conversation and choose the best answers. They draw a red circle round the letters A, B or C.

> **Check answers:**
> **1** B   **2** C   **3** B   **4** B   **5** A

F Choose answers and questions!

○ Write the following three questions on the board. Read them out, one at a time. Learners listen. Ask them to repeat each question to you.

1   *How are you, Sue?*
2   *Who cooks dinner in your house?*
3   *Where do you do your homework?*

○ Learners choose an answer for each question from the text in **E**. They draw a green square round their chosen answers.

> **Check answers:**
> **1** 1A   **2** 3C   **3** 5B

○ Write on the board 1C, 2A, 4A, 5C. In pairs, learners think of a question for these answers! For example:

1C   What's your name?
2A   Where do you play games?
4A   Whose comic is this?
5C   What's Mrs Pat like?

○ Ask 2–3 pairs to role play asking and answering their questions.

G Listen and answer!

○ Say: *Imagine another teacher is asking questions now. Listen and answer her questions. Say 'Hello and Goodbye' to her too!* Read the questions. Pause between each question so learners can answer it. It doesn't matter if their answers are all different!

Hello!
My name's Anna. What's your name?
How old are you?
Let's talk about school. Who do you play with at school?
What sports do you play?
What's your classroom like? Is it big or small?
OK. Thank you and goodbye.

50   Well done!

Pronunciation practice /aɪ/. See A.

Equipment needed

- Audio 50B.
- Coins and counters. See C.
- Copy of poem in A.

A Say what you see in the pictures. Find words that sound the same.

- Wave at the class and say: *Hello! Hi, everyone!* Write *Hi!* on the board and say *Hi!* again. The class replies, *Hi!*

  Point to your eye and say: *My eye! Tell me more words like 'Hi', 'my' and 'eye'.* **Suggestions** (ending in /aɪ/)**:** *buy, by, fly, try, dry, why.* Mime 'buy' and 'fly' and 'drying your hair'. Write 'buy' on the board and ask for another word that sounds like this but which only has two letters (by). Put 'W' on the board followed by a question mark to elicit 'why'.

- Write all these rhyming words on the board and point out the different ways we spell the sound /aɪ/.

- Learners draw circles around each word they find in the word wheel. They put up their hands when they have finished. Wait for everyone then ask: *How many words did you find in the circle?* (10) *How many pictures are there in A?* (10) Ask different learners to each say one of the words in the word wheel. (age, farm, sail, aunt, dry, hurt, loud, break, grass, eight) Learners write these words in a column in their notebooks.

- Learners decide what the word for each picture is (whale, fly, skirt, cage, glass, plate, cloud, plant, arm, lake) and write each picture word next to it's rhyming word to show ten rhyming pairs in their notebooks.

Check answers:

whale/sail, fly/dry, skirt/hurt, cage/age, glass/grass, plate/eight cloud/loud, plant/aunt, arm/farm, lake/break.

- Ask which rhyming pairs have the same way of spelling the end sound (fly/dry, cage/age, glass/grass, cloud/loud, arm/farm) and which rhyming pairs spell the sound differently (whale/sail, skirt/hurt, plate/eight, plant/aunt, lake/break).

Extension for more advanced learners:

- Create poems. Write on the board:

  The children in our class
  are sitting on the grass
  and fishing in a lake
  in our school lunch break.

  Learners read this and repeat it chorally.

  Ask: *Would you like to do this in your lunch break?*

- Draw a green circle around 'class' and 'grass' and a red circle around 'lake' and 'break'. Ask: *Do the ends of the words in the green circle sound the same?* (yes) *Do the ends of the words in the red circle sound the same?* (yes)

- Brainstorm more Movers and Starters rhyming words:

  Suggestions: black/Jack, man/ran, grey/play, cake/snake, train/plane, car/star, park/shark, bread/head, egg/leg, sea/pea, jeans/beans, swim/Jim, kicks/six, kite/right, bike/like, rice/mice, sock/rock, dog/frog, boat/goat, house/mouse, funny/sunny, brother/mother, etc.

- In groups of 3–4, learners choose two pairs of rhyming words and try to write a short four-line poem. They could use the rhyming pairs practised in A or choose two others. They could write their poem on paper and illustrate it as a group before reciting it in class, or learners could use computers and computer images to collectively produce a class book of poems.

  Further suggestions:

I often sail	I know a man
with my favourite whale	who ran and ran
now that I'm eight.	and then went for a swim
It's great!	with Jim.

  I like to plant
  flowers with my aunt
  and sit and drink tea
  under her tree.

B ▶ Listen and tick the box.   Listening **4**

Movers tip

Encourage candidates to try and answer all the questions in the Listening (and in the Reading and Writing), even if their answers are guesses. They may guess correctly and get an extra mark!

- Say: *These children have to do tests. What different kinds of tests must they do? Look at the pictures. Guess!*

  Suggestions: spelling tests, reading tests, writing tests, listening tests, grammar tests, vocabulary tests, speaking tests, music tests etc.

  Ask: *Do you sometimes have to do tests? What kind of tests do you have to do? What was your last test? Which tests are you good at? Which tests are more difficult?*

- Point to the example and ask one learner to read out the question. (*Which is Daisy?*) Point to the three pictures and say: *One of these girls is called Daisy. The three girls are doing different things in the pictures. Listen carefully. Is Daisy the girl who goes sailing? Is Daisy someone who likes reading things? Or is Daisy the girl who is good at swimming?*

- Play the example on the audio. Learners listen. Ask another learner to read out the question again then say: *Daisy doesn't go … ?* (sailing) *and she isn't good at … ?* (swimming). *Daisy likes … ?* (reading things on the computer). Learners put a tick in box B. Ask: *What kind of test did Daisy do yesterday?* (a listening test)

- Say: *Now listen and tick the right answers.* Play the audio for 1–5 twice.

Check answers:

1 C **2** A **3** B **4** A **5** B

- Ask: *What was the last thing you read about on the internet / had to write about? Was it fun? Why/why not?*

Audioscript

C Play the game! Stepping stones.

○ Say: *Before we play 'Stepping Stones', we can play 'Stop me and finish the words!'*

○ Dictate some of the following words letter by letter (10–12 words will probably be enough). Learners listen and write the letters in their notebooks.

If a learner thinks they know the word you are spelling, they put up their hand, call *Stop!* and say the remaining letters. They get a point for every remaining letter they say. Make sure all the words you choose are written in full on the board.

Words to spell:

address	breakfast	building	carefully
circus	country	downstairs	elevator
example	granddaughter	ground	hundred
hungry	island	kitten	message
moustache	naughty	nothing	pineapple
pretty	right	sandwich	sauce
thirsty	vegetable	video	weather
website	Wednesday	yesterday	zebra

○ Learners look at the words on the board and, working in pairs, find answers to the following questions. Give learners time between each question to find answers and either write them in their notebooks or to tell others in the class.

Suggestions: *Which word is / words are the longest/shortest?*
Which word do you think is the most difficult to spell/say?
How many words are adjectives / nouns / verbs?
How many words have the letter 'g'/'e' in them?
Do you know what all these words mean? Which one don't you understand?
Which is your favourite word? Why?

○ Say: *Now we can play 'Stepping Stones'.* Teach learners this useful language for the game: Pick up the coin. Toss the coin. Is it heads or tails? It's your turn.

○ Demonstrate this game with learners. Toss a coin. Ask: *Is it heads or tails?* Ask a learner to come and see. Say: *For heads, you can move to the next stone. For tails, you can move up three stones.*

○ Learners work in pairs or small groups (maximum five learners per group). They toss the coin and move to the next stone for heads and up three stones for tails. They write a word for each stepping stone they land on, using the information in the clue. The answer always starts with the stepping stone's letter. (For example: stepping stone **a** and its clue: *not before* = after)
If they cannot think of a word, they miss one turn.

○ They can choose to move back one or three stepping stones (depending on whether the coin showed heads or tails) if they want to get to a different letter. If they land on a letter they have already written a word for, they stay there until the next turn.

○ If they land on *3 places with water*, they have to write three words; if they land on *4 places in a town* they write four words; and if they land on *5 things you can see in the countryside* they write five words.

○ The pair or group that has written words for the most letters are the winners.

Note: There is sometimes more than one possible answer.

Optional extension:

At the end of the game, learners exchange lists. Ask for suggestions for the different letters and write these on the board. Learners receive a point for each word.

Check answers:

a after **b** beautiful **c** curly **d** dirty **e** exciting **f** forest
g good/great **h** hot **i** inside **j** jungle **k** kitchen **l** last
m mountain **n** naughty **o** open **p** playground/park **q** quiet
r round **s** strong **t** top **u** upstairs **v** village **w** worse
y yesterday **z** zoo

3 places with water: *bath, bathroom, kitchen, lake, pool, river, shower, sea, waterfall*

4 places in a town: *bus station/stop, café, car park, cinema, circus, hospital, library, market, roads, park, (swimming) pool, shop, shopping/sports centre, square, supermarket, store, school, streets*

5 things you can see in the countryside: *farm, field, flower, forest, grass, lake, river, mountain, plant, rock, tree, waterfall*

Goodbye!

Demonstrate shaking hands with one learner if that is acceptable in your classroom.

Say: *Right! It's the end of your book. Stand up everyone!* Learners stand. *Shake hands with the classmates who are next to you, and behind you and in front of you. Now clap your hands and let's all say, 'Brilliant! Well done, everyone!'*

Learners clap their hands and congratulate themselves in chorus!

4 Your hair looks great!

10 People in our street

Is your street in the town centre?	My street is/isn't ....
Is your street long or short?	My street is ....
Is your street quiet or noisy?	It's a .... street.
Are there lots of houses or flats in your street?	There are .... houses ....
Are there any gardens in your street?	There are/aren't ....
How many people live in your street?	About .... people ....
Is there a bus stop in your street?	There is/isn't ....
Are there any shops in your street?	There are/aren't ....
Why do you like your street?	I like my street because ....

19   What's the matter?

He fell off his skateboard by the gates to the park.	He hit his leg with his tennis racket in tennis practice.
He climbed to the top of a tree but fell and hurt his arm.	He dreamed about flying in the sky and woke up and fell out of bed!
He went for a ride but had to stop very quickly. He fell off his bike!	In his hockey game, another player hit him with the ball.
He kicked a football with no shoes on and hurt his foot!	He roller skated too quickly around the lake and fell into the water!

23   The world around us

Can you answer these questions about our world?

1 What's the biggest country? ....
2 What's the smallest country? ....
3 What's the tallest mountain? ....
4 What's the longest river? ....
5 What's the biggest sea? ....
6 What's the biggest lake? ....
7 What's the biggest city? ....
8 What's the biggest island? ....
9 What's the highest waterfall? ....
10 What's the biggest forest? ....

How much do you know about your country?

1 What's the biggest city? ....
2 What's the longest river? ....
3 What's the tallest mountain? ....
4 What's the biggest lake? ....
5 What's the tallest building? ....

What famous things do people come to see in your country?

....
....
....
....
....
....

24   Travelling, texting, phoning

Things we have in common.

Answer, then ask the other people in your group these questions.

Do you like dolphins? .... chocolate? .... shopping? ....

Can you hop? .... sing? .... skip? ....

What do you do at the weekend? ....

Where do you go after school? ....

Where do you live? ....

How many brothers have you got?   ....

sisters ....

cousins ....

What do you eat for breakfast? .... for lunch? .... for dinner? ....

What's your favourite colour? .... band? .... film? ....

food? .... place? .... website? ....

Now complete these sentences.

Everyone ....

Three of us ....

but one of us ....

Two of us ....

and two of us ....

Some of us ....

Only one of us ....

25   Which one is different?

(A) Learner A

Make five groups of three words. Then add another word to each group.
Then add one word which is different to each group.

> tennis racket, pop star, town, waterfall, sentence, cook, letter,
> village, lake, wave, city, skateboard, swimsuit, word, nurse

1 ....

2 ....

3 ....

4 ....

5 ....

---

25   Which one is different?

(B) Learner B

Make five groups of three words. Then add another word to each group.
Then add one word which is different to each group.

> rainbow, son, toothbrush, bath, earache, noodles, cloud,
> daughter, toothache, pie, star, fries, cough, aunt, shower

1 ....

2 ....

3 ....

4 ....

5 ....

26   Guess who lives here?

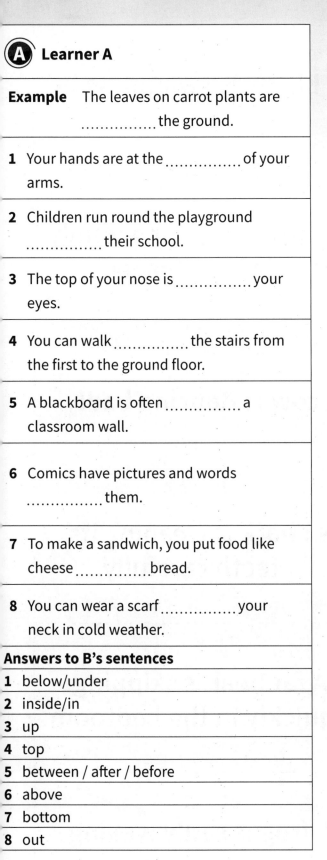

(A) Learner A

Example   The leaves on carrot plants are
.... the ground.

1   Your hands are at the .... of your
    arms.

2   Children run round the playground
    .... their school.

3   The top of your nose is .... your
    eyes.

4   You can walk .... the stairs from
    the first to the ground floor.

5   A blackboard is often .... a
    classroom wall.

6   Comics have pictures and words
    .... them.

7   To make a sandwich, you put food like
    cheese .... bread.

8   You can wear a scarf .... your
    neck in cold weather.

Answers to B's sentences

1	below/under
2	inside/in
3	up
4	top
5	between / after / before
6	above
7	bottom
8	out

(B) Learner B

Example   The leaves on carrot plants are
.... the ground.

1   The rooms in a basement are ....
    the ground.

2   Teeth are small and white. They are
    .... our mouth.

3   You can go .... to the top floor
    quickly in a lift.

4   The roof on the .... of our house
    is grey.

5   Most schools have a short break
    .... lessons.

6   You can sometimes see a rainbow
    .... your head on wet and sunny
    days.

7   In stories, pirates often find treasure at
    the .... of the sea.

8   Dolphins are animals that love jumping in
    and .... of water.

Answers to A's sentences

1	end
2	outside/at
3	between
4	down
5	on
6	inside/in
7	between / in / inside
8	around / round / on

An elephant is skating slowly.	A big fly is swimming in a cup.
A monkey is eating a banana carefully.	A parrot is singing loudly in the shower.
A kangaroo is laughing loudly.	A cow is dancing badly.
A rabbit is jumping quickly.	A shark is cleaning its teeth carefully.
A lion is painting a wall slowly.	A fat bear is skipping quickly in the bedroom.
A panda is carefully holding a box of eggs.	A frog is sadly waving goodbye.

30   About me

What's the best sport to play?

.... do you do sport? Every day?

.....................'s the best place to go and do sport?

Which sports do you like watching?

> How often   Where

.... do you use a computer?

What's your favourite website?

How do you write on your computer? Do you use a keyboard?

.... computer games and apps do you like?

> How often   Which

.... do you go away on holiday?

.... do you like going on holiday?

What do you do on holiday?

Who do you go on holiday with?

> How often   Where

What's your favourite food?

.... is the best cook in your family?

.... kind of fruit juice do you like?

Which foods don't you like?

> What   Who

.... do you go to school?

Which is your favourite school day?

What do you do in the school break?

.... children are there in your class?

> How   How many

Where is your home?

.... rooms are there in your house?

Which is your favourite room at home?

.... do you watch TV?

> Where   How many

31 Why is Sally crying?

Sometimes when I'm tired …	The best thing to drink when you're thirsty …
… is a glass of water.	… I sleep after lunch.
… because they're very dirty.	Please go to the bathroom and wash your hands …
Would you like another blanket on your bed …	… because it's very cold today.
Oh dear! The dog's wet again.	Can you get me an old towel?
Are you hungry?	Shall I make you a chicken sandwich?

32 Mary goes shopping

Look at the picture.
Ask and answer your partner about your pictures.

32 Mary goes shopping

Look at the picture.
Ask and answer your partner about your pictures.

35   What a morning!

What a terrible morning! Every day, I wake up at 7 o'clock, but today I woke up at 8 o'clock!

I didn't have a shower. I put my clothes on quickly. I didn't have breakfast.

I ran out of the house but I didn't take my coat. I didn't say goodbye to my parents.

I ran to the bus stop but I couldn't catch the bus. I saw it, but it didn't stop.

All my friends and classmates were on the bus.

I had to walk to school in the rain.

I was very tired and my feet hurt.

I got to school, but my teacher was angry when she saw me.

She wasn't happy because I didn't have any books or homework!

42 An exciting week for Alex!

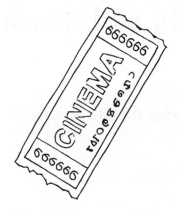

48 We want to do this one day

A Learner A

Read the questions. What are your friend's answers?

Questions	.................'s answers
1 Are you frightened of spiders?	
2 Do you often go and see your grandparents?	
3 Have you got a baseball cap?	
4 Do you enjoy watching scary movies?	
5 Is a kiwi your favourite fruit?	
6 Did you get any text messages yesterday?	
7 Would you like to learn another sport?	
8 Can you ride a bike?	
9 Would you like to have a pet snake?	
10 Could you swim when you were six?	
11 Did you score any goals last weekend?	
12 Are you hungry now?	

48 We want to do this one day

B Learner B

Read the questions. What are your friend's answers?

Questions	.................'s answers
1 Are you good at making model toys?	
2 Do you often travel by ship?	
3 Have you got a book about a famous person?	
4 Do you like going for a swim?	
5 Is hockey your favourite sport?	
6 Did you phone any of your friends yesterday?	
7 Would you like to learn more about elephants?	
8 Can you cook noodles?	
9 Would you like to be a dentist?	
10 Could you read and write when you were six?	
11 Did you send any texts last night?	
12 Are you thirsty now?	

Listening

Part 1

5 questions

Listen and draw lines. There is one example.

Paul   **Peter**   **Jane**   **Vicky**

Clare   **Nick**   **Mark**

Listening

Part 2
5 questions

Listen and write. There is one example.

The bus station

Example	Name	Charlie ....Lake............
1	Age:	....
2	Address:	27 .... Street
3	Day comes to bus station:	....
4	Meets his:	....
5	Where going:	to the .... centre

Listening

Part 3

Listen to Daisy telling her grandson, Jim, about her favourite things. Where did Daisy get each thing?

Listen and write a letter in each box. There is one example.

	a plant	B
	a poster	☐
	a board game	☐
	glasses	☐
	a teddy bear	☐
	a donkey	☐

Listening

Part 3

A

B

C

D

E

F

G

H

Listening

Part 4

5 questions

Listen and tick (✔) the box. There is one example.

What does May want for lunch?

A ☐   B ✔   C ☐

1 What did Kim get for his birthday?

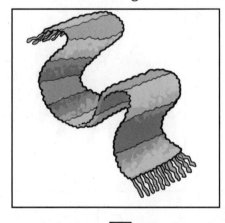

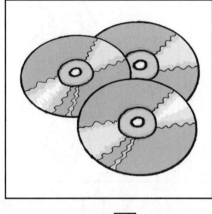

A ☐   B ☐   C ☐

2 What did Mary do at the weekend?

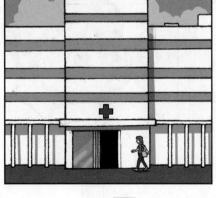

A ☐   B ☐   C ☐

Listening

Part 4

3 Where does Sam's father work?

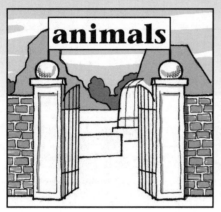

A ☐

B ☐

C ☐

4 What is Ben drawing?

A ☐

B ☐

C ☐

5 What is the matter with Jim?

A ☐

B ☐

C ☐

Listening

Listen and colour and write. There is one example.

Audioscript

Hello. This is the Cambridge Movers Practice Listening Test.

Part 1

Look at Part 1. Now look at the picture. Listen and look. There is one example.

Woman:	Look! There are lots of children at the swimming pool today!
Girl:	Yes, I know everyone here. They're all my classmates, Mum.
Woman:	Are they? Who's that girl? The one who's jumping into the water?
Girl:	Oh, that's Jane. She's very good at swimming.
Woman:	I love her long black hair!

Can you see the line? This is an example. Now you listen and draw lines.

One

Woman:	Who's that boy, there?
Girl:	The boy who's sitting at the round table?
Woman:	Yes. The one with the drink in his hand and the really curly hair.
Girl:	His name's Peter. He's one of my best friends.

Two

Girl:	Everyone's having fun but something's wrong with Vicky.
Woman:	Which girl is she?
Girl:	The one who's standing next to that square table.
Woman:	Has she got a stomach-ache?
Girl:	Yes, I think, she has.

Three

Woman:	Why's that boy on the ground?
Girl:	Which one? Oh, you mean Mark! The boy next to the crocodile?
Woman:	That's right.
Girl:	I think he's really tired, that's all.

Four

Girl:	Paul's taking pictures again! Can you see him?
Woman:	Do you mean the boy who's wearing those funny long shorts?
Girl:	Yes. He likes wearing those!
Woman:	He's got a phone too. Does he take photos with that too?
Girl:	Sometimes . . . .

Five

Girl:	Oh look! There's Nick! I want to go and talk to him.
Woman:	Which boy is he?
Girl:	The one with his feet in the water!
Woman:	Do you like his black baseball cap?
Girl:	Yes, he's got lots like that.

Now listen to Part 1 again. That is the end of Part 1.

Part 2

Listen and look. There is one example.

Woman:	Hello. I work here in the bus station. Can I ask you some questions, please?
Boy:	Yes, OK.
Woman:	Thank you. Now, what's your name?
Boy:	Charlie Lake.
Woman:	Do you spell that L-A-K-E?
Boy:	Yes.

Can you see the answer? Now you listen and write.

One

Woman:	How old are you, Charlie?
Boy:	I'm twelve.
Woman:	Sorry? Did you say twelve?
Boy:	Yes. That's right.

Two

Woman:	And do you live near here?
Boy:	No. I live in the town centre. My address is 27 Pound Street.
Woman:	I don't know that street. How do you spell that? P-O-W-N-D?
Boy:	No, P-O-U-N-D.
Woman:	OK. Thank you.

Three

Woman:	How often do you come to the bus station?
Boy:	I come here every Saturday.
Woman:	Do you? In the morning or in the afternoon?
Boy:	In the morning.
Woman:	OK. I need to write that down too.

Four

Woman:	And why do you come here, Charlie?
Boy:	I come here to meet someone. My cousin!
Woman:	That's nice.
Boy:	It's not always!
Woman:	Why not? Don't you like your cousin?
Boy:	He's OK. But he breaks my things sometimes.

Five

Woman:	One last question. Where are you going now?
Boy:	To the shopping centre.
Woman:	The shopping centre?
Boy:	Yes. To get a new football.
Woman:	I see. OK. Thank you!

Now listen to Part 2 again. That is the end of Part 2.

Part 3

Listen and look. There is one example.

Daisy is telling her grandson, Jim, about her favourite things.

Where did Daisy get each thing?

Woman:	I've got lots of favourite things in my flat, Jim.
Boy:	I know, Grandma.
Woman:	Look at this pretty plant! Isn't it nice?
Boy:	Where did you get it from?
Woman:	Oh… I found it by the river. I water it every day!

Can you see the letter B? Now you listen and write a letter in each box.

Boy:	What about this?
Woman:	Oh! My little teddy bear?
Boy:	Yes.
Woman:	My mother found it in a playground. She washed it and gave it to me.
Boy:	So, did someone lose it?
Woman:	Yes. It was sad, but we gave it a happy home!

Woman:	I love this glass donkey, too. I think it's really sweet.
Boy:	Where did you get that?
Woman:	From a farm. We were there on holiday.
Boy:	It's really cool. I like it a lot.
Woman:	Yes… Me too.

Practice test

Woman: This is one of my favourite things, too.

Boy: The poster on this wall?

Woman: Yes. It's sixty years old. She was my favourite film star when I was a little girl.

Boy: Did you get it from the cinema?

Woman: No, from a market.

Boy: And these glasses? You never wear them!

Woman: I know, but I like them. I bought them from a shop in the mountains.

Boy: Oh! Did you need some new ones then?

Woman: Yes! I dropped my old ones in a car park and we couldn't fix them.

Woman: I love this old board game, too.

Boy: Wow! It looks really cool. Can we play it, Grandma?

Woman: Yes! Let's do that now! I got that from a funfair!

Boy: Brilliant!

Part 4

Look at the pictures. Listen and look. There is one example.

What does May want for lunch?

Man: Would you like some pasta for lunch, May?

Girl: We had that yesterday, Dad. Can we have something cold please?

Man: What about a salad?

Girl: Great! And can we have some rice, oh, and some sausages for dinner?

Man: Sorry! We haven't got any.

Can you see the tick? Now you listen and tick the box.

One   *What did Kim get for his birthday?*

Woman: Are these DVDs one of your birthday presents, Kim?

Boy: No, Aunt Daisy. Mum got them for Grandpa. They're his favourite old movies.

Woman: Did she get that scarf for Grandpa, too?

Boy: Yes. And a sweater for me. It's my favourite birthday present.

Two   *What did Mary do at the weekend?*

Man: Did you go ice skating at the weekend, Mary?

Girl: No, I couldn't.

Man: Did you go horse-riding, then?

Girl: No. This weekend I went to the hospital.

Man: Oh dear!

Girl: Don't worry! It was exciting! I went to see my new baby sister.

Three   *Where does Sam's father work?*

Girl: Where does your dad work, Sam? At the library?

Boy: Not now. He works at the supermarket.

Girl: Oh! I'd like to work at a zoo, one day.

Boy: Me too! I'd love to do that!

Four   *What is Ben drawing?*

Woman: What's that in your picture, Ben?

Boy: Where?

Woman: In the jungle. Is it a bat?

Boy: No. Can't you see? It's a parrot, Grandma.

Woman: Sorry! It looks more like a penguin to me!

Five   *What is the matter with Jim?*

Woman: Are you ill, Jim? Have you got a headache?

Boy: No. It's not that.

Woman: Is your ear hurting, then?

Boy: No. I've got really bad toothache.

Now listen to Part 4 again. That is the end of Part 4.

Part 5

Look at the picture. Listen and look. There is one example.

Man: Would you like to colour this picture?

Girl: Yes, please! Can I colour the cloud?

Man: OK. What colour?

Girl: Grey, because it's raining.

Man: All right.

Can you see the grey cloud? This is an example. Now you listen and colour and write.

One

Man: Now, find the cups in the picture.

Girl: There are three of them in the cupboard.

Man: Yes. Would you like to colour one of those?

Girl: All right! Which one?

Man: The biggest one. Make it orange.

Girl: OK. I've got that colour here.

Two

Girl: What now?

Man: Well, there's some fruit in this kitchen.

Girl: Oh yes. In the bowl.

Man: That's right. Lets colour the pineapple.

Girl: OK. Can I make it yellow?

Man: No, colour it pink, please.

Three

Man: I'd like you to write something now.
   Can you see the word FUN on the TV?

Girl: Yes.

Man: Great. Write FOOD after that.

Girl: So it says, Fun Food?

Man: That's right. Thank you!

Four

Man: And now, find the jacket.

Girl: The one that's on the door?

Man: Not that one. Colour the one on the back of the chair.

Girl: OK. Can I colour it purple? That's my favourite colour!

Man: It's my favourite colour too! Yes, that's fine.

Five

Girl: What shall I do now?

Man: Can you see the bottle?

Girl: The one next to the glasses? Do you mean that one?

Man: Yes. Colour that bottle green, please.

Girt   All right. This picture looks better now!

Man: That's right! It does! Thank you.

Now listen to Part 5 again.

That is the end of the Movers Practice Listening Test.

Reading and Writing

Part 1

Look and read. Choose the correct words and write them on the lines. There is one example.

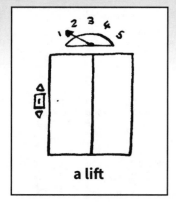

a lift

mirrors

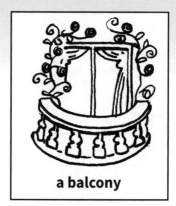

a balcony

a salad

cheese

towels

coffee

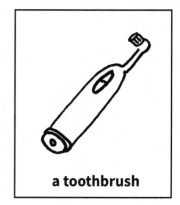

a toothbrush

Example

Some people make this for lunch with tomatoes and other kinds of vegetables.   *a salad*

Questions

1   In some apartments, you can open doors and sit outside on this.   ....

2   Farmers make this from milk and you can put it in sandwiches.   ....

3   In some large shops, people can go up or down to another floor in this.   ....

4   After a shower, you can dry your hair and body with these.   ....

5   More grown-ups than children like this hot drink.   ....

Reading and Writing

Part 2
6 questions

Read the text and choose the best answer.

Alex is talking to Mrs Cross, who lives in the house next to hers.

Example

Mrs Cross:	Hi, Alex.

Alex:	**A**	Yes, please!
	B	Brilliant, thanks!
	C	Good afternoon!

Questions

1 Mrs Cross: Where are you going now, Alex?

Alex:	**A**	It's this evening.
	B	To the village.
	C	I'm riding my bike.

Reading and Writing

Part 2

2 **Mrs Cross:** Are you going shopping for your mum?

    Alex:
- **A** Yes, that's right.
- **B** No, it's not her.
- **C** OK. Well done!

3 **Mrs Cross:** Do you have to buy a lot of things?

    Alex:
- **A** Only an apple pie.
- **B** That's my pancake.
- **C** No, it's not a kiwi.

4 **Mrs Cross:** I need to go to the the shops too. Can I come with you?

    Alex:
- **A** Yes, it's a bus.
- **B** Yes, I'd like that.
- **C** Yes, she's OK now.

5 **Mrs Cross:** I'd like to buy some chocolate ice cream!

    Alex:
- **A** What a good idea!
- **B** Whose are those?
- **C** It's now very busy.

6 **Mrs Cross:** Which is your favourite shop?

    Alex:
- **A** No, they aren't new boots.
- **B** I've got a new e-book.
- **C** Lily's sweet store!

Reading and Writing

Part 3
6 questions

Read the story. Choose a word from the box. Write the correct word next to numbers 1–5. There is one example.

city	 walk	 picnic	 surprised	 asleep

climb	 cry	 field	 wave

I'm Ben. I live in the .... *city* .... centre but last Sunday, Dad drove me to my grandparents' farm because it was my grandpa's birthday that day.

When we got there, Grandma said, 'Let's go for a **(1)** .... We've got lots of exciting things to show you, Ben!'

'I want Ben to see the new cows first!' Grandpa said. 'Come on everyone! Jump in the tractor! We can ride there in that.'

The cows were in Grandpa's biggest **(2)** .... They made lots of scary noises when they saw us but I wasn't frightened.

Then I saw a really beautiful tree. 'Can I **(3)** .... it?' I asked. 'OK,' Grandma said. 'But be careful!'

When I got to the top, I was really **(4)** .... ! 'Wow! That's so cool! I can see a waterfall!' I shouted.

'That's our favourite place, Ben!' Grandpa said. 'We can swim in the water there!

It was a fantastic day! After our swim, Grandma took a **(5)** .... out of her bag and we all had lots to eat. Grandpa's birthday cake was fantastic.

(6) Now choose the best name for this story. Tick (✓) one box.

A favourite place! ☐

Ben's biggest cow! ☐

Grandpa goes for a swim! ☐

Reading and Writing

Part 4

5 questions

Read the text. Choose the right words and write them on the lines.

Crocodiles

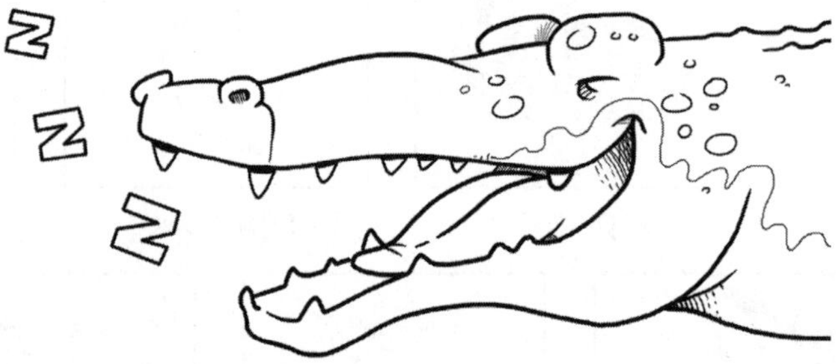

Example

Most people are frightened of crocodiles
.......*because*....... these animals have very

| | and | because | but |

1 strong tails and .... of really
big teeth!

| **1** | many | some | lots |

2 A crocodile has a funny toothbrush! It
opens its mouth and then ....
bird jumps in and takes the food out from
between its teeth!

| **2** | an | those | a |

3 Did you .... that when

| **3** | know | knows | knowing |

4 crocodiles have babies, ...
carry them very carefully in their mouths?

| **4** | it | they | we |

Crocodiles have long, fat bodies. Their legs
are short but crocodiles can move very
quickly in or out of the water.

5 .... you like to go and watch
crocodiles in a zoo one day?

| **5** | Could | Shall | Would |

Reading and Writing

Part 5

7 questions

Look at the pictures and read the story. Write some words to complete the sentences about the story. You can use 1, 2 or 3 words.

Sally's exciting day

It was a beautiful day last Friday. Sally got up and had her shower. Then she put on her school clothes and then ran downstairs to the kitchen. Sally, her brother and her parents had breakfast and talked about their day. 'I love school but it's too nice to be inside today,' she said.

Examples

Last Friday, the weather was ..... *beautiful* ......

After ..... *her shower* ....., Sally put on her school clothes.

Questions

1 Sally had breakfast with her mum, dad and ....

Reading and Writing

Part 5

Sally picked up her school things, put on her helmet, said goodbye and then rode her bike to school. When she got there, she took off her coat and went into the classroom. The classroom was very quiet. She didn't understand! 'Where are all my classmates?' she thought. Then Sally looked out of the window and saw all her school friends on the grass outside the school building.

2   Sally went to school on her ....

3   Sally was surprised that the children in her class weren't in ....

4   All Sally's .... were outside on the grass..

Reading and Writing

Part 5

Sally got up and ran to see them. 'Where were you?' asked her teacher. 'It's Friday! It's our school sports day! Look! Your class are playing basketball now and after our lunch break, it's hockey or swimming!'

'Oh yes!' Sally laughed. 'No lessons today! Brilliant!'

She ran back to the classroom, found her sports clothes and put them on. Sally enjoyed doing lots of different sports that day.

When she got home, she said to her parents, 'It was really exciting at school, today because we had lots and lots and lots of fun outside!'

5   There were no lessons on Friday because it was the ....

6   After lunch, Sally and her classmates could play ....

7   Sally told .... all about her fun day when she got home.

Reading and Writing

Part 6

6 questions

Look and read and write.

Examples

The door of this house is .... *open* ....

What's the man who's outside the garden riding?   *a motorbike*

Complete the sentences.

1   The older child is trying to help .... which is on the roof.

2   Someone is driving a huge .... along the road.

Complete the sentences.

3   What is the girl holding?   ....

4   What is the mother doing?   ....

Now write two sentences about the picture.

5   ....

6   ....

 146   Practice test

Listening

Answer key

Listening

Part 1 (5 marks)

Lines should be drawn between:

1   Peter and the boy with curly hair holding a drink at the round table.
2   Vicky and the girl standing next to the square table holding her stomach.
3   Mark and the boy lying on the ground next to the crocodile.
4   Paul and the boy taking pictures wearing funny shorts with a phone in them.
5   Nick and the boy with his feet in the water and wearing a black baseball cap.

Part 2 (5 marks)

1 12/twelve   **2** Pound   **3** Saturday   **4** cousin   **5** shopping

Part 3 (5 marks)

poster   G
board game   A
glasses   F
teddy bear   D
donkey   C

Part 4 (5 marks)

1 C   **2** B   **3** C   **4** B   **5** A

Part 5 (5 marks)

1   Colour the tallest cup orange.
2   Colour the pineapple in the bowl pink.
3   Write the word FOOD under Fun on the TV screen.
4   Colour the jacket on the back of the chair purple.
5   Colour the bottle next to the glasses green.

Reading and Writing

Part 1 (5 marks)

1   a balcony
2   cheese
3   a lift
4   towels
5   coffee

Part 2 (6 marks)

1 B   **2** A   **3** A   **4** B   **5** A   **6** C

Part 3 (6 marks)

1   walk
2   field
3   climb
4   surpised
5   picnic
6   A favourite place.

Part 4 (5 marks)

1   lots
2   a
3   know
4   they
5   Would

Part 5 (7 marks)

1   brother
2   bike
3   the/her classroom
4   classmates
5   (school) sports day
6   hockey or swimming
7   her parents

Part 6 (10 marks)

Suggested answers:

1   a/the cat/kitten
2   lorry/truck
3   a/her skateboard
4   shouting/watching the boy in the tree / standing with the girl / saying 'be careful' / carrying a bag etc

5 and **6**   (any two sentences that relate in some way to the picture)

For example:

The tree is very big.

The cat is frightened.

There is a seat in the garden.

The people are outside their house.

The boy's shoe is on the ground.

The boy is only wearing one shoe.

These people live at number 11, Quick Street.

The man on the motorbike is wearing a helmet.

The family want to help their pet cat because it's afraid.

Speaking

Examiner's Script

Part	Examiner does this:	Examiner says this:	Minimum response expected:	Back-up questions:
		Hello. My name's Jane / Ms Smith.	Hello.	
		What's your name?	Marco*.	
		How old are you, Marco?	9	Are you 9?
1	Points to **Find the differences** card.	Look at these pictures. They look the same, but some things are different. Here, there are three comics on the sofa, but here there are no comics. What other different things can you see?	Candidate describes four other differences: • big / small lamp • 2 socks / 1 sock on baby • doll / robot • rabbit in / out of the cage	Point to other differences the candidate does not mention. Give first half of response: **Here, the lamp is big, but here …**
2	Points to **Story** card. Points to the other pictures.	These pictures show a story. It's called 'Treasure under the waves'. Look at the pictures first. Dan's swimming in the sea. He's really excited. He can see a box on the sand. He's thinking, 'Is that treasure?' Now you tell the story.	(Many variations possible.) Dan's coming out of the sea. He's talking to his friends. He's pointing at the water. Dan and his friends are carrying the box. They want to find some treasure! Dan opened the box. There's no treasure inside. But there are some beautiful shells in the box!	 Is Dan in the sea now? Who's Dan talking to? What's Dan pointing at? What are Dan and his friends carrying? What do they want to find in the box? Did Dan open the box? Is there any treasure inside? What's inside the box?

Speaking

Examiner's Script

Part	Examiner does this:	Examiner says this:	Minimum response expected:	Back-up questions:
3	Points to **Odd-one-out** card. Points to the second, third and fourth sets of pictures in turn.	**Now look at these four pictures. One is different. The tablet is different.** **A lemon, a pineapple and a banana are fruit. You can eat them. You can't eat a tablet. You play games on it.** **Now you tell me about these pictures. Which one is different? (Why?)**	Candidate suggests a difference (any plausible difference is acceptable).	**Where do you wear these?** (on your feet) **And this?** (on your head) **These animals can...?** (run/walk) **And this animal...?** (can swim) **What are these girls doing?** (sports) **And this girl?** (writing)
4	Puts away all pictures.	**Now, let's talk about you and your home.** **Where do you live?** **What do you like doing at home?** **Where do you have dinner?** **Tell me more about your home.** **OK. Thank you. Goodbye.**	*in (Rome)* *playing on the computer* *(in the) living room* It's big. I live in a flat. It's in the city. Goodbye.	**Do you live in (Rome)?** **Do you like playing on the computer?** **Do you have dinner in the living room?** **Is your home big?** **Do you live in a flat?** **Is it in the city?**

Speaking

Find the differences

Speaking
Treasure under the waves

Speaking

Find the different ones

The authors and publishers would like to thank the ELT professionals who commented on the material at different stages of its development.

The authors are grateful to: Niki Donnelly of Cambridge University Press.

Anne Robinson would like to give special thanks to Adam Evans and her parents Margaret and Jim and to many, many teachers and students who have inspired her along the way. Special thanks to Cristina and Victoria for their help, patience and enthusiasm. And in memory of her brother Dave.

Karen Saxby would like to give special thanks to everyone she has worked with at Cambridge Assessment since the birth of YLE! She would particularly like to mention Frances, Felicity and Ann Kelly. She would also like to acknowledge the enthusiasm of all the teachers she has met through her work in this field. And lastly, Karen would like to say a big thank you to her sons, Tom and William, for bringing constant FUN and creative thinking to her life and work.

Freelance editorial services by Angela Janes

Design and typeset by Wild Apple Design.

Cover design by Chris Saunders (Astound).

Sound recordings by dsound Recording Studios, London

The authors and publishers acknowledge the following sources of copyright material and are grateful for the permissions granted. While every effort has been made, it has not always been possible to identify the sources of all the material used, or to trace all copyright holders. If any omissions are brought to our notice, we will be happy to include the appropriate acknowledgements on reprinting and in the next update to the digital edition, as applicable.

The authors and publishers are grateful to the following illustrators:

T = Top, B = Below, L = Left, R = Right, C = Centre, B/G = Background

Andy Elkerton (Sylvie Poggio Artists Agency) pp. 26, 116, 130, 131, 134, 136, 143; Brett Hudson (Graham-Cameron Illustration) pp. 131, 132, 133, 135, 139, 142, 144, 145, 150, 151, 152; Nigel Kitching (Sylvie Poggio Artists Agency) pp. 125, 126, 127; Pip Sampson pp. 132, 141, 142, 146; Melanie Sharp (Sylvie Poggio Artists Agency) pp. 124, 138; Jo Taylor (Sylvie Poggio Artists Agency) pp. 134, 129.